How We Know What Isn't So

The Fallibility of Human Reason in Everyday Life

—

Thomas Gilovich

THE FREE PRESS

THE FREE PRESS
A Division of Simon & Schuster Inc.
1230 Avenue of the Americas
New York, NY 10020

THE FREE PRESS and colophon are trademarks
of Simon & Schuster Inc.

First Free Press Paperback Edition 1993

Manufactured in the United States of America

27

Library of Congress Cataloging-in-Publication Data

Gilovich, Thomas.
How we know what isn't so: the fallibility of human reason in
everyday life / Thomas Gilovich.
    p. cm.
Includes bibliographical references and index.
ISBN 978-0-02-911706-4
1. Reasoning (Psychology) 2. Judgment. 3. Evidence 4. Error.
5. Critical thinking. 6. Fallacies (Logic)   I. Title.
BF442.G55   1991
153.4'3—dc20   90–26727
                                                    CIP

To Karen and Ilana

Contents

PART THREE
Examples of Questionable and Erroneous Beliefs

PART FOUR
Where Do We Go from Here?

Acknowledgments

Four people made unusually significant contributions to this work and deserve special thanks. Lee Ross commented on drafts of many of the chapters and provided a number of his uniquely illuminating insights on the phenomena at hand. Beyond that, I would like to thank Lee simply for being Lee—for being the most interesting "intuitive psychologist" I know, and for making the discussion of people and their commerce through everyday life so enjoyable. Karen Dashiff Gilovich read every word of this book and at times seemed to have something to say about nearly every one. She was in many respects my most challenging critic, but, as always, she delivered her critiques in the most loving, disarming, and helpful ways. I owe Dennis Regan and Daryl Bem a great debt for the helpful feedback they provided on earlier drafts and for their encouragement throughout the project.

Various chapters were improved by the comments of numerous people, and I would like to express my sincere thanks to all: Robert Frank, Mark Frank, David Hamilton, Robert Johnston, David Myers, James Pennebaker, Barbara Strupp, Richard Thaler, and Elaine Wethington. To protect them from blame for any wrong-headed ideas presented in this book, the usual disclaimers about ultimate responsibility apply.

Finally, I would like to thank the National Institute of Mental Health for the generous financial support that made possible much of my own research that is reported in this book, and Susan Milmoe of The Free Press for her enthusiasm and assistance during the past eighteen months.

1

Introduction

It ain't so much the things we don't know that get us into
trouble. It's the things we know that just ain't so.

Artemus Ward

It is widely believed that infertile couples who adopt a child
are subsequently more likely to conceive than similar couples
who do not. The usual explanation for this remarkable phenomenon
involves the alleviation of stress. Couples who adopt, it is said,
become less obsessed with their reproductive failure, and their
new-found peace of mind boosts their chances for success.

On closer inspection, however, it becomes clear that the remarkable phenomenon we need to explain is not why adoption increases
a couple's fertility; clinical research has shown that it does not.[1]
What needs explanation is why so many people hold this belief
when it is not true.

People who are charged with deciding who is to be admitted
to a distinguished undergraduate institution, a prestigious graduate
school, or a select executive training program all think they can
make more effective admissions decisions if each candidate is seen
in a brief, personal interview. They cannot. Research indicates
that decisions based on objective criteria alone are at least as effective as those influenced by subjective impressions formed in an
interview.[2] But then why do people believe the interview to be
informative?

Nurses who work on maternity wards believe that more babies
are born when the moon is full. They are mistaken.[3] Again, why
do they believe it if it "just ain't so?"

This book seeks to answer these questions. It examines how

[1]

questionable and erroneous beliefs are formed, and how they are maintained. As the examples above make clear, the strength and resiliency of certain beliefs cry out for explanation. Today, more people believe in ESP than in evolution,[4] and in this country there are 20 times as many astrologers as there are astronomers.[5] Both formal opinion polls and informal conversation reveal widespread acceptance of the reality of astral projection, of the authenticity of "channeling," and of the spiritual and psychic value of crystals. This book attempts to increase our understanding of such beliefs and practices, and, in so doing, to shed some light on various broader issues in the study of human judgment and reasoning.

Several things are clear at the outset. First, people do not hold questionable beliefs simply because they have not been exposed to the relevant evidence. Erroneous beliefs plague both experienced professionals and less informed laypeople alike. In this respect, the admissions officials and maternity ward nurses should "know better." They are professionals. They are in regular contact with the data. But they are mistaken.

Nor do people hold questionable beliefs simply because they are stupid or gullible. Quite the contrary. Evolution has given us powerful intellectual tools for processing vast amounts of information with accuracy and dispatch, and our questionable beliefs derive primarily from the misapplication or overutilization of generally valid and effective strategies for knowing. Just as we are subject to perceptual illusions in spite of, and largely because of, our extraordinary perceptual capacities, so too are many of our cognitive shortcomings "closely related to, or even an unavoidable cost of, [our] greatest strengths."[6] And just as the study of perceptual illusions has illuminated general principles of perception, and the study of psychopathology has enhanced our knowledge of personality, so too should the study of erroneous beliefs enlarge our understanding of human judgment and reasoning. By design, then, this book dwells on beliefs that are wrong, but in doing so we must not lose sight of how often we are right.

As these remarks suggest, many questionable and erroneous beliefs have purely cognitive origins, and can be traced to imperfections in our capacities to process information and draw conclusions. We hold many dubious beliefs, in other words, not because they satisfy some important psychological need, but because they seem to be the most sensible conclusions consistent with the available evidence. People hold such beliefs because they seem, in the words of Robert Merton, to be the "irresistible products of their own experience."[7] They are the products, not of irrationality, but of flawed rationality.

So it is with the erroneous belief that infertile couples who adopt are subsequently more likely to conceive. Our attention is automatically drawn to couples who conceive after adopting, but not to those who adopt but do not conceive, or those who conceive without adopting. Thus, to many people, the increased fertility of couples who adopt a child is a "fact" of everyday experience. People do not hold this belief because they have much of an emotional stake in doing so; they do so because it seems to be the only sensible conclusion consistent with the information that is most available to them.

Many of these imperfections in our cognitive and inferential tools might never surface under ideal conditions (just as many perceptual illusions are confined to impoverished settings). But the world does not play fair. Instead of providing us with clear information that would enable us to "know" better, it presents us with messy data that are random, incomplete, unrepresentative, ambiguous, inconsistent, unpalatable, or secondhand. As we shall see, it is often our flawed attempts to cope with precisely these difficulties that lay bare our inferential shortcomings and produce the facts we know that just ain't so.

Returning to the infertility example once again, we can readily see how the world does not play fair. Couples who conceive after adopting are noteworthy. Their good fortune is reported by the media, transmitted by friends and neighbors, and therefore is more likely to come to our attention than the fate of couples who adopt but do not conceive, or those who conceive without adopting. Thus, even putting our own cognitive and inferential limitations aside, there are inherent biases in the data upon which we base our beliefs, biases that must be recognized and overcome if we are to arrive at sound judgments and valid beliefs.

In tackling this subject of questionable and erroneous beliefs, I continue the efforts of many social and cognitive psychologists who in the past several years have sought to understand the bounded rationality of human information processing. Part I of this book, "Cognitive determinants of questionable beliefs," contains three chapters that analyze our imperfect strategies for dealing with the often messy data of the real world. Chapter 2 concerns random data and our tendency to see regularity and order where only the vagaries of chance are operating. Chapter 3 deals with incomplete and unrepresentative data and our limited ability to detect and correct for these biases. Chapter 4 discusses our eagerness to interpret ambiguous and inconsistent data in light of our pet theories and *a priori* expectations.

Although an examination of these cognitive biases is enormously helpful in understanding questionable and erroneous beliefs, the richness and diversity of such beliefs require a consideration of other factors as well. Accordingly, Part II contains three chapters on the "Motivational and social determinants of questionable beliefs." Chapter 5 locates the roots of erroneous belief in wishful thinking and self-serving distortions of reality. This chapter provides a revisionist interpretation of motivational effects by examining how our motives collude with our cognitive processes to produce erroneous, but self-serving, beliefs. Chapter 6 examines the pitfalls of secondhand information and the distortions introduced by communicators—including the mass media—who are obliged to summarize and tempted to entertain. Chapter 7 takes a psychological truism, "we tend to believe what we think others believe" and turns it around: We tend to think others believe what we believe. This chapter examines a set of cognitive, social, and motivational processes that prompt us to overestimate the extent to which others share our beliefs, further bolstering our credulity.

Part III adopts a case study approach by bringing all the mechanisms introduced in Parts I and II together in an attempt to understand the origins and durability of several widely held but empirically dubious beliefs. These include beliefs in the efficacy of untested or ineffective health practices (Chapter 8), in the effectiveness of self-defeating interpersonal strategies (Chapter 9), and in the existence of ESP (Chapter 10). These chapters necessarily tread more lightly at times, for it cannot always be said with certainty that the beliefs under examination are false. Nevertheless, there is a notable gap in all cases between belief and evidence, and it is this gap that these chapters seek to explain.

Part IV ends the book with a discussion of how we might improve the way we evaluate the evidence of everyday life, and thus how we can steer clear of erroneous beliefs.

WHY WORRY ABOUT ERRONEOUS BELIEFS?

It is a great discredit to humankind that a species as magnificant as the rhinoceros can be so endangered. Their numbers thinned by the encroachment of civilization in the first half of this century, they now face the menace of deliberate slaughter. In the last 15 years, 90% of the rhinos in Africa have been killed by poachers who sell their horns on the black market. The horns fetch a high price in the Far East where they are used, in powdered form, to reduce fevers, cure headaches, and (less commonly) increase sexual potency. As a consequence of this senseless killing, there are now only a few thousand black rhinos left in Africa, and even fewer in Asia and Indonesia.[8]

Unhappily, the rhinoceros is not alone in this plight. Six hundred black bears were killed in the Great Smoky Mountains during the last three years, their gall bladders exported to Korea where they are thought to be an effective aid for indigestion (bears, the logic runs, are omnivores and are rarely seen to be ill). To understand the severity of this slaughter, it should be noted that the entire bear population in the Great Smoky Mountains at any one time is estimated to be approximately six hundred. A recent raid of a single black-market warehouse in San Francisco uncovered 40,000 seal penises that were to be sold, predictably, for use as aphrodisiacs. The Chinese green-haired turtle has been trapped to near extinction, in part because the Taiwanese believe that it can cure cancer. The list of species that have been slaughtered in the service of human superstition could go on and on.[9]

I mention these depressing facts to provide an unconventional answer to the familiar questions of "What's wrong with a few questionable beliefs?" or "Why worry about a little superstition?" This senseless killing makes it clear that the costs of our superstitions are real and severe, and that they are paid for not only by ourselves but by others—including other species. That our mistaken beliefs about aphrodisiacs and cancer cures have brought a number of species to the brink of extinction should challenge our own species to do better—to insist on clearer thinking and the effort required to obtain more valid beliefs about the world. "A little superstition" is a luxury we should not be allowed and can ill afford.

Of course, there are other, more conventional answers to this question of what is wrong with having a few questionable beliefs, answers that focus more on the costs to the believers themselves. The most striking are those cases we all hear about from time to time in which someone dies because a demonstrably effective medical treatment was ignored in favor of some quack therapy. Consider the fate of 7 year-old Rhea Sullins.[10] Her father was once president of the American Natural Hygiene Society, which advocates "natural" cures such as fasting and the consumption of fruit and vegetable juices in lieu of drugs and other conventional treatments. When Rhea became ill, her father put her on a water-only fast for 18 days and then on a diet of fruit juice for 17 more. She died of malnutrition at the end of this regimen. I trust the reader has read about a number of similar cases elsewhere. Is there anything more pitiful than a life lost in the service of some unsound belief? As the tragedies of people like Rhea Sullins make clear, there are undeniable benefits in perceiving and understanding the world accurately, and terrible costs in tolerating mistakes.

There is still another, less direct price we pay when we tolerate flawed thinking and superstitious belief. It is the familiar problem of the slippery slope: How do we prevent the occasional acceptance of faulty reasoning and erroneous beliefs from influencing our habits of thought more generally? Thinking straight about the world is a precious and difficult process that must be carefully nurtured. By attempting to turn our critical intelligence off and on at will, we risk losing it altogether, and thus jeopardize our ability to see the world clearly. Furthermore, by failing to fully develop our critical faculties, we become susceptible to the arguments and exhortations of those with other than benign intentions. In the words of Stephen Jay Gould, "When people learn no tools of judgment and merely follow their hopes, the seeds of political manipulation are sown."[11] As individuals and as a society, we should be less accepting of superstition and sloppy thinking, and should strive to develop those "habits of mind" that promote a more accurate view of the world.

—

PART ONE

Cognitive Determinants of Questionable Beliefs

2

Something Out of Nothing

The Misperception and Misinterpretation of Random Data

The human understanding supposes a greater degree of order and equality in things than it really finds; and although many things in nature be sui generis and most irregular, will yet invest parallels and conjugates and relatives where no such thing is.

Francis Bacon, *Novum Organum*

In 1677, Baruch Spinoza wrote his famous words, "Nature abhors a vacuum," to describe a host of physical phenomena. Three hundred years later, it seems that his statement applies as well to human nature, for it too abhors a vacuum. We are predisposed to see order, pattern, and meaning in the world, and we find randomness, chaos, and meaninglessness unsatisfying. Human nature abhors a lack of predictability and the absence of meaning. As a consequence, we tend to "see" order where there is none, and we spot meaningful patterns where only the vagaries of chance are operating.

People look at the irregularities of heavenly bodies and see a face on the surface of the moon or a series of canals on Mars. Parents listen to their teenagers' music backwards and claim to hear Satanic messages in the chaotic waves of noise that are produced.[1] While praying for his critically ill son, a man looks at the wood grain on the hospital room door and claims to see the face of Jesus; hundreds now visit the clinic each year and confirm the miraculous likeness.[2] Gamblers claim that they experience hot and cold streaks in random rolls of the dice, and they alter their bets accordingly.

The more one thinks about Spinoza's phrase, the better it fits as a description of human nature. Nature does not "abhor" a vacuum in the sense of "to loathe" or "to regard with extreme repugnance" (Webster's definition). Nature has no rooting interest. The same is largely true of human nature as well. Often we impose order even when there is no motive to do so. We do not "want" to see a man in the moon. We do not profit from the illusion. We just see it.

The tendency to impute order to ambiguous stimuli is simply built into the cognitive machinery we use to apprehend the world. It may have been bred into us through evolution because of its general adaptiveness: We can capitalize on ordered phenomena in ways that we cannot on those that are random. The predisposition to detect patterns and make connections is what leads to discovery and advance. The problem, however, is that the tendency is so strong and so automatic that we sometimes detect coherence even when it does not exist.

This touches on a theme that will be raised repeatedly in this book. Many of the mechanisms that distort our judgments stem from basic cognitive processes that are usually quite helpful in accurately perceiving and understanding the world. The structuring and ordering of stimuli is no exception. Ignaz Semmelweis detected a pattern in the occurrence of childbed fever among women who were assisted in giving birth by doctors who had just finished a dissection. His observation led to the practice of antisepsis. Charles Darwin saw order in the distribution of different species of finches in the Galapagos, and his insight furthered his thinking about evolution and natural selection.

Clearly, the tendency to look for order and to spot patterns is enormously helpful, particularly when we subject whatever hunches it generates to further, more rigorous test (as both Semmelweis and Darwin did, for example). Many times, however, we treat the products of this tendency not as hypotheses, but as established facts. The predisposition to impose order can be so automatic and so unchecked that we often end up believing in the existence of phenomena that just aren't there.

To get a better sense of how our structuring of events can go awry, it is helpful to take a closer look at a specific example. The example comes from the world of sports, but the reader who is not a sports fan need not dismay. The example is easy to follow even if one knows nothing about sports, and the lessons it conveys are quite general.

THE MISPERCEPTION OF RANDOM EVENTS

"If I'm on, I find that confidence just builds. . . . you feel nobody can stop you. It's important to hit that first one, especially if it's a swish. Then you hit another, and . . . you feel like you can do anything."

—World B. Free

I must caution the reader not to construe the sentences above as two distinct quotations, the first a statement about confidence, and the second an anti-imperialist slogan. Known as Lloyd Free before legally changing his first name, World B. Free is a professional basketball player. His statement captures a belief held by nearly everyone who plays or watches the sport of basketball, a belief in a phenomenon known as the "hot hand." The term refers to the putative tendency for success (and failure) in basketball to be self-promoting or self-sustaining. After making a couple of shots, players are thought to become relaxed, to feel confident, and to "get in a groove" such that subsequent success becomes more likely. In contrast, after missing several shots a player is considered to have "gone cold" and is thought to become tense, hesitant, and less likely to make his next few shots.

The belief in the hot hand, then, is really one version of a wider conviction that "success breeds success" and "failure breeds failure" in many walks of life. In certain areas it surely does. Financial success promotes further financial success because one's initial good fortune provides more capital with which to wheel and deal. Success in the art world promotes further success because it earns an artist a reputation that exerts a powerful influence over people's judgments of inherently ambiguous stimuli. However, there are other areas—gambling games immediately come to mind—where the belief may be just as strongly held, but where the phenomenon simply does not exist. What about the game of basketball? Does success in this sport tend to be self-promoting?

My colleagues and I have conducted a series of studies to answer this question.[3] The first step, as always, involved translating the idea of the hot hand into a testable hypothesis. If a player's performance is subject to periods of hot and cold shooting, then he should be more likely to make a shot after making his previous shot (or previous several shots) than after missing his previous shot. This implies, in turn, that a player's hits (and misses) should cluster together more than one would expect by chance. We interviewed 100 knowledgeable basketball fans to determine whether this constitutes an appropriate interpretation of what people mean by the hot hand. Their responses indicated that it does: 91% thought that a player has "a better chance of making a shot after having just made his last two or three shots than he does after having just missed his last two or three shots." In fact, when asked to consider a hypothetical player who makes 50% of his shots, they estimated that his shooting percentage would be 61% "after having just made a shot," and 42% "after having just missed a shot." Finally, 84% of the respondents thought that "it is important to pass the ball to someone who has just made several shots in a row."

To find out whether players actually shoot in streaks, we obtained the shooting records of the Philadelphia 76ers during the 1980–81 season. (The 76ers are the only team, we were told, who keep records of the *order* in which a player's hits and misses occurred, rather than simple cumulative totals.) We then analyzed these data to determine whether players' hits tended to cluster together more than one would expect by chance. Table 2.1 presents the relevant data. Contrary to the expectations expressed by our sample of fans, players were *not* more likely to make a shot after making their last one, two, or three shots than after missing their last one, two, or three shots. In fact, there was a slight tendency for players to shoot better after *missing* their last shot. They made 51% of their shots after making their previous shot, compared to 54% after missing their previous shot; 50% after making their previous two shots, compared to 53% after missing their previous two; 46% after making three in a row, compared to 56% after missing three in a row. These data flatly contradict the notion that "success breeds success" in basketball and that hits tend to follow hits and misses tend to follow misses.

We also examined each player's performance record to determine

Table 2.1 Probability of Making a Shot Conditioned on the Outcome of Previous Shots for Nine Members of the 76ers

Player	P(x|ooo)	P(x|oo)	P(x|o)	P(x)	P(x|x)	P(x|xx)	P(x|xxx)	r
C. Richardson	.50	.47	.56	.50	.49	.50	.48	−.02
J. Erving	.52	.51	.51	.52	.53	.52	.48	.02
L. Hollins	.50	.49	.46	.46	.46	.46	.32	.00
M. Cheeks	.77	.60	.60	.56	.55	.54	.59	−.04
C. Jones	.50	.48	.47	.47	.45	.43	.27	−.02
A. Toney	.52	.53	.51	.46	.43	.40	.34	−.08
B. Jones	.61	.58	.58	.54	.53	.47	.53	−.05
S. Mix	.70	.56	.52	.52	.51	.48	.36	−.02
D. Dawkins	.88	.73	.71	.62	.57	.58	.51	−.14
Mean =	.56	.53	.54	.52	.51	.50	.46	−.04

NOTE: x = a hit; o = a miss. r = the correlation between the outcomes of consecutive shots

whether the number of streaks of various lengths exceeded the number to be expected if individual shots were statistically independent. Were there more streaks of, say, 4, 5, or 6 hits in a row than chance would allow? Were there more, for example, than the number of streaks of 4, 5, or 6 heads in a row that one observes when flipping coins? The relevant statistical tests indicated that there was no such tendency. A variety of additional, more complicated, analyses led to the same conclusion: A player's performance on a given shot is independent of his performance on previous shots. (It is interesting to note that an interview with eight members of the 76ers that year revealed that these *very* players believed that they tended to shoot in streaks.)

How can we reconcile the widespread belief in the hot hand with the startling disconfirmation provided by these data? Most people's first response is to insist that the belief is valid and the data are not. The hot hand exists, the argument goes, it just did not show up in our sample of data. Perhaps it did not appear because being hot is perfectly compensated for by a hot player's tendency to take more difficult shots or receive more attention by the defensive team. The hot hand may have been masked, in other words, by other phenomena that work in the opposite direction. To test such an alternative interpretation, one must examine players' performance records when the difficulty of the shot and the amount of defensive pressure have been held constant. The most direct way of doing so is to examine players' "free-throw" records—penalty shots taken in pairs from the same distance and without defensive pressure. If success promotes success, then we would expect a player's shooting percentage on his second shot to be higher after making his first shot than after missing his first. It is not. Our analysis of two seasons of free-throw statistics by the Boston Celtics indicate that the outcomes of consecutive free throws are independent. On average, the players made 75% of their second free throws after making their first, and 75% after missing their first.

Still unconvinced, a number of people have tried to salvage their belief in the hot hand by suggesting that perhaps we have not adequately captured what is meant by the term (our initial survey results notwithstanding). Perhaps players' hits and misses do not cluster together more than do heads and tails, but, unlike coin flips, the player can predict in advance whether he is likely to make the next shot. In other words, maybe the hot hand really refers to the predictability of hits and misses rather than the clustering together of success with success and failure with failure.

This too was tested and found wanting. We asked a group of college basketball players to take 100 shots from along an arc that was everywhere an equal distance from the basket. Before each shot the players chose either a risky or conservative bet corresponding to whether they felt more or less likely to make their upcoming shot. The results indicated that the players believed that they shot in streaks: They tended to make risky bets after hitting their previous shot and conservative bets after missing their previous shot. However, there was no correlation between the outcome of consecutive shots, and hence no connection between their bets and the outcome of the next shot. In other words, not only do players fail to shoot in streaks, but they cannot predict in advance whether they are likely to make a given shot. Even according to this revised definition, the hot hand does not seem to exist.

Why Players Seem *to Shoot in Streaks.* It is important to note that although a player's performance record does not contain more or longer streaks than chance would allow, it does not mean that the player's performance is chance *determined.* It is not. Whether a given shot is hit or missed is determined by a host of non-chance factors, foremost among them being the skill of the offensive and defensive players involved. However, one factor that does *not* influence the outcome, or does not have any *predictable* influence, is the outcome of the previous shot(s). That is what our research shows.

This qualification aside, why do people believe in the hot hand when it does not exist? There are at least two possible explanations. The first involves the tendency for people's preconceptions to bias their interpretations of what they see. Because people have theories about how confidence affects performance, they may expect to see streak shooting even before watching their first basketball game. This preconception could then influence their interpretation and memory of the game's events. Streaks of successive hits or misses may stand out and be remembered, while sequences of frequent alternation between the two may go unnoticed and be forgotten. Or, the common occurrence of a shot popping out of the basket after having seemingly been made might be counted as a "near miss" if the player had made his last several shots, but as evidence of being extremely cold if the player had missed his last several shots.[4] (The biasing effects of people's theories and preconceptions is discussed more thoroughly in Chapter 4.)

A second explanation involves a process that appears to be more fundamental, and thus operates even in the absence of any explicit theories people might have. Psychologists have discovered that people have faulty intuitions about what chance sequences look like.[5] People expect sequences of coin flips, for example, to alternate between heads and tails more than they actually do. Because chance produces less alternation than our intuition leads us to expect, truly random sequences look too ordered or "lumpy." Streaks of 4, 5, or 6 heads in a row clash with our expectations about the behavior of a fair coin, although in a series of 20 tosses there is a 50–50 chance of getting 4 heads in a row, a 25 percent chance of five in a row, and a 10 percent chance of a streak of six. Because the average basketball player makes about 50% of his shots, he has a reasonably good chance of looking like he has the hot hand by making four, five, or even six shots in a row if he takes 20 shots in a game (as many players do).

To determine whether this general misconception of the laws of chance might be responsible for the belief in the hot hand, we showed basketball fans sequences of X's and O's that we told them represented a player's hits and misses in a basketball game. We also asked them to indicate whether each sequence constituted an example of streak shooting. For instance, one of the sequences was OXXXOXXXOXXOOOXOOXXOO, a sequence in which the order of hits and misses is perfectly random.* Nevertheless, 62% of our subjects thought that it constituted streak shooting.

Note that although these judgments are wrong, it is easy to see why they were made. The sequence above does *look* like streak shooting. Six of the first eight shots were hits, as were eight of the first eleven! Thus, players and fans are not mistaken in what they see: Basketball players do shoot in streaks. But the length and frequency of such streaks do not exceed the laws of chance and thus do not warrant an explanation involving factors like confidence and relaxation that comprise the mythical concept of the hot hand. Chance works in strange ways, and the mistake made by players and fans lies in how they interpret what they see.

The Clustering Illusion. The intuition that random events such as coin flips should alternate between heads and tails more than they do has been described by statisticians as a "clustering illusion." Random distributions seem to us to have too many clusters or streaks of consecutive outcomes of the same type, and so we have difficulty accepting their true origins. The term illusion is well-chosen because, like a perceptual illusion, it is not eliminated by repeated examination.[6]

Consider the picture of St. Louis's Gateway Arch depicted in Figure 2.1.[7] The arch is one of the world's largest optical illusions: It appears to be much taller than it is wide, although its height and base are equal in length. More important, even when one is told that the height and base are equal, they still do not seem to be. The illusion cannot be overcome simply by taking another look; only an objective measurement will do. (The reader is encouraged to make the necessary measurements.)

The reaction of the professional basketball world to our research on the hot hand is instructive in this regard. Do those close to the game give up their belief in the hot hand when confronted

* The sequence is random in the sense that there is no correlation between the outcomes of consecutive shots. The number of adjacent shots with the same outcome (i.e., xx or oo) in the sequence is equal to the number of adjacent shots with different outcomes (i.e., xo or ox).

with the relevant data? Hardly. Red Auerbach, the brains behind what is arguably the most successful franchise in American sports history, the Boston Celtics, had this to say upon hearing about our results: "Who is this guy? So he makes a study. I couldn't care less." Another prominent coach, Bobby Knight of the 1987 NCAA champion Indiana Hoosiers, responded by saying ". . . there are so many variables involved in shooting the basketball that a paper like this really doesn't mean anything." These comments are not terribly surprising. Because a truly random arrangement of hits and misses contains a number of streaks of various lengths, the belief in the hot hand should be held most strongly by those closest to the game. Furthermore, simply hearing that the hot hand does not exist, or merely taking another look at the game is not sufficient to disabuse oneself of this belief. It is only through the kind of objective assessment we performed that the illusion can be overcome.

Judgment by Representativeness. In the grand scheme of things, whether or not basketball players shoot in streaks is not particularly important. What is important is the suggestion—conveyed with unusual clarity by the basketball example—that people chronically misconstrue random events, and that there may be other cases in which truly random phenomena are erroneously thought to be ordered and "real." If so, we arrive at the more critical question of why people expect random sequences to alternate more than

Figure 2.1 Gateway Arch

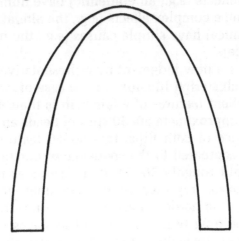

they do. Why, beyond noting that human nature abhors a vacuum, do people fall prey to the clustering illusion?

The best explanation to date of the misperception of random sequences is offered by psychologists Daniel Kahneman and Amos Tversky, who attribute it to people's tendency to be overly influenced by judgments of "representativeness."[8] Representativeness can be thought of as the reflexive tendency to assess the similarity of outcomes, instances, and categories on relatively salient and even superficial features, and then to use these assessments of similarity as a basis of judgment. People assume that "like goes with like": Things that go together should look as though they go together. We expect instances to look like the categories of which they are members; thus, we expect someone who is a librarian to resemble the prototypical librarian. We expect effects to look like their causes; thus, we are more likely to attribute a case of heartburn to spicy rather than bland food, and we are more inclined to see jagged handwriting as a sign of a tense rather than a relaxed personality.

Judgment by representativeness is often valid and helpful because objects, instances, and categories that go together often do in fact share a resemblance. Many librarians fit the prototype of a librarian—after all, the prototype came from somewhere. Causes often resemble their effects: All else being equal, "bigger" effects require "bigger" causes, complex effects stem from complex causes, etc. It is the *overapplication* of representativeness that gets us into trouble. All else is not always equal. Not all librarians are prototypical; Some big effects (e.g., an epidemic) have humble causes (e.g., a virus) and some complex effects (e.g., the alteration of a region's ecological balance) have simple causes (e.g., the introduction of a single pesticide).

It is easy to see how judgment by representativeness could contribute to the clustering illusion. In the case of coin flipping, one of the most salient features of a fair coin is the set of outcomes it produces—an approximate 50–50 split of heads and tails. In examining a sequence of coin flips, this 50–50 feature of the coin is automatically compared to the sequence of outcomes itself. If the sequence is split roughly 50–50, it strikes us as random because the outcome appears representative of a random generating process. A less even split is harder to accept. These intuitions are correct, but only in the long term. The law of averages (called the "law of large numbers" by statisticians) ensures that there will be close to a 50–50 split after a large number of tosses. After only a few tosses, however, even very unbalanced splits are quite likely. There is no "law of small numbers."

The clustering illusion thus stems from a form of over-generalization: We expect the correct proportion of heads and tails or hits and misses to be present not only globally in a long sequence, but also locally in each of its parts. A sequence like the one shown previously with 8 hits in the first 11 shots does not look random because it deviates from the expected 50–50 split. In such a short sequence, however, such a split is not terribly unlikely.

Misperceptions of Random Dispersions. The hot hand is not the only erroneous belief that stems from the compelling nature of the clustering illusion. People believe that fluctuations in the prices of stocks on Wall Street are far more patterned and predictable than they really are. A random series of changes in stock prices simply does not look random; it seems to contain enough coherence to enable a wily investor to make profitable predictions of future value from past performance. People who work in maternity wards witness streaks of boy births followed by streaks of girl births that they attribute to a variety of mysterious forces like the phases of the moon. Here too, the random sequences of births to which they are exposed simply do not look random.

The clustering illusion also affects our assessments of spatial dispersions. As noted earlier, people "see" a face on the surface of the moon and a series of canals on Mars, and many people with a religious orientation have reported seeing the likeness of various religious figures in unstructured stimuli such as grains of wood, cloud formations, even skillet burns. A particularly clear illustration of this phenomenon occurred during the latter stages of World War II, when the Germans bombarded London with their "vengeance weapons"—the V-1 buzz bomb and the V-2 rocket. During this "Second Battle of London," Londoners asserted that the weapons appeared to land in definite clusters, making some areas of the city more dangerous than others.[9] However, an analysis carried out after the war indicated that the points of impact of these weapons were randomly dispersed throughout London.[10] Although with time the Germans became increasingly accurate in terms of having a higher percentage of these weapons strike London, within this general target area their accuracy was sufficiently limited that any location was as likely to be struck as any other.

Still, it is hard not to empathize with those who thought the weapons fell in clusters. A random dispersion of events often does not look random, as Figure 2.2 indicates. This figure shows the points of impact of 67 V-1 bombs in Central London.[11] Even after learning the results of the proper statistical analysis, the points do not look randomly dispersed. The lower right quadrant looks devastated and the upper left quadrant also looks rather hard hit; the upper right and lower left quadrants, however, appear to be relatively tranquil. We can easily imagine how the presence of special target areas could have seemed to Londoners to be an "irresistible product of their own experience."

A close inspection of Figure 2.2 sheds further light on why people "detect" order in random dispersions. Imagine Figure 2.2 being bisected both vertically and horizontally, creating four quadrants of equal area. As already discussed, this results in an abundance of points in the upper-left and lower-right quadrants, and a dearth of points in the other two areas. In fact, the appropriate statistical test shows this clustering to be a significant departure from an independent, random dispersion.* In other words, when the dispersion of points is carved up in this particular way, non-chance clusters can be found. It is the existence of such clusters, no doubt, that creates the impression that the bombs did not fall randomly over London.

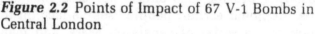

Figure 2.2 Points of Impact of 67 V-1 Bombs in Central London

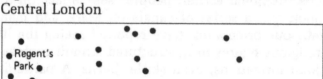

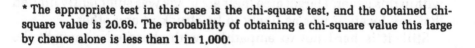

* The appropriate test in this case is the chi-square test, and the obtained chi-square value is 20.69. The probability of obtaining a chi-square value this large by chance alone is less than 1 in 1,000.

But why carve the map this way? (Indeed, why conduct the statistical analysis only on the data from this particular area of London?) Why not bisect this figure with two diagonal lines? Bisected that way, there are no significant clusters.

The important point here is that with *hindsight* it is always possible to spot the most anomalous features of the data and build a favorable statistical analysis around them. However, a properly-trained scientist (or simply a wise person) avoids doing so because he or she recognizes that constructing a statistical analysis retrospectively capitalizes too much on chance and renders the analysis meaningless. To the scientist, such apparent anomalies merely suggest hypotheses that are subsequently tested on other, *independent* sets of data. Only if the anomaly persists is the hypothesis to be taken seriously.

Unfortunately, the intuitive assessments of the average person are not bound by these constraints. Hypotheses that are formed on the basis of one set of results are considered to have been proven by those very same results. By retrospectively and selectively perusing the data in this way, people tend to make too much of apparent anomalies and too often end up detecting order where none exists.

CEMENTING OUR MISPERCEPTIONS WITH CAUSAL THEORIES

The main thrust of these examples, and the major point of this chapter, lies in the inescapable conclusion that our difficulty in accurately recognizing random arrangements of events can lead us to believe things that are not true—to believe something is systematic, ordered, and "real" when it is really random, chaotic, and illusory. Thus, one of the most fundamental tasks that we face in accurately perceiving and understanding our world—that of determining whether there is a phenomenon "out there" that warrants attention and explanation—is a task that we perform imperfectly.

Furthermore, once we suspect that a phenomenon exists, we generally have little trouble explaining *why* it exists or what it means. People are extraordinarily good at ad hoc explanation. According to past resarch, if people are erroneously led to believe that they are either above or below average at some task, they can explain either their superior or inferior performance with little difficulty.[12] If they are asked to account for how a childhood experience such as running away from home could lead during adulthood to outcomes as diverse as suicide or a job in the Peace Corps, they can do so quite readily and convincingly.[13] To live, it seems, is to explain, to justify, and to find coherence among diverse outcomes, characteristics, and causes. With practice, we have learned to perform these tasks quickly and effectively.

A dramatic illustration of our facility with ad hoc explanation comes from research on split-brain patients. In nearly all of these patients, language ability is localized in the left cerebral hemisphere, as it is in most people. The one difference between split-brain patients and other individuals is that communication between the two hemispheres is prevented in the split-brain patient because of a severed corpus callosum. Imagine, then, that two different pictures are presented to the two hemispheres of a split-brain patient. A picture of a snow-filled meadow is presented to the nonverbal right hemisphere (by presenting it in the left visual field). Simultaneously, a picture of a bird's claw is presented to the verbal left hemisphere (by presenting it in the right visual field). Afterwards, the patient is asked to select from an array of pictures the one that goes with the stimuli he or she had just seen.

What happens? The usual response is that the patient selects two pictures. In this instance, the person's left hand (controlled by the right hemisphere) might select a shovel to go with the snow scene originally presented to the right hemisphere. At the same time, the right hand (controlled by the left hemisphere) might select a picture of a chicken to go with the claw originally presented to the left hemisphere. Both responses fit the relevant stimulus because the response mode—pointing—is one that can be controlled by each cerebral hemisphere. The most interesting response occurs when the patient is asked to explain the choices he or she made. Here we might expect some difficulty because the verbal response mode is controlled solely by the left hemisphere. However, the person generally provides an explanation without hesitation: "Oh, that's easy. The chicken claw goes with the chicken and you need a shovel to clean out the chicken shed."[14] Note that the real reason the subject pointed to the shovel was not given, because the snow scene that prompted the response is inaccessible to the left hemisphere that must fashion the verbal explanation. This does not stop the person from giving a "sensible" response: He or she examines the relevant output and invents a story to account for it. It is as if the left hemisphere contains an explanation module along with, or as part of, its language center—an explanation module that can quickly and easily make sense of even the most bizarre patterns of information.[15]

This work has important implications for the ideas developed in this chapter. It suggests that once a person has (mis)identified a random pattern as a "real" phenomenon, it will not exist as a puzzling, isolated fact about the world. Rather, it is quickly explained and readily integrated into the person's pre-existing theories and beliefs. These theories, furthermore, then serve to bias the person's evaluation of new information in such a way that the initial belief becomes solidly entrenched. Indeed, as the astute reader has probably discerned, the story of our research on the hot hand is only partly a story about the misperception of random events. As the common response to our research makes clear, it is also a story about how people cling tenaciously to their beliefs in the face of hostile evidence. In Chapter 4 we return to the subject of how people's theories and expectations influence their evaluation of evidence.

MISUNDERSTANDING INSTANCES OF STATISTICAL REGRESSION

An important lesson taught in nearly every introductory statistics course is that when two variables are related, but imperfectly so, extreme values on one of the variables tend to be matched by less extreme values on the other. This is the regression effect. The heights of parents and children are related, but the relationship is not perfect—it is subject to variability and fluctuation. The same is true of a student's grades in high school and in college, a company's profits in consecutive years, a musician's performance from concert to concert, etc. As a consequence, very tall parents tend to have tall children, but not as tall (on average) as they are themselves; high school valedictorians tend to do well in college, but not as well (on average) as they did in high school; a company's disastrous years tend to be followed by more profitable ones, and its banner years by those that are less profitable. When one score is extreme, its counterpart tends to be closer to the average. It is a simple statistical fact.*

The concept of statistical regression is not terribly difficult, and most people who take a statistics course can learn to answer correctly the standard classroom questions about the heights of fathers and sons, the IQs of mothers and daughters, and the SAT scores and grade point averages of college students. People have more difficulty, however, acquiring a truly general and deep understanding that whenever *any* two variables are imperfectly correlated, extreme values of one of the variables are matched, on the average, by less extreme values of the other. Without this deeper understanding, people encounter two problems when they venture out in the world and deal with less familiar instances of regression.

First, people tend to be insufficiently conservative or "regressive" when making predictions. Parents expect a child who excels in school one year to do as well or better the following year; shareholders expect a company that has had a banner year to earn as much or more the next. In each case, the predicted performance is simply matched to initial performance without taking into account the likely effects of regression. This tendency for people's predictions to be insufficiently regressive has been implicated in the high rate of business failures, in disastrous personnel hiring decisions, and

* To understand why regression occurs, consider the relation between a person's scores on the Scholastic Aptitude Test (SAT) on two occasions. Each score can be thought of as a reflection of the person's true ability level plus some "chance error" that either improves or lowers the observed result (e.g., some answers may have been mere guesses that turned out to be correct or incorrect, the room might be unusually noisy or quiet, the person might have slept poorly or well the previous evening, etc.). A very high score is more likely to be the result of a less extraordinary true ability that has been helped by chance error, than of an even more extraordinary true ability that has been hurt by it—simply because there are more of the former than the latter (truly extraordinary ability is rare by definition). As a consequence, an extraordinarily high score at one time will tend to be less extreme the next time because it is unlikely to be paired again with such a favorable chance error. To see this more clearly, consider the case in which someone receives the highest score possible on the SAT, 800 points. Because those who receive such scores cannot score any higher the next time, their scores on a subsequent test will either be the same (the person has true 800 "aptitude") or lower (the person has less "aptitude" but was lucky the first time). On average, then, the SAT scores of those getting an 800 the first time will be lower than 800 the second. Analogous logic explains why those who do poorly the first time tend to do better the second.

in non-conservative risk estimates made by certified public accountants.

A particularly striking demonstration of people's insensitivity to regression effects was provided by an experiment in which the participants were asked to predict the grade-point averages (GPAs) of ten hypothetical students on the basis of one of two types of information.[16] Some were given information that is perfectly predictive of GPA (the targets' GPA not in "raw" form such as "4.0," but in "percentile" form such as "99th percentile"). Others were given information that was described as less diagnostic of GPA (the targets' score on a test of sense of humor). Statistical theory dictates that the better one's basis of prediction, the less regressive one needs to be. Thus, those who based their estimates on the perfectly predictive information need not have been regressive at all; in contrast, the estimates based on the students' sense of humor should have been regressed considerably (i.e., a nearly-average GPA should have been predicted for each student, regardless of the student's score on the relatively uninformative test of sense of humor).

That is not what happened. The predictions made by the respondents in the two groups were nearly identical, and only minimally regressive. Students who supposedly scored at the 90th percentile, for example, were predicted to have the same GPA, regardless of whether their percentile ranking referred to their GPA or their sense of humor. The regression effect was just not incorporated into the participants' predictions.

This tendency to make non-regressive predictions, like the clustering illusion, can be attributed to the compelling nature of judgment by representativeness. In this case, people's judgments reflect the intuition that the prediction ought to resemble the predictor as much as possible, and thus that it should deviate from the average to the same extent. The most representative son of a 6'5" father is one who is 6'5" himself—a height that is reached by only a minority of such fathers' sons. Once again, judgment by representativeness produces overgeneralization. In this case, people correctly recognize that if variables x and y are related, the value of x is helpful in predicting y, and that therefore relatively extreme values of y should be predicted for extreme values of x (e.g., we expect tall parents to have tall children, and our expectation is usually confirmed). However, this intuition is often taken too far, and the predictions made about y tend to be *as extreme* as the input variable x rather than regressed toward the average of y (e.g., few parents who are 6'5" have children as tall as they are).

A second, related problem that people have with regression is known as the regression fallacy. The regression fallacy refers to the tendency to fail to recognize statistical regression when it occurs, and instead to "explain" the observed phenomena with superfluous and often complicated causal theories. A lesser performance that follows a brilliant one is attributed to slacking off; a slight improvement in felony statistics following a crime wave is attributed to a new law enforcement policy. The regression fallacy is analogous to the clustering illusion: Both represent cases of people extracting too much meaning from chance events. By developing elaborate explanations for phenomena that are the predictable result of statistical regression, people form spurious beliefs about phenomena and causal relations in everyday life.

Examples of erroneous beliefs produced by the regression fallacy pervade many walks of life. There are many such examples in the sports world, for instance, one of the best being the widespread belief in the "*Sports Illustrated* jinx." Many individuals associated with the world of athletics believe that it is bad luck to be pictured on the cover of *Sports Illustrated* magazine.[17] Doing so is thought to spell doom for whatever success was responsible for getting oneself or one's team on the cover in the first place. Olympic medalist Shirley Babashoff, for example, reportedly balked at getting her picture taken for *Sports Illustrated* before the 1976 Olympics because of her fear of the jinx (she was eventually persuaded to pose when reminded that a cover story on Mark Spitz had not prevented him from winning seven gold medals in the previous Olympic games).

It does not take much statistical sophistication to see how regression effects may be responsible for the belief in the *Sports Illustrated* jinx. Athletes' performances at different times are imperfectly correlated. Thus, due to regression alone, we can expect an extraordinarily good performance to be followed, on the average, by a somewhat less extraordinary performance. Athletes appear on the cover of *Sports Illustrated* when they are newsworthy—i.e., when their performance is extraordinary. Thus, an athlete's superior performance in the weeks preceding a cover story is very likely to be followed by somewhat poorer performance in the weeks after. Those who believe in the jinx, like those who believe in the hot hand, are mistaken, not in what they observe, but in how they interpret what they see. Many athletes do suffer a deterioration in their performance after being pictured on the cover of *Sports Illustrated*, and the mistake lies in citing a jinx, rather than citing regression as the proper interpretation of this phenomenon.

The regression fallacy also plays a role in shaping parents' and teachers' beliefs about the relative effectiveness of reward and punishment in producing desired behavior and learning. Psychologists have known for some time that rewarding desirable responses is generally more effective in shaping behavior than punishing undesirable responses.[19] However, the average person tends to find this fact surprising, and punishment has been the preferred reinforcer for the majority of parents in both modern society[19] and in earlier periods.[20] One explanation for this discrepancy between common practice and the recommendation of psychologists is that regression effects may mask the true effectiveness of reward, and spuriously boost the apparent effectiveness of punishment. Rewards are most likely to be given following another person's extraordinarily good performance. However, regression guarantees that on the average such extraordinary performances will be followed by deterioration. The reward will thus appear ineffective or counter-productive. In contrast, because bad performances tend to be followed by improvement, any punishment meted out after a disappointing performance will appear to have been beneficial. Regression effects, in other words, serve to "punish the administration of reward, and to reward the administration of punishment."[21]

An intriguing demonstration of this phenomenon was provided by an experiment in which the participants played the role of a teacher trying to encourage a hypothetical student to arrive for school on time at 8:30 A.M.[22] A computer displayed the "student's" arrival time, which varied from 8:20 to 8:40, for each of 15 consecutive days, one at a time. On each day, the participants were allowed to praise, reprimand, or issue no comment to the student. Predictably, the participants elected to praise the student whenever he was early or on time, and to reprimand him when he was late. The student's arrival time, however, was pre-programmed and thus was not connected to the subject's response for the previous day. Nevertheless, due to regression alone, the student's arrival time tended to improve (to regress toward 8:30) after he was punished for being late, and to deteriorate (again, by regressing to 8:30) after being praised for arriving early. As a result, 70% of the subjects concluded that reprimand was more effective than praise in producing prompt attendance by the student. Regression effects teach us specious lessons about the relative effectiveness of reward and punishment.

CODA

Perhaps the reader has anticipated how the two difficulties discussed in this chapter—the clustering illusion and the regression fallacy—can combine to produce firmly-held, but questionable beliefs. In particular, they may combine to produce a variety of superstitious beliefs about how to end a bad streak or how to prolong a good one. A modest "streak" of good or bad performance may be assigned too much significance initially, making its likely regression even more salient and in even greater need of explanation. An episode I witnessed during a recent trip to Israel provides a good example.

A flurry of deaths by natural causes in the northern part of the country led to speculation about some new and unusual threat. It was not determined whether the increase in the number of deaths was within the normal fluctuation in the death rate that one can expect by chance. Instead, remedies for the problem were quickly put in place. In particular, a group of rabbis attributed the problem to the sacrilege of allowing women to attend funerals, formerly a forbidden practice. The remedy was a decree that subsequently barred women from funerals in the area. The decree was quickly enforced, and the rash of unusual deaths subsided—leaving one to wonder what the people in this area have concluded about the effectiveness of their remedy.[23]

Examples like this illustrate how the misperception of random sequences and the misinterpretation of regression can lead to the formation of superstitious beliefs. Furthermore, these beliefs and how they are accounted for do not remain as isolated convictions, but serve to bolster or create more general beliefs—in this case about the wisdom of religious officials, the "proper" role of women in society, and even the existence of a powerful and watchful god.

3

Too Much from Too Little

The Misinterpretation of Incomplete and Unrepresentative Data

They still cling stubbornly to the idea that the only good answer is a yes *answer. If they say, "Is the number between 5,000 and 10,000?" and I say* yes, *they cheer; if I say* no, *they groan, even though they get exactly the same amount of information in either case.*

John Holt, *Why Children Fail*

"I've seen it happen." "I know someone who did." "You see it all the time." What these statements have in common is that they are often cited in support of a person's beliefs. "I know horoscopes can predict the future, because I've seen it happen." "I am convinced you can cure cancer with positive thinking because I know somebody who whipped the Big C after practicing mental imagery." "Of course there's a second-year slump, you see it all the time." Sometimes these statements are offered as justifications for the speaker's own beliefs; at other times they are designed to convince the listener of some important truth. In either case, they represent a conviction that a particular belief is warranted in light of the evidence presented.

Such convictions are on the right track. Evidence of the type mentioned in these statements is certainly *necessary* for the beliefs to be true. If a phenomenon exists, there must be some positive evidence of its existence—"instances" of its existence must be visible to oneself or to others. But it should be clear that such evidence is hardly *sufficient* to warrant such beliefs. Instances of cancer remission in patients who practice mental imagery do not constitute sufficient evidence that mental imagery helps ameliorate cancer (after all, some people get better without practicing visualization and some who practice it do not get better). Unfortunately, people do not always appreciate this distinction between necessary and sufficient evidence, and they can be overly impressed by data that, at best, only *suggests* that a belief may be true. The main thrust of this chapter is that this willingness to base conclusions on incomplete or unrepresentative information is a common cause of people's questionable and erroneous beliefs. Because people often fail to recognize that a particular belief rests on inadequate evidence, the belief enjoys an "illusion of validity"[1] and is considered, not a matter of opinion or values, but a logical conclusion from the objective evidence that any rational person would make.

THE EXCESSIVE IMPACT OF CONFIRMATORY INFORMATION

Many of the beliefs we hold are about *relationships* between two variables. A belief that our dreams are prophetic is really a belief about the relationship between dream content and life events. A belief that increased military spending by the U.S. was partly responsible for the recent changes in Eastern Europe is really a belief about the linkage between U.S. defense appropriations and Soviet foreign and domestic policy. Indeed, a belief in streak shooting or the hot hand (see Chapter 2) is really a belief about the relationship between the outcomes of successive shots.

Most of these relationships, and the evidence necessary to assess their validity, can be represented in the 2×2 table familiar to most social scientists. Consider once again the common belief that infertile couples who adopt a child are subsequently more likely to conceive than those who do not. The evidence relevant to this belief can be represented in the layout at the top of page 31.

In this layout, "a" represents the number of couples who adopt and then conceive, "b" represents the number who adopt and do not conceive, etc. To adequately assess whether adoption leads to conception, it is necessary to compare the probability of concep-

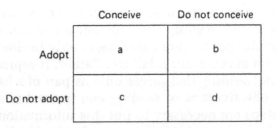

tion after adopting a/(a+b), with the probability of conception after not adopting, c/(c+d). There is now a large literature on how well people evaluate this kind of information in assessing the presence or strength of such relationships.[2] According to this research, although people sometimes perform such "covariation" tasks with considerable accuracy, there are as many or more occasions in which they perform poorly. A major culprit in people's poor performance seems to be an over-reliance on instances that confirm the existence of a relationship—cells "a" and "d." In fact, many judgments seem to be influenced almost exclusively by the information contained in cell "a." In the example above, people are most influenced by the number (and salience) of couples who adopt and subsequently conceive. In so doing, people implicitly confuse necessary and sufficient evidence: They seem to be reasoning that if there are a fair number of such positive cases, then the phenomenon must exist, or the relationship must be valid.

In one of the most direct demonstrations of this phenomenon, two groups of people were asked different versions of the same question. One group was asked to assess whether practicing the day before a tennis match is related to winning the match, and a second group was asked to assess whether practicing the day before the match is related to *losing*. The participants were asked to indicate what information, from cells a, b, c, & d above, they thought was necessary to adequately assess whether such a relationship existed. The results were quite revealing: Those testing whether practice leads to winning emphasized the number of times players practiced and won; those testing whether practicing leads to *losing* emphasized the number of times players practiced and lost.[3]

The most likely reason for the excessive influence of confirmatory information is that it is easier to deal with cognitively. Consider someone trying to determine whether cloud seeding produces rain. An instance in which cloud seeding is followed by rain is clearly relevant to the issue in question—it registers as an unambiguous success for cloud seeding. In contrast, an instance in which it rains in the absence of cloud seeding is only indirectly relevant— it is neither a success nor a failure. Rather, it represents a consequence of *not* seeding that serves only as part of a baseline against which the effectiveness of seeding can be evaluated. Additional cognitive steps are necessary to put this information to use.

Non-confirmatory information can also be harder to deal with because it is usually framed negatively (e.g., it rained when we did *not* seed), and we sometimes have trouble conceptualizing negative assertions. Compare, for example, how much easier it is to comprehend the statement "All Greeks are mortals" than "All non-mortals are non-Greeks." Thus, one would expect confirmatory information to be particularly influential whenever the disconfirmations are framed as negations. The research literature strongly supports this prediction. People are particularly swayed by the information in "cell a" of the 2×2 table discussed above when the two variables in question are "asymmetric." Asymmetric variables are those in which one level of the variable is simply the absence of the other, such as whether it rains or not, or whether a couple has adopted or not. Symmetric variables, on the other hand, are those in which both levels are defined by the *presence* of some attribute or set of attributes, like whether a person is male or female, or whether a university is publicly or privately funded. The influence of confirmatory information is particularly strong when both variables are asymmetric because in such cases three of the four cells contain information about the *nonoccurrence* of one of the variables, and, once again, such negative or null instances have been shown to be particularly difficult to process.[4] As Francis Bacon noted long ago, "It is the peculiar and perpetual error of the human understanding to be more moved and excited by affirmatives than negatives."[5]

With respect to the formation of erroneous beliefs, the implications of people's difficulties in detecting covariation should be clear. By placing too much emphasis on positive instances, people will occasionally "detect" relationships that are not there. For many of the real-world phenomena that are of greatest interest, one is sure to encounter many positive instances even when there is no relationship at all between the two variables. Although there is surely no validity to the common belief that we are more likely to need something once we have thrown it away, examples of acute longing for a discarded possession may be easy to come by. By letting necessary evidence "slip by" as sufficient evidence, people establish an insufficient threshold of what constitutes adequate support for a belief, and they run the risk of believing things that are not true.

The Tendency to Seek Confirmatory Information. People exhibit a parallel tendency to focus on positive or confirming instances when they *gather,* rather than simply evaluate, information relevant to a given belief or hypothesis. When trying to assess whether a belief is valid, people tend to seek out information that would potentially confirm the belief, over information that might disconfirm it. In other words, people ask questions or seek information for which the equivalent of a "yes" response would lend credence to their hypothesis. To illustrate this tendency, consider an experiment in which participants were given a set of four cards, each of which has a letter or number on the side facing up—A, B, 2, and 3. The participants were told that each card had a letter on one side and a number on the other, and they were asked to determine, by judiciously turning over the proper cards, whether "all cards with a vowel on one side have an even number on the other." (The reader is encouraged to take a moment to consider which cards should be turned over.)

A common response was to turn over the "A" and "2" cards. These cards were presumably chosen because of their potential to provide evidence consistent with the hypothesis. However, turning over the "2" card was uninformative because it could *only* confirm the hypothesis (a vowel on the other side would confirm it and a consonant would be irrelevant to it). The "3" card was rarely turned over, on the other hand, even though it was potentially at least as informative as any other because of its potential to invalidate the hypothesis in one quick step (a vowel on the other side guarantees that not all cards with vowels on one side have an even number on the other).[6]

This experiment is particularly informative because it makes it abundantly clear that the tendency to seek out information consistent with a hypothesis need not stem from any *desire* for the hypothesis to be true. The people in this experiment surely did not care whether all cards with vowels on one side had even numbers on the other; they sought information consistent with the hypothesis simply because it seemed to them to be the most relevant to the issue at hand.*

The intuition that positive instances are somehow more informative than disconfirmations can also be seen in the quotation by Holt that began this chapter. In that example, elementary school students who had 20 questions to identify an unknown number between 1 and 10,000 cheer when the teacher tells them "yes, it is between 5,000 and 10,000," but groan when he says "no, it is not between 5,000 and 10,000," even though the latter response is just as informative as the former. Their difficulty in recognizing the relevance of the latter response is no doubt due to the extra cognitive step that is required to put it to use—a statement that the number is not between 5,000 and 10,000 must be converted to a mental representation that it *is* between 1 and 5,000.

A number of investigators have examined the extent to which this tendency to seek out confirmatory information governs people's hypothesis-testing strategies in everyday social life.[7] In the most common procedure used in these experiments, participants are asked to determine whether a target person possesses a certain trait (e.g., extroversion) by selecting a set of questions to ask the target from a list of questions provided by the experimenter. Much of this research, as we might expect, indicates that people some-

---

* Interestingly, it has been shown that people can do much better at this task— i.e., they are more likely to turn over the correct cards, and *only* the correct cards—if it is embedded in just the right substantive context. For instance, suppose you are trying to test the rule, "everyone who drinks alcohol is over 21 years old." In front of you are 4 cards with a person's age on one side and what he or she is drinking on the other. The four cards are "drinking beer," "drinking Coke," "25 years old," and "16 years old." Which would you examine? Most people correctly turn over the cards "drinking beer" and "16 years old," and do not show a preoccupation with potentially confirmatory information by turning over the "25 years old" card. [See P. W. Cheng & K. J. Holyoak (1985) Pragmatic reasoning schemas. *Cognitive Psychology, 17,* 391–416; P. W. Cheng & K. J. Holyoak (1989) On the natural selection of reasoning theories. *Cognition, 33,* 285–313; L. Cosmides (1989) The logic of social exchange: Has natural selection shaped how humans reason? Studies with the Wason selection task. *Cognition, 31,* 187–276.]

This improved performance is not obtained by embedding the task in just *any* context, but mainly in those that invoke the idea of "permission"—e.g., a person must be over 21 years old to be permitted to drink alcohol. The fact that there are *some* domains in which people are not preoccupied with confirmations, of course, does not undermine the general finding that people often test their hypotheses by seeking out potentially confirmatory information.

times perform quite well at this task. They seem sensitive to which questions discriminate most effectively between, say, introverts and extroverts, and they often prefer to ask questions that are the most discriminative.[8]

Nevertheless, it is also clear that people sometimes perform this task rather poorly by being too inclined to ask questions for which a positive response would confirm the hypothesis.[9] When trying to determine if a person is an extrovert, for example, people prefer to ask about the ways in which the target person is outgoing; when trying to determine if a person is an introvert, people are more inclined to ask about the ways in which the target is socially inert.

Although a tendency to ask such one-sided questions does not guarantee that the hypothesis will be confirmed, it can produce an erroneous sense of confirmation for a couple of reasons. First, the specific questions asked can sometimes be so constraining that *only* information consistent with the hypothesis is likely to be elicited. For example, in one widely-cited study,[10] one of the questions that the participants were fond of asking when trying to determine if a person was an extrovert was: "What would you do if you wanted to liven things up at a party?" A question such as this one is clearly biased against disconfirmation: Even the most inner-directed individual has been to a party or two and can at least *discuss* how to liven one up if explicitly asked to do so. By asking such constraining questions, it is difficult for anyone, including introverts, not to sound extroverted. In fact, the experimenters in this study tape-recorded the responses of the target individuals who were asked the questions selected by the "interviewer" subjects. These tapes were then played for a group of judges. The targets who were asked questions by interviewers who were testing whether they were extroverted impressed the judges as being more extroverted than those who were asked questions by interviewers who were testing whether they were introverted. In other words, the participants tended to ask questions that produced a spurious confirmation of their initial hypotheses.

Furthermore, even if such constraining questions are not asked, a tendency to ask confirmatory questions can still produce a spurious sense of confirmation if the likelihood of a positive response to the question is high whether or not the hypothesis is true. Suppose, for example, that you want to determine if an individual is introverted, and so you ask about a characteristic that might confirm your hypothesis: "Do you sometimes feel that it is hard for you to really let yourself go at a party?" The person's response is unlikely to be truly informative because most people, extroverts as well as introverts, would answer the same way—yes, *sometimes* it is hard to *really* let go. For the sake of illustration, suppose that 50% of the people in the world are introverts and 50% are extroverts. Suppose also that 90% of the introverts would say that it is hard for them to really let themselves go, and that 70% of the *extroverts* would also say so. Under these conditions, the question asked is indeed diagnostic of introversion (90% of the introverts would respond affirmatively as opposed to 70% of the extroverts), and it is hardly constraining (one can easily respond by saying, "No, I don't find it hard to let myself go."). Nevertheless, because an affirmative response is likely whether the hypothesis is true (90%) or false (70%), one is likely to conclude too often that the person is introverted. In this case, one would do so 80% of the time—(90% + 70%)/2—when the actual likelihood that a person is introverted given a positive response to this question is 56%—(90%/2)/[(90% + 70%)/2].

A similar tendency to seek out hypothesis-confirming evidence seems to exist when people search their own memories for relevant evidence, rather than asking questions of another person. In one study, participants read a story about a woman who behaved in a number of prototypically introverted and extroverted ways.[11] Two days later, half of the participants were asked to assess the woman's suitability for a job in real estate sales (a job thought to demand considerable extroversion) and the other half were asked to assess her fitness for a job as a librarian (a job thought to demand introversion). As part of their assessment, the participants were asked to recall examples of the woman's introversion and extroversion. The particular job the woman was seeking strongly affected the evidence that the participants could recall: Those asked to assess the woman's suitability for an extroverted job recalled more examples of the woman's extroversion; those asked to assess her suitability for an introverted job recalled more examples of her introversion.

Still further evidence that people tend to seek out confirmatory evidence comes from research that was designed to investigate a very different problem—namely, the psychological basis of perceived similarity.[12] As part of this research, one group of participants was asked which two countries are more similar to one another, East Germany and West Germany, or Sri Lanka and Nepal. Most of them said that East and West Germany are more similar. A second group of participants, however, was asked which two countries are more *different* from one another, East Germany and West Germany, or Sri Lanka and Nepal. The majority likewise said that East and West Germany are more dissimilar. This leads to the seemingly impossible conclusion that East and West Germany are both more similar and more dissimilar than Sri Lanka and Nepal. How can that be?

The accepted interpretation of these results is that judgments of similarity are primarily determined by features that two entities share. Because people know more about East and West Germany than they do about Sri Lanka and Nepal (people in the Western world, that is), they can think of more things they have in common, and so they seem more similar. Judgments of dissimilarity, on the other hand, are primarily determined by features that are *not* shared by the two entities—i.e., by those features that are *distinctive* to one or the other. Again, because people know more about East and West Germany than Sri Lanka and Nepal, it is easier to think of ways in which they differ from one another, and so they are seen as more dissimilar as well.

With respect to the focus of this chapter, it seems that once again people engage in a search for evidence that is biased toward confirmation. Asked to assess the similarity of two entities, people pay more attention to the ways in which they are similar than to the ways in which they differ. Asked to assess dissimilarity, they become more concerned with differences than with similarities. In other words, when testing a hypothesis of similarity, people look for evidence of similarity rather than dissimilarity, and when testing a hypothesis of dissimilarity, they do the opposite. The relationship one perceives between two entities, then, can vary with the precise form of the question that is asked.

THE PROBLEM OF HIDDEN OR ABSENT DATA

The research described thus far indicates that we do not adequately assess the validity of our hypotheses or beliefs because we do not fully utilize all of the information available to us. As we shall see, this tendency is compounded by the fact that there are many times when important information is simply unavailable.

To make this clear, consider an expansion of the 2x2 table discussed earlier. In this expansion, depicted in Figure 3.1, the x-axis represents performance on some "selection" criterion and the y-axis represents performance on some "outcome" criterion. For example, the x and y axes could represent the performance of job applicants in interviews and their subsequent performance on the job, high-school students' SAT scores and their college GPAs, or scientists' grant-evaluation scores and the subsequent success of their research programs.[13]

Each of the points in Figure 3.1 represents an individual's performance on the selection and outcome criteria. In this case, there is a substantial correlation between people's performances on the two criteria, as seen by the lower-left to upper-right drift of the points (captured by the tilted ellipse). Note that some performances on the selection criterion are sufficiently high to warrant predictions of subsequent success and to earn admission to some special status—those who excel in an interview gain employment, and those who score high on the SAT are admitted to exclusive colleges. Similarly, some performances on the outcome criterion are sufficiently high that they are considered successes—new employees who work out well and contribute to the organization, or college

Figure 3.1 Initial Selection and Subsequent Performance

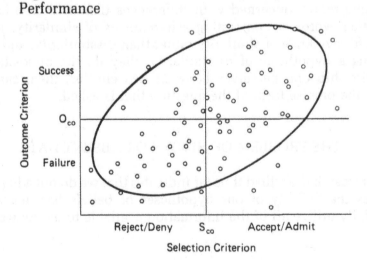

students who study hard, get good grades, and contribute to the intellectual atmosphere of their colleges.

The vertical line at S_{co} represents the cutoff between those scores on the selection criterion that warrant predictions of future success and those that warrant predictions of failure. The horizontal line at O_{co} represents the cutoff between actual successes and failures. The four quadrants that emerge comprise the familiar 2x2 table that permits an assessment of whether predicted success or failure is related to actual success or failure. In other words, does the selection test predict actual performance? To answer this question, it is necessary to compare the success rate among those for whom success was predicted (the two quadrants on the right) with the success rate among those for whom it was not (the two on the left).

The important point here is that many times we *cannot* carry out such a comparison even if we appreciate how important such a comparison is. Those who do not score high enough on the selection criterion are not allowed to perform, and so we cannot determine how many of them would have succeeded. Those who create bad impressions in interviews do not land jobs, those with low SAT scores do not go to elite colleges, and those with poor grant scores are confined to nickel-and-dime research. Without information about how members of the "rejected" group would have performed had they not been rejected, the only way to evaluate the effectiveness of the selection test is to look at the success rate among those who are "accepted"—a comparison that is inadequate to do the job. If the base rate of success is high—i.e., if there would have been a large number of successes even among those who fell below the cutoff on the selection criteria—one can erroneously conclude that the selection criterion is effective even if it is completely unrelated to performance. Such erroneous conclusions are particularly likely whenever the talent pool of applicants is sufficiently strong, so that nearly everyone—regardless of their performance on the selection criterion—would succeed. If only the best people apply to a company, school, or funding organization, the "gatekeepers" in such institutions are likely to look around at all of their successful selection decisions and conclude that their procedures for hiring employees, admitting students, and disseminating funds are extremely effective. However, without knowing more about how well the rejected applicants would have performed, such conclusions rest on shaky ground.

Another factor that can make a selection criterion appear spuri-ously effective is that the mere fact of being in the "accepted" group can give a person a competitive advantage over those who were rejected. Some of those who receive research grants go on to have more productive careers than some who were less fortunate, not because their research ideas were any better, but because the grant enabled them to examine their ideas more thoroughly. Some of the students who score well enough on the SAT to be admitted to a prestigious college go on to become professionally successful men and women partly because of the superior intellectual environment their high scores allowed them to experience.

The hazards of drawing conclusions solely from the performance of those in the accepted group can be seen most clearly by comparing Figure 3.1 with Figure 3.2. In Figure 3.1 the data from all four cells of the 2x2 table are presented—the subsequent performances of those who were accepted as well as the performances that *would have been turned in* by those below the cut-off had they not been rejected. Furthermore, because everyone in this depiction is "admitted," there are no competitive advantages enjoyed by a subset of the population. In Figure 3.2, however, the picture is much different. In this, more realistic depiction, information about how well the rejected group would have performed is absent, so there is no baseline against which to evaluate the effectiveness of the selection criterion. In addition, the competitive advantage that stems from being in the accepted group serves to artificially raise each person's score on the outcome criterion. This is depicted by the upward shift in all of the points (from the white to the black dots), and an upward shift in the half-ellipse that tracks these points.

The net effect of these two processes is that nearly all of the observations fall in the upper-right quadrant, representing predicted successes that are vindicated by actual success. The observations that might have fallen in the two lefthand quadrants are simply unavailable, and many of those that would have fallen in the lower-right area have been artificially shifted into the upper-right, success/success quadrant. In the specific case represented in Figures 3.1 and 3.2, the result is that an effective selection criterion appears to be even more effective than it actually is. In other cases, the same processes can make a completely worthless selection criterion appear to have some value.

The scheme depicted in Figures 3.1 and 3.2, it should be noted, also clarifies when decision makers will *avoid* making overly-optimistic assessments of their ability to make accurate selection decisions. In particular, decision makers may be immune to the "illusion of validity" in domains in which they are not shielded from the subsequent performances of those they rejected. Sometimes our decision to reject someone comes back to haunt us. Baseball executives who underestimate a player's potential and trade him to another team do not remain blissfully unaware of their misjudgment: The mistake becomes apparent when the player returns as an opponent and torments his former team. Similarly, talent scouts in the music industry are often haunted by the meteoric rise to fame of someone they thought "didn't have it." Research has shown that decision-makers' assessments of their abilities are fairly well-calibrated in domains such as these in which "the cream always rises to the top" and the decision maker becomes aware of his or her mistakes.[14]

The scheme depicted in Figures 3.1 and 3.2 is really quite general, and applies not only to the evaluation of selection criteria, but to the assessment of policy more generally. A fundamental difficulty with effective policy evaluation is that we rarely get to observe what would have happened if the policy had not been put into

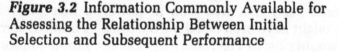

Figure 3.2 Information Commonly Available for Assessing the Relationship Between Initial Selection and Subsequent Performance

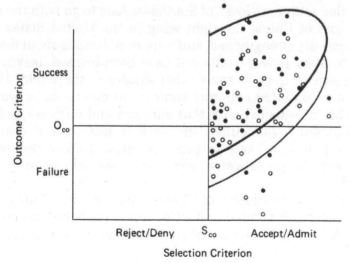

Outcome Criterion

Success

O_{co}

Failure

Reject/Deny S_{co} Accept/Admit

Selection Criterion

effect. Policies are not implemented as controlled experiments, but as concerted actions. Not knowing what would have happened under a different policy makes it enormously difficult to distinguish positive or negative outcomes from good or bad strategies. If the base rate of success is high, even a dubious strategy will seem wise; if the base rate is low, even the wisest strategy can seem foolish. Returning to baseball for just a moment, this idea explains why late-inning "relief" pitchers tend to make or break managers' careers. If a manager without a good reliever goes to his bullpen late in the game and his team's lead is squandered, the fans bemoan his decision to change pitchers. If, mindful of his ineffective bullpen, he leaves a tiring pitcher in the game too long and loses, he is criticized for that too. It is hard to look good when you only have two options and both of them are bad.

This idea is illustrated even more clearly by considering a specific policy that is widely viewed as a fiasco—the United States' military intervention in Viet Nam. The actions taken there were clearly disastrous: After the loss of more than 50,000 American lives and incalculable devastation to Southeast Asia, Viet Nam now exists as a unified, communist country. However, it is interesting to speculate about what lessons we would have learned and whether we would have been any more pleased with the outcome had we employed a different strategy. At least from the standpoint of the Democratic Party that was then in power, a non-interventionist strategy might have been equally disastrous. A unified, communist regime would exist in Viet Nam, a Democratic administration would be saddled with the "loss" of Southeast Asia to go with the party's earlier loss of China, the right wing in the United States would be enormously strengthened, and important lessons about the limits of our military power would not have been learned, leaving us to lose American lives in some other theater of the world. Had we pursued a non-interventionist strategy, in other words, we might be terribly dissatisfied with *that* outcome and wish we had acted more forcefully. Sometimes the deck is just stacked against us and any policy is likely to produce unsatisfactory results. That can be hard to see, however, when only one policy can be implemented.

The problem of hidden or absent data has also clouded many people's thoughts about the effectiveness of the Scholastic Aptitude Test (SAT) in predicting students' success in college. The SAT has been criticized as a poor predictor of college success because the relationship between SAT scores and college GPAs among students in most universities is quite modest (the correlation coefficient is generally about 0.2). Note, however, that students with very different SAT scores tend not to enroll in the same schools: Those with high scores attend the most prestigious institutions and those with lower scores attend less renowned schools. Thus, students with very different SAT scores are never assessed together, and so the correlation between SAT scores and GPAs within a university cannot tell us how students with very different SAT scores would perform in the same environment. All that the modest correlation between SAT's and GPA's can tell us, then, is that the SAT does not make very fine discriminations—someone who gets, say, a 610 cannot be counted on to get a higher GPA than someone who receives a 570.

But perhaps the test can make gross discriminations with greater accuracy. Maybe someone who gets a 610 can indeed be counted on to get better grades than someone who receives a 410. If so, we would expect there to be a much higher correlation between SAT's and GPAs among a group of students with a wide range of SAT scores. There is. There are a few schools that have an open enrollment (and thus do not admit only the best prospects), but that, due to their location, still attract many students with very high SATs. Among these more heterogeneous students, correlations as high as .6 to .7 have been observed.[15] Students with high SAT scores are indeed more likely to do well in college than those with low SAT scores. By looking only at the restricted data from schools with the usual patterns of enrollment, many people have failed to recognize the true effectiveness of the SAT (in terms of making gross discriminations between applicants). The problem of absent data has thus served to misdirect much of the discussion of whether to use the SAT in admissions decisions.*

Moving away from the domain of policy evaluation, it should be clear that the problem of hidden or absent data also affects the

---

* Note that this discussion addresses only one of the criticisms of the SAT exam—that it supposedly does not adequately predict college GPA. As a proper analysis of the problem makes clear, this criticism is misguided. However, there are other criticisms of the SAT exam that this analysis does not address, such as whether the test is culturally biased and whether college GPA is really the most desireable measure of college performance.

kinds of inferences we draw and the beliefs we have about everyday social life. Oftentimes, the lifestyles we lead, the roles we play, and the positions we occupy in a social network deny us access to important classes of information and thus distort our view of the world. At large research universities where there is less informal contact between students and faculty than one would like, professors learn early on that unless they are careful, it is easy to be exposed mainly to the alibis and complaints of the most difficult students and rarely see the more successful and more pleasant students who make teaching so gratifying. Similarly, the experience of therapists who treat alcoholics appears to predispose many of them to expect the worst from even the most temperate drinking. We can occasionally overcome our limited exposure to relevant data, but doing so is difficult: It requires that we not only recognize the existence of a class of information to which we have not been exposed, but that we accurately characterize what that information is like.

SELF-FULFILLING PROPHECIES
AS A SPECIAL CASE OF THE HIDDEN DATA PROBLEM

There is a special version of the hidden data problem that arises whenever our expectations lead us to act in ways that fundamentally change the world that we observe. When this happens, we often accept what we observe at face value, with little consideration of how things might have been different if we had acted differently. Sociologist Robert Merton used the term "self-fulfilling prophecy" to describe this phenomenon, and he gave the example of how a false rumor of a bank's insolvency can generate a panic that creates the very insolvency that was initially feared.[16]

There are several aspects of self-fulfilling prophecies that warrant further analysis and discussion. First, because self-fulfilling prophecies have received so much attention, there is some danger that their impact can be exaggerated. Not all prophecies are self-fulfilling. As psychologist Robyn Dawes has noted, some can even be self-negating, as when a reckless driver claims that "nothing bad can happen to me."[17] For a prophecy to be self-fulfilling, there must be some mechanism that translates the expectation into confirmatory action.

An informative example of the limits of self-fulfilling prophecies is provided by an experiment in which the participants played numerous rounds of a standard "prisoner's dilemma" game.* After hearing the rules of the game, the participants were asked to articulate their opinion of the proper orientation toward the game. Some ("cooperators") stated that they thought the point of the game was to cooperate with one's partner in order to maximize their joint outcomes. Others ("competitors") said that they thought the purpose was to compete strategically with one's partner in order to maximize one's own individual outcomes.

The cooperators and competitors were not equally successful in having their views of the game confirmed. If a cooperator was paired with another cooperator, they quickly began making mutually beneficial, cooperative moves. When paired with a competitor, the cooperator was forced into more competitive actions in order to avoid consistent losses. Competitive players, in contrast, always ended up in a cut-throat game: When paired with another competitor, the game quickly settled into an internecine struggle; when

---

* The Prisoner's Dilemma is the most widely researched experimental game used to study conflict and "social dilemmas." In the original version, two partners have committed a crime and are interrogated separately by the district attorney (A. Rapoport & A. Chammah [1965] *Prisoner's dilemma.* Ann Arbor: University of Michigan Press). The DA has only enough evidence to convict the two suspects of a lesser offense, so he offers each a chance to confess privately in order to "get the goods" on the other. If one suspect confesses and the other does not, the one who confesses will be granted immunity and the one who does not will receive a harsh sentence of, say, 10 years. If neither confesses, they each receive the penalty for the lesser offense—say, 1 year. If both confess, they each receive a moderate penalty of 5 years.

The participants in a Prisoner's Dilemma experiment must decide whether they would confess (and thus "defect" from or compete with their partner) or not (and thus cooperate with their partner). Note that it is always better for a person to defect, regardless of what his or her partner does (doing so gives the player 5 years rather than 10 if his or her partner confesses, and 0 years rather than 1 if his or her partner does not confess). However, if both players confess, their fate (5 years each) is clearly much worse than if both do not confess (1 year each).

Subsequent versions of the Prisoner's Dilemma Game have maintained its basic structure but have changed the scenario and the "payoffs" so that participants can play many rounds of the game (with the same or different partners) and gain or lose different sums of money as a function of the combination of "cooperative" or "competitive" choices made.

paired with a cooperator, their own actions forced the potential cooperator to become competitive out of self-defense.[18] Thus, because competitive behavior creates more of a demand for the other person to respond in kind than does cooperation, a competitive person's belief that the world is full of selfish opportunists will almost always be confirmed, whereas the less gloomy orientation of cooperative individuals will not. Sadly, negative prophecies are often more readily fulfilled.

Another, often-neglected point about the limits of self-fulfilling prophecies is that they usually serve to exaggerate a belief that contains a kernel of truth, rather than create one that is completely erroneous. Rumors of insolvency generally plague banks that are in fact having difficulty. Suppositions that a student might be exceptionally gifted are generally made about students who do in fact have superior intellectual talent. This point often goes unnoticed because of the logic behind the experiments that have examined self-fulfilling prophecies: To show that a teacher's expectations can influence students' achievement, for example, it is imperative that the teacher be given different expectations about students who are in fact equal in achievement. Any subsequent differences in performance can then be confidently attributed to the teacher's expectations. In the real world, however, expectations are not generated randomly, but by cues from the environment. Thus, self-fulfilling prophecies generally turn little effects into big effects, rather than create effects from scratch.

A final point to be made about self-fulfilling prophecies is that there are really two kinds—true self-fulfilling prophecies and *seemingly*-fulfilled prophecies. True self-fulfilling prophecies are like those already discussed in which a person's expectation elicits the very behavior that was originally anticipated. Behaving in an unfriendly and defensive manner because you think someone is hostile will generally produce the very hostility that was originally feared. Seemingly-fulfilled prophecies, on the other hand, refer to expectations that alter another person's world, or limit another's responses, in such a way that it is difficult or impossible for the expectations to be *disconfirmed*. Thus, the expectancy is confirmed, not by the target person actively conforming to some expectancy, but by the target having little opportunity to disconfirm it. If someone thinks that I am unfriendly, for example, I might have little chance to correct that misconception because he or she may steer clear of me. The absence of friendliness on my part could then be construed as unfriendliness. When little-league baseball players are thought to be incompetent, they are only allowed to play where the ball is rarely hit (for little leaguers, in right field), and thus they have few opportunities to overcome their unfortunate reputation. The continued absence of any positive contributions can then easily be mistaken for an absence of talent rather than an absence of opportunity.

This type of expectancy effect is obviously a special case of the hidden data problem described above. A perceiver's expectation can cause him or her to behave in such a way that certain behaviors by the target person cannot be observed, making what is observed a biased and misleading indicator of what that person is like. The employers, college admissions officers, and grant review panelists discussed earlier are all potential victims of seemingly-fulfilled prophecies: Their own actions guarantee that they will rarely receive a challenge to their negative assessments of job applicants, potential students, and research proposals. The research on people's hypothesis-testing strategies that was discussed earlier also provides a good example of a seemingly-fulfilled prophecy: By asking people they suspected to be extroverts what they do to liven things up at a party, one compels them to talk about their most sociable leanings and thus is prevented from observing much in the way of introversion.

The existence of seemingly-fulfilled prophecies implies that negative first impressions should generally be more stable (i.e., less subject to change) than positive first impressions. If we find another person unpleasant initially, we try to avoid that person as much as possible, and he or she will have a difficult time disabusing us of our negative assessment. If we like another person, on the other hand, we seek out his or her company and thereby give him or her ample opportunity to ruin our hopes and expectations.[20] This can sound rather grim, but it does have a positive flip-side: It suggests that our negative assessments of other people are less likely than our positive assessments to be correct, and we should give our foes another chance.

From the perspective of trying to understand questionable and erroneous beliefs, it should be clear that the impact of self-fulfilling prophecies is similar to that of the confirmatory search strategies and hidden data problem described earlier. All of these processes serve to provide us with incomplete and unrepresentative samples of information from which we draw conclusions and evaluate beliefs. Unless we recognize these sources of systematic distortion and make sufficient adjustments for them, we will surely end up believing some things that just aren't so.

4

Seeing What We Expect to See

The Biased Evaluation of Ambiguous and Inconsistent Data

I'll see it when I believe it.

Slip of the tongue by psychologist Thane Pittman

Life is a series of trade-offs. For every benefit gained, there is usually some cost. If we increase our speed on most tasks, we generally lose accuracy; to increase precision, we must slow down. If a successful business expands, it is likely to suffer a decline in the informality and access to the boss that may have been a large part of its initial success. Human beings are blessed with unsurpassed intelligence, but biologists tell us that getting the large brains responsible for that intelligence through the narrow birth canal requires that we be born prematurely and that we suffer an unusually long infancy of uncommon helplessness as a result.[1]

Trade-offs are apparent in everyday judgment and reasoning as well. When making judgments and decisions, we employ a variety of informal rules and strategies that simplify fundamentally difficult problems and allow us to solve them without excessive effort and stress. These strategies are generally effective, but the benefit of simplification is paid for at the cost of occasional *systematic* error. There is, in other words, an ease/accuracy trade-off in human judgment.

The tendency to make judgments by "representativeness" that

[49]

was described in Chapter 2 is a good example. Among other things, to reiterate, representativeness leads to the belief that causes resemble their effects: Big effects should have big causes, complex effects should have complex causes, and so on. This assumption contains some truth, and so it generally facilitates causal reasoning by narrowing the number of potential causes to consider. But not all causes resemble their effects (again, tiny viruses cause enormous epidemics), and an over-reliance on this assumption can lead people to ignore important causal relations and to "detect" some that are not there. Thus, the very same principle that permits us to make judgments with apparent ease and considerable success can also be responsible for some of our systematic errors.

No feature of human judgment and reasoning illustrates this trade-off of advantage and disadvantage better than the tendency for our expectations, preconceptions, and prior beliefs to influence our interpretation of new information. When examining evidence relevant to a given belief, people are inclined to see what they expect to see, and conclude what they expect to conclude. Information that is consistent with our pre-existing beliefs is often accepted at face value, whereas evidence that contradicts them is critically scrutinized and discounted. Our beliefs may thus be less responsive than they should to the implications of new information.

APPROPRIATE AND INAPPROPRIATE BIAS

At first blush, such uneven treatment of new information strikes most people as completely unjustified and potentially pernicious. It conjures up images, for example, of closed-minded people disregarding a person's individual characteristics in deference to some invalid ethnic, gender, or occupational stereotype; it brings to mind examples of individuals and groups blindly adhering to outmoded dogma. To be sure, the tendency to evaluate evidence in a biased manner can have deleterious consequences and, as we shall see, it serves to bolster a great many questionable and erroneous beliefs. On closer inspection, however, the question of how impartial we should be in evaluating information that confirms or refutes our preconceptions is far more subtle and complicated than most people realize.

The issue is complex because it is also inappropriate and misguided to go through life weighing all facts equally and reconsidering one's beliefs anew each time an antagonistic fact is encountered. If a belief has received a lifetime of support, it is perfectly justified to be skeptical of an observation or report that calls the belief into question, but to readily accept evidence that supports its validity. The skepticism of scientists who doubted the reports of cold fusion was entirely appropriate because it was based upon a solid theoretical foundation that specified what events are likely and unlikely, possible and impossible. Each of us is equally justified in looking askance at claims about UFO's, levitations, and miracle cancer cures. Events that challenge a broadly-based and time-tested body of knowledge should be treated cautiously; those that fit with pre-existing knowledge can be accepted more freely. To clarify with a rather extreme example, consider two headlines: "Soviet Republic Votes for Secession," and "Statue of Elvis found on Mars." Surely we need not treat the two reports with equal seriousness.

As soon as we accept the legitimacy of treating new information unevenly, however, we worry about it being taken too far. How do we distinguish between the legitimate skepticism of those who scoffed at cold fusion, and the stifling dogma of the seventeenth-century clergymen who, doubting Galileo's claim that the earth was not the center of the solar system, put him under house arrest for the last eight years of his life? In part, the answer lies in the distinction between skepticism and closed-mindedness. Many scientists who were skeptical about cold fusion nevertheless tried to replicate the reported phenomenon in their own labs; Galileo's critics refused to look at the pertinent data. Equally important, however, is the foundation on which a person's pre-existing beliefs and theories rest. We are justified in allowing our beliefs and theories to influence our assessments of new information in direct proportion to how plausible and well-substantiated they are in the first place. One need not feel concerned about quickly dismissing a purported levitation because our faith in the inexorable effect of gravity has been built up by a lifetime of consistent experience. Well-supported beliefs and theories have earned a bit of inertia, and should not be easily modified or abandoned because of isolated antagonistic "facts." In marked contrast, many ethnic, gender, and occupational stereotypes are particularly troublesome because they often rest on such flimsy or non-existent evidence to begin with.

All of this is to say that the question of how even-handed we should be in evaluating evidence is rather complex. Not all bias is a bad thing; indeed, a certain amount is absolutely essential.

The power and flexibility with which we reason depends upon our ability to use context, generic knowledge, and pre-existing information to disambiguate and extract meaning from new information—and, to some degree, to bias our interpretation of evidence. Consider, for example, the newspaper headline, "Mondale's offensive looks hard to beat."[2] Nothing in the words themselves allows us to determine whether it is referring to Mondale's campaign strategy or to his physical appearance. Nevertheless, our pre-existing knowledge of what is and is not plausible allows us to quickly and effortlessly draw the correct conclusion.

Note, however, that it has proven extremely difficult to program even the most advanced computers to make such "simple" inferences.[3] Thus, without this ability to use context and expectations to "go beyond the information given,"[4] we would be unintelligent in the same way that computers with superior compututional capacity are unintelligent. As dysfunctional as they may be on occasion, our theories, preconceptions, and "biases" are what make us smart.

THE PATH OF BIAS

Ambiguous Information. Our expectations can bias our evaluation of new information in two ways, depending largely on whether or not the information is ambiguous. Truly ambiguous information is often simply perceived in a way that fits our preconceptions. Consider how the stimulus "ℬ" is differently perceived in the context of "12, ℬ, 14" versus "A, ℬ, C." Similarly, the same smile can look warm and friendly when it is worn by someone we like, but smug or sinister when worn by someone we consider untrustworthy.

A particularly interesting example of how our expectations can influence what we see involves people's negative associations to the color black and how they can influence the perceived aggressiveness of someone wearing black clothing. The "bad guys" have worn black hats since the invention of motion pictures, and psychological research has shown that film directors who employ this tactic are capitalizing on a very basic psychological phenomenon: Surveys conducted in a wide range of cultures reveal that black is seen as the color of evil and death in virtually all corners of the world.

This negative association leads to several interesting results in the domain of professional sports. When my colleague Mark Frank and I asked a group of respondents to rate the appearance of professional football and hockey uniforms, they judged those that were at least half black to be the most "bad," "mean," and "aggressive" looking. These perceptions influence, in turn, how specific actions performed by black-uniformed teams are viewed. We showed groups of trained referees one of two videotapes of the same aggressive play in a football scrimmage, one with the aggressive team wearing white and one with it wearing black. The referees who saw the black-uniformed version rated the play as much more aggressive and more deserving of a penalty than those who saw the white-uniformed version. The referees "saw" what this common negative association led them to expect to see. As a result of this bias, it is not surprising to learn that teams that wear black uniforms in these two sports have been penalized significantly more than average during the last two decades.[5]

Unambiguous Information. Our expectations can also slant our evaluations of unambiguous information, but in a rather different manner. In evaluating more clear-cut information, our perceptions are rarely so distorted that information that completely contradicts our expectations is seen as supportive. Nor do we simply ignore contradictory information and pay attention only to that which supports our preconceptions. Rather, our expectations have their effects through the way we subject inconsistent information to more critical scrutiny than consistent information; through the way we seek out additional information only when the initial outcomes are inconsistent with our expectations; and—more generally— through the way we assign meaning to new information. People place a premium on being rational and cognitively consistent, and so they are reluctant to simply disregard pertinent evidence in order to see what they expect to see and believe what they expect to believe. Instead, people subtly and carefully "massage" the evidence to make it consistent with their expectations. (A similar argument is made in Chapter 5 about the biasing effects of our *motivations*).

This point is effectively illustrated by a study in which proponents and opponents of the death penalty were exposed to evidence concerning the deterrent efficacy of capital punishment.[6] Both groups read summaries of the procedures, results, and critiques of two relevant studies. One study provided evidence supporting the deterrent efficacy of capital punishment and the other provided evidence against. For half the participants, the study supporting capital punishment compared homicide rates in the same state before and after capital punishment, and the study refuting its deterrent efficacy compared homicide rates in different states, some with capital punishment and others without. For the other participants, the type of studies supporting and refuting capital punishment was reversed. Thus, for both proponents and opponents of capital punishment, half of them had their expectations supported by one type of study and opposed by the other, and the other half were exposed to the opposite pattern of data.

The results of this experiment were striking. The participants considered the study that provided evidence consistent with their prior beliefs—regardless of what type of study that was—to be a well-conducted piece of research that provided important evidence concerning the effectiveness of capital punishment. In contrast, they uncovered numerous flaws in the research that contradicted their initial beliefs. The net effect of these two results was that the participants' attitudes became polarized: Exposure to a mixed body of evidence made both sides even *more* convinced of the fundamental soundness of their original beliefs.

Now consider what the participants in this experiment did *not* do. They did not miscontrue the evidence against their position as being more favorable than it really was. They correctly saw hostile findings as hostile findings. Nor did the participants simply ignore these negative results. Instead, they carefully scrutinized the studies that produced these unwanted and unexpected findings, and came up with criticisms that were largely appropriate. Rather than ignoring outright the evidence at variance with their expectations, the participants cognitively transformed it into evidence that was considered relatively uninformative and could be assigned little weight. Thus, the participants' expectations had their effect not through a simple process of ignoring inconsistent results, but through a more complicated process that involved a fair amount of cognitive effort.

This point is illustrated even more directly by research conducted in my own laboratory on the tendency of gamblers to evaluate outcomes in a biased manner.[7] This research began with the question of why gamblers persist in such an unrewarding enterprise. Why do gamblers believe, despite all their previous losses, that success is just around the corner? One might have predicted that they do so by remembering their successes and forgetting or repressing their failures. However, the actual state of affairs is more complicated. Gamblers do revise their personal histories of success and failure, but they do so in a way that is more subtle, and rather interesting.

The most direct evidence for this claim comes from a study in which people who had bet on professional football games provided tape-recorded accounts of their thoughts about the outcomes of their bets. (Their thoughts were recorded in the guise of keeping a record for themselves to help them make additional bets later in the season.) An analysis of their comments indicated that they spent more time discussing their *losses* than their wins. Furthermore, the kind of comments made about wins and losses were quite different. The bettors tended to make "undoing" comments about their losses—comments to the effect that the outcome would have been different if not for some anomalous or "fluke" element (". . . it was just luck. Their quarterback got hurt during the game and that probably led to their defeat."). In contrast, they tended to make "bolstering" comments about their wins—comments indicating that the outcome either should have been as it was, or should have been even more extreme in the same direction ("I don't think you can put the blame on losing the quarterback. He is an exceptional quarterback, but so is their backup"). By carefully scrutinizing and explaining away their losses, while accepting their successes at face value, gamblers do indeed rewrite their personal histories of success and failure. Losses are often counted, not as losses, but as "near wins."

One consequence of the greater amount of time the bettors spent scrutinizing their losses is particularly noteworthy: They remembered their losses better than their wins when tested three weeks later. This contradicts everyday intuition as well as a good deal of psychological theorizing that would have us believe that people remain confident in the possibility of future success by selectively remembering their successes and forgetting their failures.[8]

The studies of gambling and of capital punishment demonstrate that we do not generally treat information at variance with our beliefs as lightly as is sometimes thought, although such information *is* dealt with in such a way that it has relatively little impact on our beliefs. Rather than simply ignoring contradictory information, we often examine it particularly closely. The end product of this intense scrutiny is that the contradictory information is either considered too flawed to be relevant, or is redefined into a less damaging category. Opponents of the death penalty come to view evidence supporting the deterrent efficacy of capital punishment as hopelessly deficient and uninformative. Gamblers come to see negative outcomes not as losses that signal the difficulty of ever coming out ahead, but as near-wins that call for just a little strategic fine-tuning.

BIASED EVALUATION OF SCIENTIFIC FINDINGS

Gamblers and partisans of the capital punishment debate are not the only ones who fail to treat supportive and antagonistic information evenhandedly. Scientists have been known to do the same when evaluating evidence relevant to their fields. The methodological critiques and publication recommendations of peer reviewers, for example, have been shown to be greatly affected by whether the results of a study support or oppose the reviewer's own theoretical orientation.[9] Every experimental psychologist I know is much more likely to run an additional experiment if the results of an initial study refute a favored hypothesis than if the results support it. More vividly, the history of scientific attempts to relate brain size or body shape to intelligence, personality, and (often by implication) "social worth" is riddled with examples of investigators vigorously challenging and reinterpreting unanticipated results while glossing over similar flaws and ambiguities in more comfortable findings. The French craniologist Paul Broca could not accept that the German brains he examined were on average 100 grams heavier than his sample of French brains. As a consequence, he adjusted the weights of the two brain samples to take into account extraneous factors such as overall body size that are related to brain weight. However, Broca never made a similar adjustment for his much-discussed difference in the brain sizes of men and women.[10] The "criminal anthropologist" Cesare Lombroso supported his thesis about the primitive and animalistic nature of criminals and "lower races" by citing numerous examples of their insensitivity to pain—examples that he construed as courage and bravery when exhibited by a privileged European.[11]

Although the history of science contains numerous examples of an investigator's expectations clouding his or her vision and judgment, the most serious of these abuses are overcome by the discipline's insistence on replicability and the public presentation of results. Findings that rest on a shaky foundation tend not to survive in the intellectual marketplace. To a lesser extent, the same is true with regard to beliefs formed in everyday life: Some of our most erroneous beliefs are weeded out by the corrective influence of our peers and society at large (although see Chapter 7 for a discussion of the limits of this phenomenon in everyday life). The biggest difference between the world of science and everyday life in protecting against erroneous beliefs is that scientists utilize a set of formal procedures to guard against the sources of bias and error discussed in this book—a set of procedures of which the average person is insufficiently aware, and has not adequately adopted in daily life. Scientists employ relatively simple statistical tools to guard against the misperception of random sequences discussed in Chapter 2. They utilize control groups and random sampling to avoid drawing inferences from incomplete and unrepresentative data (Chapter 3). They use "blind" observers as one way of eliminating the influence of the biased evaluation processes discussed in this chapter.*

But perhaps the most fundamental safeguard of the scientific enterprise is the requirement that the meaning of various outcomes be precisely specified (in advance if possible) and objectively determined. If a scientist sets out to test the ability of subliminal self-help tapes to improve the productivity of salespeople, he or she would doubtless focus on actual sales volume, and would ignore the claims of enhanced confidence, improved poise, and increased energy from those who were exposed to the tapes. (If such testimonials were to be used at all, it would be as suggestions for further hypotheses that would themselves be subjected to rigid test.) This kind of precise specification of what constitutes "success" and "failure" is something we rarely do in everyday life, and consequently our preconceptions often lead us to interpret the meaning of various outcomes in ways that favor our initial expectations. If we are interested in informally testing the effectiveness of vitamin C with the data of our own experience, it may be wise to specify

---

*A blind observer is a person who is unaware of either the hypothesis under investigation or the specific condition of the experiment that is being run at any given time (e.g., treatment or control group). Because the observer is blind in this way, his or her expectations about what "should" happen in the experiment cannot bias his or her behavior.

in advance that "success" or "improvement" be defined as a reduction in the number of days with a cold. If not, we run the risk of reading too much into every moment's respite from post-nasal drip or any temporary reduction in our fever-induced nagging of loved ones.

To stretch this idea a bit further (and pursue a theme introduced earlier), the methods of science protect an investigator from juggling the meaning of different results by deliberately making the investigator rigid and "unintelligent" in the same way that computers are rigid and unintelligent. Experimental results, like the input to a computer, must fall into certain pre-specified slots according to pre-specified rules or they are not processed at all. As scientists, we willingly sacrifice some "intelligence" and flexibility for the benefit of objectivity.

This is not to suggest, of course, that all of science is such a rigid, constrained process. A distinction must be made between the processes involved in generating versus testing ideas; between what philosophers of science have referred to as the "context of discovery" and the "context of justification." In the context of discovery, "anything goes" in science as in everyday life; it is in the context of justification that scientists become more conservative. As Sir Peter Medawar has noted, science works ". . . in a rapid reciprocation of guesswork and checkwork, proposal and disposal, conjecture and refutation."[12] Flashes of inspiration are followed by rigorous test. When asked on a talk show to explain the secret of his success, two-time Nobel Laureate Linus Pauling once replied that ". . . you need to have a lot of ideas, and then you have to throw away the bad ones." Much of the scientific enterprise can be construed as the use of formal procedures for determining when to throw out bad ideas, a set of procedures that we might be well advised to adopt in our everyday lives. We humans seem to be extremely good at generating ideas, theories, and explanations that have the ring of plausibility.[13] We may be relatively deficient, however, in evaluating and testing our ideas once they are formed. One of the biggest impediments to doing so is our failure to realize that when we do not precisely specify the kind of evidence that will count as support for our position, we can end up "detecting" too much evidence for our preconceptions.

Another way of stating this is that our expectations can often be confirmed by any of a set of "multiple endpoints" after the fact, some of which we would not be willing to accept as criteria for success beforehand.[14] When a psychic predicts that "a famous politician will die this year," it is important to specify then and there the range of events that will constitute a success. Otherwise, we are likely to be overly impressed by various tenuous connections between the prediction and any of a number of subsequent events. Suppose Armand Hammer dies within the year: Is that a successful prediction? (He is an industrialist rather than a politician, but he has served as this country's ambassador-without-portfolio to Moscow for several generations.) Or suppose the President is shot in an unsuccessful assassination attempt: Does that count? Without specifying the meaning of all possible outcomes, the test is no longer objective, and we run the risk that our initial hypotheses will receive apparent support too easily.

The problem of multiple endpoints is most severe when the subject under investigation is inherently fuzzy and hard to define. For instance, suppose someone claims that day care during infancy hinders "personal adjustment" in later life. Well, what is "personal adjustment" and how does one measure it? The number of friends during adolescence? Academic success? Happiness with chosen career? It is at times such as these, when the meaning of the phenomenon under investigation is unclear, that our preconceptions have their greatest effect. Any measure of personal adjustment that supports our initial beliefs is likely to be seized upon as the "true" test. In contrast, if someone were to claim that day care during infancy hinders subsequent "scholastic achievement," there is less flexibility in how it should be defined (although some remains) and therefore less latitude for our preconceptions to exert an effect.

An interesting analogue of the problem of multiple endpoints is what could be called the problem of "variable windows." The essence of a number of beliefs is that certain events tend to happen within some (unspecified) period of time. The belief that things "happen in threes" is a perfect example: Many people believe that events like plane crashes, serial-killing sprees, or birth announcements tend to occur in triplets. It is almost certainly the case, however, that these beliefs are mere superstitions that stem from the tendency to allow the occurrence of the third event in the triplet to *define* the period of time that constitutes their "happening together." If three plane crashes occur in a month, then the period of time that counts as their happening together is one month. If the third plane crash does not happen for another month, the relevant period of time is stretched to two months. By allowing the window of opportunity to be sufficiently flexible, such beliefs can *only* be confirmed.

MULTIPLE ENDPOINTS AND MULTI-FACETED EXPECTATIONS

People often comment on the resemblance between a newborn baby and one or both of the parents. "He has his mother's eyes." "She sure has that Gilovich nose." Interestingly, these same observations are often made when the child, unknown to the observer, has been adopted. Even when there is no genetic connection between parent and child, it is still possible to detect, from the vast number of possible features, a few striking similarities.

This phenomenon illustrates a particularly common result of the problem of multiple endpoints that gives rise to a specific class of erroneous belief. Certain beliefs or suppositions imply a similarity between two entities: A child should look like his or her parents, identical twins should behave alike, or a personality description ought to resemble the person it describes. However, if the two entities are sufficiently complex, then mapping one onto the other will almost certainly produce a number of points of overlap, and the expectation will appear to be confirmed.

One of the best examples of this phenomenon is the "Barnum effect," named after circus entrepreneur P. T. Barnum because it was he who said "there's a sucker born every minute." The Barnum effect refers to the tendency for people to accept as uncannily descriptive of themselves the same generally worded assessment, as long as they believe it was written specifically for them on the basis of some "diagnostic" instrument such as a horoscope or personality inventory. Consider the following description:

> You have a strong need for other people to like you and for
> them to admire you. At times you are extroverted, affable, and
> sociable, while at other times you are introverted, wary, and
> reserved. You have a great deal of unused energy which you
> have not turned to your advantage. While you have some person-
> ality weaknesses, you are generally able to compensate for them.
> You prefer a certain amount of change and variety and become
> dissatisfied when hemmed in by restrictions and limitations.
> You pride yourself on being an independent thinker and do
> not accept other opinions without satisfactory proof. You have

a tendency to be critical of yourself. Some of your aspirations tend to be pretty unrealistic.[15]

If you see yourself in that description, you are not alone. Many people who read it are convinced that it reveals unusual insight into their personality. What they fail to realize, however, is that: 1) In such a multi-faceted description there is bound to be *some* overlap with one's own characteristics, and 2) the statements that fit the best are so general that they are bound to ring true. They are nothing more than "one size fits all" assessments that apply to virtually everyone.*

There are numerous examples of beliefs that stem partly from this process. As we shall see later on (Chapter 10), it affects people's beliefs about the prophetic nature of dreams and the meaningfulness of coincidence. It has also played a role in at least a couple of scientific controversies. Some of the early claims about the biological basis of personality touted the amazing similarities between identical twins reared apart without properly controlling for the problem of multiple endpoints. Similarly, the claim that stress causes cancer is often buttressed by noting specific traumas that occurred shortly before the onset of an individual cancer. However, because we all experience various traumas from time to time, it is almost always possible to link the cancer to some particular traumatic episode.**

SOME THOUGHTS ON THE RECALL OF SUCCESS AND FAILURE, AND CONSISTENT AND INCONSISTENT INFORMATION

Folk wisdom tells us that people maintain confidence in their prospects for future success in part by selectively recalling how they have performed in the past: People supposedly remember their

---

* Fittingly, P. T. Barnum also said that a good circus, like these bogus personality descriptions, should have "something for everybody."
** This is not to suggest that these two beliefs are false. Indeed, both have been subsequently supported by more rigorous evidence: Identical twins do tend to have somewhat similar personalities (see R. Plomin. Special section on developmental behavior genetics. *Child Development*, 1983, *54*, 331–55), and stress can in fact lead to cancer (see L. S. Sklar, & H. Anisman, Stress and Cancer. *Psychological Bulletin*, 1981, *89*, 369–406). Note, however, that our confidence in the validity of these beliefs must rest on this more carefully collected evidence, and not on common anecdotal accounts that are subject to the problem of multiple endpoints.

successes and forget their failures. Likewise, it is commonly believed that people are more inclined to remember information that
supports their beliefs than information that contradicts them. Francis Bacon, Charles Darwin, and Sigmund Freud are among the
many wise observers of the human condition who have described
these tendencies as manifest features of everyday life. Darwin, for
example, in a statement that reflects his characteristic care and
attention to detail, said that he ". . . followed a golden rule, namely
that whenever a new observation or thought came across me, which
was opposed to my general results, to make a memorandum of it
without fail and at once; for I had found by experience that such
facts and thoughts were far more apt to escape from the memory
than favourable ones."[16] According to Darwin and others, favorable
information is seized upon and well remembered; unfavorable information is ignored and forgotten.

The thrust of much of the present chapter, however, can be considered to be somewhat at variance with these ideas. I have argued
that people often resist the challenge of information that is inconsistent with their beliefs not by ignoring it, but by subjecting it to
particularly intense scrutiny. I have also described the results of
an experiment in which people were more likely to remember
their losses than their wins.[17] Furthermore, research that has examined people's ability to remember information about other people
has often found that it is the information that *conflicts* with a
person's general impression of someone that is particularly
memorable.[18] How can these results be reconciled with the consensus of folk wisdom and the insights of such sage observers as
Bacon, Darwin, and Freud?

In essence, this question boils down to the issue of when, as
folk psychology suggests, people remember favorable information
better than unfavorable information, and when, as some of the
findings reported earlier suggest, this pattern is reversed. A satisfactory answer to this question requires a distinction between what
could be called "one-sided" and "two-sided" events. Two-sided
events are those that stand out and register as events regardless
of how they turn out. If a person bets on a sporting event and
expects to win, both outcomes (a win or a loss) have emotional
significance for the individual, both outcomes are likely to be noticed, and both will register as events. The outcome of a sporting
event, then, can be considered a two-sided event. The results of
buying a stock, going on a date, or taking a vacation are also two-

sided: Whether favorable or unfavorable, the outcome stands out in one's experience and registers as an event.

I suspect that the predictions of folk psychology are not particularly applicable to such two-sided events. Because both outcomes stand out equally from the stream of experience, they are likely to be equally well remembered. In fact, there are certain two-sided events for which the unfavorable or unanticipated outcome is likely to be *more* memorable because it produces thought and rumination about "what might have been." As we have seen, this appears to be why gamblers remember their losses better than their wins. This occurs in other areas as well: The high school athlete remembers nothing more clearly than the potential touchdown pass that skidded off his fingertips, the participant in a spelling bee can never forget the word that ousted her from the tournament, and fishermen are all too willing to recount their experience with "the one that got away." Similarly, recent research indicates that the member of a married couple who "loses" an argument remembers the fight with greater clarity.[19] And, as any student of psychology can tell you, there is the "Zeigarnik effect," or the tendency for people to remember interrupted tasks better than those that have been completed.[20]

But what about the claim of folk wisdom that people are particularly inclined to remember favorable or expected outcomes? This idea may fare better when applied to one-sided events. One-sided events are those that stand out and are mentally represented as events only when they turn out one way. Consider, for example, the set of experiences that might produce and maintain the belief that "the phone always rings when I'm in the shower." If the phone rings while showering, it will stand out and register as an event by virtue of the conflict that arises in deciding whether to answer it, by virtue of the chills and discomfort that are experienced while racing—dripping wet—to the phone, and by virtue of the frustration that is felt when it is picked up and only a dial tone is heard. In contrast, if the phone does not ring while showering, it is unlikely to register as an event. Nothing happened. Logically, such a nonoccurrence is just as much an event as an occurrence, but phenomenologically it is not.

It may be that it is these one-sided events to which folk wisdom best applies, and information consistent with our beliefs is better recalled. Because only one outcome is likely to be noticed, only one has much chance of being recalled. ("Memory," *New York*

Times writer Daniel Goleman aptly notes, "is attention in the past tense."[21]) Furthermore, although there are some important exceptions that will be described below, it may also be the case that with such one-sided events it is more often the side that supports a person's beliefs and matches his or her expectations that is likely to stand out. If I believe that my dreams are prophetic, it is my prophetic dreams that are eventful; if I believe that strange things happen during a full moon, it is the bizarre events that stand out. Consequently, people tend to remember the times when the phone rings while they are in the shower, somebody is murdered during a full moon, or someone's cancer goes into remission after a visit to a faith healer.

How then to distinguish one-sided and two-sided events? To examine this distinction in more detail, it is necessary to identify various sub-classes of one-sided and two-sided events, and to consider their implications for the kind of information that people tend to recall.

Confirmations and Non-confirmations. One clearly important factor involves the difference between confirmations and non-confirmations. Many beliefs or expectations are such that only events that confirm the belief stand out, because only the confirmations remind the person of the original expectation. If you go to a fortune teller and are told that you will someday have twins, having twins will almost certainly jar your memory and make you recall the long-forgotten prophecy. Furthermore, once having linked the prophecy and the confirmation, they will be hard to forget. Having a single child, on the other hand, is less likely to be linked to the original prediction. The birth of a single child is a non-event (with respect to the original prediction, that is!) and so the failed prophecy is unlikely to be recalled. Also, the birth of a single child does not directly disconfirm the prophecy; it simply fails to confirm it. It could still occur on a subsequent pregnancy.

Thus, one way in which commonsense psychology is correct (in that information that supports our beliefs is indeed particularly memorable) is that confirmatory events are in fact much more memorable than non-confirmatory events. Support for this contention comes from a study in which participants read the diary of a hypothetical student who believed in the prophetic nature of dreams. The student explained, on the first day of the diary, that she wanted to conduct an informal test of this belief by writing down her dreams each night, recording the most significant events that occurred that day, and checking whether there was any connection between the two. The investigators arranged the diary so that on half the subsequent days the previous night's dream was paired with a confirmatory event and on the other half there was no confirmation. When subsequently asked to recall as many of the dreams as they could, the participants were much more likely to remember the dreams that had been confirmed than those that were not confirmed.[22]

So commonsense psychology is correct: Events that confirm a person's expectations are indeed better remembered, at least in comparison to those "non-events" that fail to confirm them. But are there other ways in which folk wisdom is correct? Are there circumstances in which confirmations are not only better remembered than non-confirmations, but better remembered than actual *contradictory* information?

Focused and Unfocused Expectations. To address this question, it is necessary to introduce another variable that determines whether events are one-sided or two-sided—whether the original expectation is "temporally focused" or "temporally unfocused." Consider once again the example of somebody who bets on a sporting event. The expectation in this case (that one will win, let's say) is temporally focused because the outcome will occur at a particular time known in advance. The person's attention is drawn to what occurs at that particular time, and so either outcome is almost certain to be noticed. Thus the event is also two-sided. As with two-sided events generally, the expected outcome is unlikely to be any more memorable that the unexpected outcome.

In contrast, consider the expectation that a dream will prove to be prophetic. The expectation in this case is temporally unfocused because a relevant outcome can occur at any time—that day, the next day, a week later, etc. The person's attention, then, is not automatically drawn to all relevant outcomes. Rather, it is necessary for the person to extract relevant outcomes from the ongoing stream of experience, and events that confirm the original expectation may have an advantage. Thus, the outcomes relevant to such unfocused expectations tend to be one-sided, and the person may be more likely to recall events that are consistent with his or her expectations.

This distinction between focused and unfocused expectations was examined in an experiment similar to the one described above in which the participants read the diary of a student who believed in the prophetic nature of dreams. As before, the student indicated on the first day that she would write down each night's dream and the most significant events of the day, and then determine whether there was any connection between the two. This study, however, differed from the previous one in two important ways. First, half of the dreams were paired with confirmatory events and the other half were paired with *contradictory* events. For instance, a dream such as "I dreamt of gorgeous sunshine," might be paired with a confirmatory event such as "I sat on the deck of the student union and soaked up the rays," or a contradictory event like "It was so cold and blustery all day that I was almost blown down the library slope."

The second difference between this study and the previous experiment was that in this case each participant read one of two versions of the diary. In the *unfocused* version, each day's diary entry began with a description of the previous night's dream, and the event that either confirmed or contradicted the dream was written in some unpredictable location of the text. Thus, the participants' attention was not focused on one particular location, and so they had to find the relevant events in the larger body of text. In the *focused* version, in contrast, the confirmatory or disconfirmatory events were always listed at the end of each day's entry, and they were set off from the rest of the text and labelled "the most significant event of the day." Thus, the participants knew exactly where to look for the relevant information, and their attention was presumably drawn equally to confirmatory and contradictory events.

As predicted, those in the *focused* condition recalled the confirmatory and disconfirmatory events equally well. Those in the *unfocused* condition, on the other hand, recalled three times as many of the confirmatory events. Thus, when outcomes are temporally focused, the events are two-sided in the sense that both outcomes are equally noticed and remembered. When the outcomes are temporally unfocused, in contrast, the events tend to be one-sided, and the events that confirm a person's expectations tend to draw more attention and remain in memory.[23]

Outcome Asymmetries and One-sided Events. The two experiments just described demonstrate that whether an expectation is confirmed or remains unconfirmed, and whether an expectation is temporally focused or unfocused, are important determinants of whether an outcome is one or two-sided. This, in turn, influences the kind of information that is likely to be recalled. In addition, there are a number of asymmetries between possible outcomes that make some events inherently one-sided and thus strongly influence what is recalled.

i. Hedonic asymmetries. One entrance to the Psychology Department at Cornell University is a set of six doors that are open during all but the wee hours of the night. For an unknown reason, however, the person who unlocks the doors each morning often fails to unlock one of the six, and the one that remains locked varies randomly from day to day. Because I approach the building from different directions on different occasions, the door through which I enter also varies haphazardly from time to time. It stands to reason, then, that I should happen to pick the locked door only occasionally, say, once in six entries if one door really were left locked each morning. Objectively, I acknowledge that that must be the case. Subjectively, however, it seems that the custodian has an uncanny ability to overlook the very door I happen to select later that day. I "always" seem to select the locked door!

As this example suggests, one of the most powerful determinants of whether various outcomes are one or two-sided is whether the potential outcomes differ in their hedonic or instrumental consequences. Outcomes are two-sided if both produce the same intensity (if not the same kind) of emotion, or if both necessitate further action on the part of the individual. Many times, however, only one of the outcomes arouses much affect or demands further action, making the outcomes one-sided. My entrance to the Psychology Department is a good example: A locked door that one wants to pass through arouses anger, and the frustration and delay make the event stand out in one's experience. Passing through an unlocked door, on the other hand, requires no effort, gives rise to no emotion, and goes unnoticed. Consequently, the encounters with a locked door dominate my memory. Similar processes are no doubt responsible for a host of folk beliefs such as "it always rains right after you wash the car," "you usually seem to need something just after you've thrown it away," "the elevator (or the bus) always seems to be heading in the wrong direction," and, as mentioned previously, "the phone tends to ring when you're in the shower."

The belief that "the bus always seems to be heading in the wrong direction" is particularly interesting in this regard because of an important asymmetry between positive and negative events: Certain kinds of negative events can accumulate in ways that positive events cannot. I can become convinced that all the buses are headed in the wrong direction by observing quite a number headed the wrong way before I encounter one going in my direction. Note that the opposite cannot happen: Unless I have difficulty boarding, I never observe several going my way before I discover one headed in the opposite direction. If a bus is going in my direction, I take it. Because of this asymmetry, we can experience a certain kind of "bad streak," but not a complementary streak of good fortune. To those who fail to recognize this fact, events can sometimes seem to be conspiring against them.

Asymmetries in hedonic and instrumental consequences can also lead to the formation and maintenance of beliefs that can have more serious consequences, such as those that induce marital conflict. Many people claim that their spouses "never" do the chores or tasks they have agreed to do. While the claim is surely justified in some cases, in others it may stem from the fact that the spouse's failure to wash the dishes, clean the counter, or do the laundry arouses resentment and anger, and can have immediate instrumental consequences such as the need to do the tasks oneself. When the tasks are performed on time, however, the world runs smoothly and there is little to notice. Similar processes operate in the common belief among couples that they are "out of sync"—it seems one always wants to stay home and watch TV when the other needs to socialize, one wants to make love when the other "needs some space," one is upbeat when the other is morose, etc. Here too, there may be an inherent asymmetry in the salience of relevant events that can make things seem more out of sync than they really are. Wanting to do something when the other does not is frustrating, and it can occupy the contents of one's mental life for some time. Examples of asynchrony are therefore easily brought to mind. But again, when a couple's passions, preferences, or moods coincide, things go smoothly and the events can be less noteworthy. Furthermore, even when they do stand out, they tend to do so by virtue of the quality of the events themselves, and not by virtue of the synchrony that produced them. They are categorized and remembered as instances of laughter, passion, or fun, and not as instances of synchrony.

ii. Pattern asymmetries. A second variable that makes some events one-sided is whether there is an asymmetry in the numerical, spatial, or temporal pattern produced by the various outcomes.

Many people report that when they wake up in the middle of the night, their digital clocks indicate that it is something like 2:22, 3:33, or 1:23 "too often." This is no doubt because such outcomes stand out—in a way that 3:51 or 2:47 does not—as a result of the pattern or "unit" that is formed. Indeed, a great deal of numerology depends upon certain coincidences being imbued with special meaning because events such as these are so salient and memorable that they seem more common than they really are. Similarly, the widespread beliefs (discussed in Chapter 2) that basketball players shoot in streaks or that gamblers get "on a roll" stem in part from analogous processes: A run of several hits or misses in a row, or a burst of consecutive winning bets, are so much more noteworthy and memorable than a mixture of hits and misses, or losses and wins.

To continue with sports for a moment, how many times have we heard baseball announcers state that "the player who makes a great play in the field to end an inning tends to be the one who comes to bat first the next inning." Of course this cannot really be the case (unless we are willing to believe that an effect can precede its cause), but every time there is such an occurrence we are sure to notice it. Occasions when someone else leads off the next inning escape our attention.

There's a similar origin to some of the remarkable similarities alluded to earlier in the character or life histories of identical twins who are reunited after having been separated at birth. A match on some characteristic or dimension creates a pattern, a unit, a focus of attention; a mismatch, unless terribly egregious, generally does not. The similarities between twins are noticed and remembered, and the dissimilarities pass us by.

Asymmetries in pattern are not limited to those that are spatial, temporal, or numerical, or to the inherent difference between matches and mismatches. Some derive from their relation to broader theories that we hold. Popular superstition informs us that the period of the full moon is an unusually dangerous time of the month. Consequently, any homicide, suicide, or accident during that time will command our attention and be linked to the full moon—*even if we do not believe in the superstition*. Similar events during other periods of the month will be thought of exclusively as what they are, and not as tragedies that happened in the *absence* of a full moon. This asymmetry leaves us with a distorted view of the relevant evidence and appears to lend empirical support to groundless superstition. Likewise, we notice when a crime is committed by someone on drugs or by a member of an ethnic minority. A link forms in our heads. But when the criminal is drug-free and a member of the majority, we focus on the crime itself and not on the absence of drugs or the perpetrator's mainstream ethnicity.

iii. "Definitional" asymmetries. Certain events are one-sided almost by definition. The outcomes relevant to the belief that "I can always tell when someone has had a facelift" is one example. Those that one detects lend support to the belief, but those that go undetected are simply that—undetected. They do not disconfirm the belief except in those rare instances in which an unsuspected person reveals that he or she has secretly undergone such surgery. The belief held by many people, including many clinicians, that a person can only overcome some problem (drinking, drug abuse, procrastination, etc.) after hitting "rock bottom" follows a similar pattern. Because there is no real definition of what constitutes "rock bottom," it is hard to know what a disconfirmation of this belief would look like. Evidence that is inconsistent with the belief cannot stand out and is not remembered. The belief that people cannot profit from advice unless they are "truly ready" to receive it follows a similar logic. If the person benefits from the advice, he was obviously ready; if the advice is unheeded, however, the person must not have been "in the right place" to receive it. The very nature of the belief makes it impossible for it to be disconfirmed.

iv. Base-rate departures. Perhaps the most common determinant of whether an event is one-sided is the base-rate frequency of the different possible outcomes. When certain outcomes occur frequently enough, they become part of our experiential background and go unnoticed. Departures from normality, in contrast, can generate surprise and draw attention. The unexpected can sometimes be unusually memorable.

Consider cases of cancer remission. Sadly, people who are diagnosed as having certain forms of cancer rarely recover. An instance in which someone does recover, therefore, is rather noteworthy, particularly if the person did anything unconventional to try to effect a cure (such as visiting a faith healer or travelling to Mexico for Laetrile therapy). Because we do not expect people to get better, we hardly notice any time someone tries an unconventional treatment and it fails; when such treatments are successful, in contrast, the outcome violates our expectations and stands out in our memory.

Similarly, people's beliefs in certain "jinxes" are partly due to the vividness of outcomes that depart from the base rate. People will often say things such as, "I hope I don't jinx him, but Fred has never picked a losing stock." It is easy to see how a concern about jinxing someone might arise. If a person has experienced such a large number of positive outcomes that it is worthy of comment, an additional success is not, by itself, terribly noteworthy. A subsequent failure, on the other hand, violates the typical pattern of success and thus stands out in the person's experience. Examples of earlier jinxes are therefore easy to recall.

One of the most interesting classes of events that depart from the baserate and thus stand out in everyday experience is what sociologist Erving Goffman referred to as "negatively eventful actions," or those actions and customs that are so common and automatic that we only become aware of them when someone fails to honor them.[24] All of us have a preferred distance that we like to maintain from others—a "personal space" that governs the physical closeness of our interactions. Few of us, however, are aware of the precise dimensions or even the existence of such a bubble until someone invades it. It is only when someone violates the spacing norm that we even notice that it exists. Similarly, we tend to face forward in an elevator, pass fellow pedestrians on the right, and talk to people of different status with different styles of speech. All of this occurs with minimal awareness until we encounter someone who fails to uphold the norms.

Goffman's negatively eventful actions are perfect examples of one-sided events: The outcome is perceived as an event only when it comes out one way. Although the "expectations" in Goffman's examples are generally vague and unarticulated, it is the *disconfir-mations* that tend to stand out. Interestingly, these kinds of disconfirmations tend not to undermine a person's pre-existing beliefs. A norm violation of the type Goffman describes certainly does not diminish one's expectations about how people will behave in the future. If anything, it strengthens those expectations by making them more explicit.

These asymmetries of pattern, hedonic consequences, etc., as well as one-sided events more generally, all serve to distort the evidential record that a person consults to evaluate the validity of various beliefs. For the most part, these asymmetries tend to accentuate information that is consistent with a person's expectations and pre-existing beliefs. As a result, people tend to see in a body of evidence what they expect to see. What people expect to see, furthermore, is often what they want to see, and so the biasing effect of their preconceptions is often exacerbated by the biasing effect of their preferences and motives. This latter effect serves as the subject of the next chapter.

Motivational and Social Determinants of Questionable Beliefs

5

Seeing What We Want to See
Motivational
Determinants of Belief

Man prefers to believe what he prefers to be true.

Francis Bacon

If you are like me, you have spent more time than you care to admit wondering who you would want to be if you could be somebody else. Sometimes I play this game alone, simply by trying to think of someone I might rather be. Although I am aware that other people might take one look at my life and quickly generate a host of promising candidates, I have always been struck by how difficult it is to think of any acceptable possibilities. Somehow I can always think of reasons why I would rather be myself than, say, John Updike, Warren Beatty, or Ted Koppel.

In another version of this game, I ask other people whether they would trade places with a particular person. I generally try to pick a person who is right on the borderline—one about whom the decision to trade lives should be truly difficult. Thus, I might start with the likes of Updike, Beatty, or Koppel, expecting to find a readiness to exchange lives, and then move down the list of candidates to the more difficult and informative choices. Again, I am intrigued by how quickly one reaches the other person's point of hesitation. The Updikes, Beattys, and Koppels do not elicit the expected swift willingness to trade; instead they bring forth the kind of hesitation indicative of truly tough decisions.

Why are people so reluctant to switch lives with others? To

some extent, the answer lies in the inherent ambiguity of the game. What does it mean to trade places with another person? Do you become that other person, or do you remain yourself and simply occupy the other person's station in life? If it's the latter, can you truly remain yourself while living under such radically different circumstances? Questions like these raise the worry that changing places with someone else ultimately entails the death of oneself, a fate we all want to avoid.

The difficulty of finding someone with whom we are willing to exchange lives can also be understood as a particular instance of a phenomenon known to economists and decision theorists as the "reluctance to trade" or the "endowment effect."[1] Ownership creates an inertia that prevents people from completing many seemingly-beneficial economic transactions. What one side is willing to give up tends to loom larger to that side than to the side receiving it, with the result that agreements with which both sides would be happy are difficult to achieve. In the present context, what one gains in money, fame, and respect by becoming an Updike, Beatty, or Koppel has surprisingly little weight compared to whatever idiosyncratic losses are involved in giving up one's former existence.

Finally, and perhaps most interestingly, the reluctance to trade places with someone else is also partly due to the tendency to overestimate our own value in the "market" of compelling lives. We are capable of believing the most flattering things about ourselves, and many scholars have argued that we do so for no other reason than that we want them to be true. If we think we are brighter, healthier, and more esteemed than is actually the case, it is not so surprising that we are reluctant to trade places with people of undeniable fame, wealth, and achievement.

This chapter deals with this tendency for people to believe, within limits, what they want to believe. As the discussion will make clear, much of the empirical research and theoretical analysis on this topic has dealt with how our wishes influence our beliefs in one particular domain—our beliefs about ourselves. There is ample evidence indicating that we tend to make optimistic assessments of our own abilities, traits, and prospects for future success. This chapter will critically evaluate the work in this and other areas, and discuss how this "wish to believe" can lead to the formation of erroneous beliefs.

Empirical Support for the Wish to Believe. The idea that we tend to believe what we want to believe has been around for a long time, and considerable evidence consistent with this notion has accumulated. As we saw in Chapter 4, those who prefer to believe that capital punishment is an effective deterrent to murder find support for such a belief in an equivocal body of evidence; those who prefer to believe that it is *not* an effective deterrent find support for *their* position in the same body of evidence. Similarly, a study of the public's reaction to the Kennedy-Nixon debates in 1960 revealed that those who were pro-Kennedy thought that Kennedy had won the debates, whereas those who were pro-Nixon thought that their man had won.[2] Voters, furthermore, generally exaggerate the extent to which their candidate is favored by others, and thus tend to overestimate their candidate's chances of winning an election.[3]

However, most of the evidence indicating that people tend to believe what they want to believe comes from research on people's assessments of their own abilities, and their explanations of their own actions. One of the most documented findings in psychology is that the average person purports to believe extremely flattering things about him or herself—beliefs that do not stand up to objective analysis. We tend to believe that we possess a host of socially desirable characteristics, and that we are free of most of those that are socially undesirable. For example, a large majority of the general public thinks that they are more intelligent,[4] more fair-minded,[5] less prejudiced,[6] and more skilled behind the wheel of an automobile[7] than the average person. This phenomenon is so reliable and ubiquitous that it has come to be known as the "Lake Wobegon effect,"[8] after Garrison Keillor's fictional community where "the women are strong, the men are good-looking, and all the children are above average." A survey of one million high-school seniors found that 70% thought they were above average in leadership ability, and only 2% thought they were below average. In terms of ability to get along with others, *all* students thought they were above average, 60% thought they were in the top 10%, and 25% thought they were in the top 1%![9] Lest one think that such inflated self-assessments occur only in the minds of callow high-school students, it should be pointed out that a survey of university professors found that 94% thought they were better at their jobs than their average colleague.[10] Also, people tend to think that they are more likely than their peers to experience a variety of favorable events like owning a home or earning a large salary, but less likely to experience aversive events like getting divorced or suffering from lung cancer.[11] Recent public opinion polls indicate that although only 25% of the population believes that the country as a whole will be better off financially in the coming year, 54% nevertheless think that *they* will do better.[12]

People are also prone to self-serving assessments when it comes to apportioning responsibility for their successes and failures. In numerous studies across a wide range of situations, people have been found to attribute their successes to themselves, and their failures to external circumstances.[13] People also tend to make more charitable attributions about their performance than do observers of their performance. Athletes tend to attribute their victories to themselves, but to blame their losses on bad officiating and bad luck.[14] Students who perform well on an examination generally think of it as a valid measure of their knowledge; those who fail tend to think of it as arbitrary and unfair.[15] From the other side of the instructional podium, teachers tend to attribute a student's success to the quality of instruction the student received, but they tend to attribute a student's failure to the student's lack of ability or effort.[16] Academicians whose attempts to publish have been rejected often attribute their bad fortune to factors beyond their control, like an unfortunate choice of reviewers; those who have their manuscripts accepted, in contrast, rarely acknowledge any parallel good fortune in the selection of reviewers.[17]

Mechanisms Underlying Self-serving Beliefs. The results of these investigations are clear and consistent: We are inclined to adopt self-serving beliefs about ourselves, and comforting beliefs about the world. The interpretation of these results, however, is extremely controversial. Many psychologists believe these phenomena stem from truly motivational processes: We hold such self-serving beliefs because they satisfy important psychological needs or motives, such as the motive to maintain self-esteem.[18] Others believe that such beliefs, although clearly self-serving, are the product of purely cognitive mechanisms.[19] By this account, a perfectly rational person, unaffected by needs and motives, might nevertheless arrive at such self-serving attributions and self-assessments, and such comforting beliefs about the world.

Indeed, with a little thought one can see how the results discussed above could result purely from cognitive processes. The tendency to believe that we are more likely than our peers to experience positive events, for example, may result from our being more aware of our own efforts to bring about such experiences than we are of analogous efforts by others. We thus seem to ourselves, even when we are trying to be perfectly objective, to be relatively likely to experience positive outcomes. The tendency for people to attribute success internally and failure externally can likewise be explained without reference to self-esteem motives. If a person tries to succeed at something, then any success is at least partly due to his or her efforts and thus warrants some internal attributional credit. Failure, on the other hand, generally defies one's efforts and intentions, and therefore necessitates looking elsewhere, often externally, for its cause. Even an unbiased attributor, then, might exhibit an asymmetrical pattern of attributions for success and failure because success is so much more tightly connected than failure to intention and effort. Furthermore, consider a person who has had a lifetime of experience indicating that she is adept at mathematics. Is she not justified in attributing her failure to solve a mathematical puzzle during an experiment to the difficulty of the puzzle or the unfamiliarity of the setting, rather than to a sudden loss of mathematical acumen?

To what, then, should we attribute these self-serving patterns of beliefs and attributions? Are they the result of the "interference" of needs and motives, or are they the product of "cooler" cognitive processes? Do they come from the heart or the mind? Those who favor a cognitive interpretation argue that since any apparent demonstration of a motivational bias can be explained solely in terms of dispassionate cognitive processes, we should not invoke motivational mechanisms to explain these phenomena. Cognitive explanations, we are told, are more parsimonious.[20]

There are a couple of points to be made about this issue. First, cognitive explanations are *not* inherently more parsimonious than motivational ones. They can, and do, involve as many assumptions as motivational accounts. Cognitive mechanisms are more parsimonious only if one adopts a model of the human organism in which a motivational system overlays, and occasionally interferes with, a more fundamental cognitive system. But it is an open question whether the cognitive system should be considered primary.[21] Given a model in which the motivational system is more fundamental, motivational explanations would be more parsimonious.

The second point to be made about this motivation-versus-cognition controversy is that it is in many ways a false issue. There is little reason to believe that our self-serving biases result exclusively from one or the other, and even less reason to believe that there will ever be a truly definitive test that will decide between the two accounts. Indeed, when we closely examine how our motivational biases might operate, the two explanations begin to blend rather closely. To the extent that there is a motivational "engine" responsible for our self-serving biases and beliefs, it is one that delivers its effects through processes that look suspiciously cognitive. Our desire to believe comforting things about ourselves and about the world does not mean that we believe willy-nilly what we want to believe; such flights of fantasy are reined in by the existence of a real world and the need to perceive it accurately. Rather, our motivations have their effects more subtly through the ways in which we cognitively process information relevant to a given belief. What evidence do we consider? How much of it do we consider? What criteria do we use as sufficient evidence for a belief? Cognition and motivation collude to allow our preferences to exert influence over what we believe.

Essentially the same point has been articulated by social psychologist Ziva Kunda, who argues that people are indeed more likely to believe things they want to believe, but that their capacity to do so is constrained by objective evidence and by their ability ". . . to construct a justification of their desired conclusion that would persuade a dispassionate observer. They draw the desired conclusion only if they can muster up the evidence necessary to support it."[22] It is informative in this respect that people generally think of themselves as objective.* People rarely think that they hold a particular belief simply because they want to hold it, the evidence be damned. This sense of objectivity can nevertheless be illusory: Although people consider their beliefs to be closely tied to relevant evidence, they are generally unaware that the same evidence could be looked at differently, or that there is other, equally pertinent evidence to consider. As Kunda describes it, ". . . people do not realize that the [inferential] process is biased by their goals, that they are only accessing a subset of their relevant knowledge, that they would probably access different beliefs and [inferential]

---

*Indeed, this would make a particularly good item for a demonstration of the "Lake Wobegon effect": Asked to assess how objective or unbiased he or she is, the average person would no doubt rate him or herself above average.

rules in the presence of different goals, and that they might even be capable of justifying opposite conclusions on different occasions."[23]

Our motivations thus influence our beliefs through the subtle ways we choose a comforting pattern from the fabric of evidence. One of the simplest and yet most powerful ways we do so lies in how we frame the very question we ask of the evidence. When we prefer to believe something, we may approach the relevant evidence by asking ourselves, "what evidence is there to support this belief?" If we prefer to believe that a political assassination was not the work of a lone gunman, we may ask ourselves about the evidence that supports a conspiracy theory. Note that this question is not unbiased: It directs our attention to supportive evidence and away from information that might contradict the desired conclusion. Because it is almost always possible to uncover *some* supportive evidence, the asymmetrical way we frame the question makes us overly likely to become convinced of what we hope to be true.

Kunda and her students have collected evidence indicating that our preferences lead us to test hypotheses that are slanted toward confirmation in precisely this way. In one study, participants were led to believe that either introversion or extroversion was related to academic success.[24] Not surprisingly, those who were led to believe that introversion was predictive of success thought of themselves as more introverted than those who were led to believe that extroversion was associated with success. More important, when asked to recall autobiographical events relevant to introversion/extroversion, those who were led to believe in the importance of introversion recalled more incidents of introversion, and they did so with greater speed. Those who were led to believe in the value of extroversion, in contrast, recalled more incidents of extroversion, and they did so more quickly. By establishing a preference for one of these traits, the ease of generating evidence consistent with that trait was facilitated. It seems that the preference led participants to formulate and test an asymmetrical hypothesis that was biased toward confirmation.

A second way in which our motives influence the kind of evidence we entertain involves whose opinions, expert or otherwise, we consult. We can often anticipate other people's general beliefs and overall orientations, and thus can predict with some accuracy their views on a particular question. By judiciously choosing the right people to consult, we can increase our chances of hearing what we want to hear. Smokers can discuss their habit's health risks with other smokers; Nixon fans can explore the "real meaning" of the Watergate scandal with those of similar ideological bent. There are a number of physiologists at Cornell who differ in their assessments of the importance of dietary fat as a determinant of serum cholesterol and arteriosclerosis. This variability in expert opinion gives members of the Cornell community an opportunity to find support for whatever eating practices they wish. Those who need to justify the lost opportunities brought on by an austere diet can talk with someone willing and able to describe the latest studies testifying to the evils of dietary fat; those with an appetite for Continental cuisine can talk with someone eager to discuss the critical flaws of those very same studies. We seek opinions that are likely to support what we want to be true.

People's preferences influence not only the *kind* of information they consider, but also the *amount* they examine. When the initial evidence supports our preferences, we are generally satisfied and terminate our search; when the initial evidence is hostile, however, we often dig deeper, hoping to find more comforting information, or to uncover reasons to believe that the original evidence was flawed. By taking advantage of "optional stopping" in this way, we dramatically increase our chances of finding satisfactory support for what we wish to be true.[25]

Consider a student who has performed poorly on an exam and wants desperately to believe that the test was unfair. The student may initially seek support for this interpretation by trying to recall specific questions that were ambiguous. If examples of ambiguity can be found, the student rests his case: the exam was unfair. If no such examples can be recalled, however, the search for supportive evidence continues. Maybe other students thought it was unfair! Again, if a number of like-minded others can be found, the test is deemed to be unfair; if not, then still further evidence is sought. Perhaps the student will think of all the things he learned in the course that were *not* tested, and therefore conclude that the test was unfair because it did not adequately cover all the course material. By considering a number of different sources of evidence and declaring victory whenever supportive data are obtained, the person is likely to end up spuriously believing that his or her suspicion is valid.

To illustrate further, consider a discussion I recently heard between two prominent psychologists concerning the severity of the AIDS risk among the heterosexual, non-drug-using population. One was arguing that the risks were overstated, whereas the other thought they were indeed so severe that they would soon bring about widespread changes in social life as we know it. Their opinions, furthermore, mirrored their preferences. One fervently wanted the sexual revolution to continue, and the other, someone who has lived a happy, monogamous life for some time, would just as soon see this era pass (in his words, "AIDS is not God's punishment for licentiousness, but His way of reducing dissonance for sexual monogamy"). How did their divergent preferences influence how they arrived at, and how they justified, their ultimate beliefs? It is doubtful that their predilections led them simply to see things their way, with little attention to the relevant evidence. The consequences of ignoring reality are too great (indeed, in this case potentially fatal) for such a cavalier regard for the way things really are. However, their preferences did influence the kind of evidence each considered, as well as the *amount* they considered.

The person worried about the end of the sexual revolution began the discussion by noting the small number of drug-free heterosexuals in the United States who have contracted AIDS and assumed that that was decisive. Jarred out of premature security, however, by the other person's statistics regarding AIDS transmission among heterosexuals in central and east Africa, he was momentarily concerned. But only momentarily. He proceeded to dig deeper into the matter, eventually finding solace in the fact that the state of public health in central Africa is so different from that in the United States that such information is not terribly informative. ("So many people there have open sores due to untreated venereal disease that of course AIDS is readily transmitted heterosexually.")

The important point here is that although evidence and reality constrain our beliefs, they do not do so completely. For nearly all complex issues, the evidence is fraught with ambiguity and open to alternative interpretation. One way that our desires or preferences serve to resolve these ambiguities in our favor is by keeping our investigative engines running until we uncover information that permits a conclusion that we find comforting.

More generally, it is clear that we tend to use different criteria to evaluate propositions or conclusions we desire, and those we abhor. For propositions we want to believe, we ask only that the evidence not force us to believe otherwise—a rather easy standard to meet, given the equivocal nature of much information. For propositions we want to resist, however, we ask whether the evidence *compels* such a distasteful conclusion—a much more difficult standard to achieve. For desired conclusions, in other words, it is as if we ask ourselves, *"Can* I believe this?", but for unpalatable conclusions we ask, *"Must* I believe this?" The evidence required for affirmative answers to these two questions are enormously different. By framing the question in such ways, however, we can often believe what we prefer to believe, and satisfy ourselves that we have an objective basis for doing so.

Optimistic Self-assessments and Self-based Definitions of Ability. To consider a particularly intriguing example of how we juggle criteria to arrive at comforting conclusions, let us return to the previously discussed tendency for people to make unduly favorable assessments of their own abilities. Recall that, on average, people think of themselves as being much better than average. Part of the reason, it seems, is that different people use different criteria to evaluate their standing on a given trait—criteria that work to their own advantage. As economist Thomas Schelling explains, ". . . everybody ranks himself high in qualities he values: careful drivers give weight to care, skillful drivers give weight to skill, and those who think that, whatever else they are not, at least they are polite, give weight to courtesy, and come out high on their own scale. This is the way that every child has the best dog on the block."[26] By basing our definitions of what constitutes being, say, athletic, intelligent, or generous on our own idiosyncratic strengths on these dimensions, almost all of us can think of ourselves as better than average and have some "objective" justification for doing so.

Several recent experiments indicate that such self-based definitions of ability are largely responsible for this "Lake Wobegon effect." First, it has been shown that people are particularly inclined to think of themselves as above average on ambiguous traits—those for which the definition of what constitutes excellence can most readily be construed in self-serving ways. People rate themselves more favorably on amorphous traits like sensitivity and idealism (at the 73rd percentile, on average) than on relatively straightforward traits like thriftiness and being well-read (48th percentile). Further evidence was obtained in an experiment in which a group of university students was asked to rate the importance of a variety of academic skills (e.g., public speaking, math) and personal characteristics (e.g., creativity, meticulousness) in terms of how important they are in determining success in college. The students were also asked to rate their own standing on these characteristics. As expected, the students tended to think that the characteristics at which they excelled were most important in determining what constitutes a successful college student. Finally, it has been shown that the tendency for people to think of themselves as above average is reduced—even for ambiguous traits—when people are required to use specific definitions of each trait in their judgments.[27]

This research effectively illustrates how we juggle different criteria to arrive at conclusions we favor.* As strong as our wishes or motives may sometimes be, they rarely lead us simply to see the world the way we would like to see it. To do so would invite pathology. It would require that we pay an excessively high price in cognitive inconsistency and in the ability to get along effectively in the world. Instead, we accomplish the same motivational goals more subtly by skewing the meaning we assign to the information we take in from the world. There are alternative ways of interpreting or "framing" what we encounter around us, and we seem to be fairly adept at finding a frame that is comforting. (Indeed, some evidence has accumulated that people who habitually fail to put the most favorable cast on their circumstances run the risk of depression.[28]) It is in these relatively subtle shifts of criteria and interpretation that many of the most significant effects of the wish to believe can be found.

EPILOGUE: BELIEFS AS POSSESSIONS

A supplementary perspective on how our preferences influence what we believe can be obtained by considering a useful metaphor offered by psychologist Robert Abelson, who argues that "beliefs

---

* Although this self-serving juggling of criteria can be attributed—as it is above—to the motive to see ourselves in a favorable light, it is important to note that this phenomenon can be explained in purely cognitive terms as well. In particular, people may use their own strengths as the basis of what constitutes success in a given domain because, after a lifetime of basing their actions on what they do well, those elements at which they excel simply come to mind more readily and thus figure more prominently in their assessments. These two rival explanations are not mutually exclusive, of course, and the most important point is that both processes result in people believing what they would prefer to believe.

are like possessions."[29] We acquire and retain material possessions because of the functions they serve and the value they offer. To some extent, the same can be said of our beliefs: We may be particularly inclined to acquire and retain beliefs that make us feel good.

As Abelson notes, the similarity between beliefs and possessions is captured in our language. First of all, a person is said to "have" a belief, and this ownership connotation is maintained throughout a belief's history, from the time it is "obtained" to the time it is "discarded." We describe the formation of beliefs with numerous references to possession, as when we say that "I *adopted* the belief," "he *inherited* the view," "she *acquired* her conviction," or, if a potential belief is rejected, "I don't *buy* that." When someone believes in something, we refer to fact that "she *holds* a belief," or "he *clings* to his belief." When a belief is "given up," we state that "he *lost* his belief," "she *abandoned* her convictions," or "I *disown* my earlier stand."

This metaphor sharpens our understanding of the formation and maintenance of beliefs in a number of ways. First, we are quite possessive and protective of our beliefs, as we are of our material possessions. When someone challenges our beliefs, it is as if someone criticized our possessions. We might no longer associate with that person, or we might seek solace and confirmation from others with similar beliefs. As with possessions, in other words, "one shows off one's beliefs to people one thinks will appreciate them, not to those who are likely to be critical."[30] Alternatively, we might respond to a challenge or criticism by thinking of compensatory features ("True, it is not very stylish, but I bought it for the gas mileage."/"True, the raw statistics might seem to contradict me, but if you look at the intangibles. . . ."); or by shielding it from public view ("Maybe we should move the watercolor from the living room to the upstairs bedroom."/"My beliefs work for me, why should I have to justify them to those people?").

The metaphor also applies to how our beliefs fit together. We carefully choose furniture and works of art that do not clash, just as we try to avoid the dissonance produced by incompatible beliefs. If, over time, we find that our decor does not make a single, coherent statement, we might hold a garage sale and start anew. A similar phenomenon is observed when one undergoes an ideological conversion (such as joining a cult) and many of one's earlier convictions are discarded to make room for new beliefs.

For the purposes of this chapter, however, the most telling analogue between beliefs and possessions involves the tension between desire and constraint. We are tempted to buy as many of the best things in life that we can. As much of today's world makes clear, the thirst for material possessions is hard to quench. But few of us can afford everything we desire. We have a budget, and some things are just too expensive. So we do without.

The same can be said of our beliefs. There are things we are sorely tempted to believe; to do so would be tremendously gratifying. To simply acquire many of these comforting beliefs, however, would extract too high a price in rationality and cognitive consistency. So not all are acquired, at least not as is. But if we could just view them from a slightly more flattering perspective, if we could just take the evidence in a little here and let it out a little there—if we could get them on sale!—we just might buy them.

6

Believing What We Are Told
The Biasing Effects of Secondhand Information

What ails the truth is that it is mainly uncomfortable, and often dull. The human mind seeks something more amusing, and more caressing.

H. L. Mencken

Among the most widely known studies in the history of psychology is the conditioning of "Little Albert."[1] As most students of psychology have been told many times, every time the nine-month-old Albert came near a white rat, Watson and Raynor made a frighteningly loud noise behind Albert's head by banging a metal bar with a hammer. Albert subsequently exhibited a strong fear of the rat even when it was no longer paired with the sound, a fear that did not readily diminish over time. Albert also exhibited a milder, but still pronounced, fear of a number of objects that had many of the same features as the rat, such as a rabbit, a white glove, cotton balls, and a white beard. The results of this experiment are often presented as evidence of how people can develop phobias of seemingly harmless objects, and of how our acquired fears can generalize to other, similar entities.

Although the story of Little Albert serves as a convenient vehicle for communicating some important ideas about the acquisition and modification of human emotional behavior, it suffers from a very serious flaw: Many of the events that are often described in secondhand accounts of this story never occurred.[2] The experimenters did indeed manage to make Albert afraid of the rat by pairing its presence with the loud noise seven times at the beginning of the experiment, a fear that remained strong five days later during a follow-up test. At that time, Albert also exhibited a strong fear of a rabbit, a dog, and a sealskin coat, a less pronounced "negative reaction" to a Santa Claus mask and to Dr. Watson's hair, a mild response to the cotton balls, and a very favorable reaction to a set of wooden blocks and to the hair of Watson's assistants.

After another five days, however, Albert showed such a slight reaction to the rat that the experimenters decided "to freshen the reaction" to it by presenting it with the loud noise once again; something they also did for the first time with the rabbit and the dog (thereby making them useless as stimuli in subsequent tests of generalization). Finally, when tested after another 31 days, Albert exhibited fear when touching the rat, the rabbit, the dog, the sealskin coat, and the Santa Claus mask. However, Albert also *initiated* contact with the very same rabbit and coat. After this final set of tests, Albert's mother removed him from the hospital in which the study was conducted, and he was no longer available for subsequent assessment.

The actual details of Watson and Raynor's study make it clear that Albert's fear of the rat was not so intense, nor did it generalize as readily to other entities, as is often claimed in textbook accounts of this landmark study in the history of psychology. Eysenck, for example, claimed that "Albert developed a phobia for white rats and indeed for all furry animals."[3] However, the contention that Albert developed a rat phobia is hard to reconcile with his mild reaction to the rat during the second test period, a reaction described by the experimenters as: "Fell over to the left side, got up on all fours and started to crawl away. On this occasion there was no crying, but strange to say, as he started away he began to gurgle and coo, even while leaning far over to the left side to avoid the rat." His reported fear of "all furry animals" has also been exaggerated, given that his reaction to such animals was assessed only with respect to the rabbit and the dog (and even they, recall, were directly paired with the noise during the second test session). Indeed, the range of entities to which Albert's fear reportedly generalized is the most frequently misrepresented result of the study. Different texts have made Albert afraid of a cat,[4] a white glove,[5] the fur neckpiece or fur coat of Albert's mother,[6] and even a teddy bear.[7] Finally, in what may be the most intriguing distortion, a number of texts have re-written the ending of the tale, claiming that Albert's fear had been eliminated by a "re-conditioning" procedure, sometimes described in detail, at the end of the experiment.[8]

Why has the story of Little Albert been so frequently distorted, and why has it been distorted in the precise way that it has? There is little doubt that many of these distortions were introduced because they make the tale of Little Albert into a "good story." There are numerous aspects of what constitutes a good story, several of which are illustrated by the accounts of Albert's experiences at the hands of Watson and Raynor. These accounts tell a simple, coherent tale of how phobias can be acquired, a tale with a tidy (even happy) ending. This chapter discusses these and other elements of what constitutes a good narrative.

More to the point, however, this chapter also examines how this need or desire to tell a good story can distort the accuracy of information we receive secondhand, and thus bias some of the most important information upon which we base our beliefs. Much of what we know in today's world comes not from direct experience, but from what we read and what others tell us. An ever-higher percentage of our beliefs rest on a foundation of evidence that we have not collected ourselves. Therefore, by shedding light on the ways in which secondhand information can be misleading, we can better understand a common source of questionable and erroneous beliefs.

TELLING A GOOD STORY

To understand what constitutes a good story, it is necessary to examine the needs of the speaker and listener, and the goals they try to achieve in their interaction.* Because communication or con-

---

*This analysis is not meant to be an exhaustive account of the goals people try to fulfill in the process of communication. I discuss only those goals that are most likely to introduce bias and distortion into the content of the communication. For a more complete account of the goals of conversation and communication, the reader should consult D. Cushman & G. C. Whiting "An approach to communication theory: Toward consensus on rules." *Journal of Communication* 1972, 22, 217–38; H. P. Grice, "Logic and conversation." In P. Cole & J. Morgan (Eds.), *Syntax and semantics* (Vol. 3). New York: Academic Press, 1975; or J. R. Searle,

versation is a reciprocal process, it is not surprising that many of the needs and goals of the speaker and listener are complementary. This is well illustrated by one of the most basic goals of communication, to ensure that the act of communication is "justified." For the speaker, this means, among other things, that his or her message should be worthy of the listener's attention; for the listener, it means that the interaction must in some way be worthwhile. To satisfy this basic goal, it is necessary that certain preconditions be met. The message should be understandable (i.e., not assume too much knowledge on the part of the listener), and yet not be laden with too many needless details (i.e., not assume too *little* knowledge on the part of the listener).[9]

Sharpening and Leveling. For the purpose of understanding the formation of erroneous beliefs, it is important to note that satisfying even these very basic enabling conditions can introduce distortion in what is communicated. Classic studies by psychologists F. C. Bartlett[10] and Gordon Allport and Leo Postman[11] demonstrate that when people are given a message to relay to someone else, they rarely convey the message verbatim. The limits of human memory and the implicit demand that the listener not be burdened with too many details constrain the amount and kind of information that is transmitted. What the speaker construes to be the gist of the message is emphasized or "sharpened," whereas details thought to be less essential are de-emphasized or "leveled." Secondhand accounts often become simpler and "cleaner" stories that are not encumbered by minor inconsistencies or ambiguous details.

The case of Little Albert is a good example. Albert did develop some fear of the rat, and his fear did generalize somewhat to other

---

(1969) *Speech acts: An essay in the philosophy of language.* Cambridge, England: Cambridge University Press.

The reader should also understand that this section deals with verbal and written communication rather broadly defined—from face-to-face conversation to the dissemination of information through print and broadcast media. One consequence of this focus is that certain words are used *very* broadly. For example, the word "speaker" is intended to refer to any of a host of different "transmitters," such as writers, broadcasters, or the person doing the talking in face-to-face conversation. Similarly, the words "communication," "conversation," and "interaction" are sometimes used interchangeably, as are the words "listener" and "audience."

entities. However, the evidence for both the extent of his fear and the amount of generalization was rather inconsistent and hard to interpret. Because these inconsistencies interfered with the main story about classically conditioned anxiety, many authors managed to set them aside. Watson's original report mentioned that Albert's fear had to be "freshened" after a few days, and that the loud noise was directly paired with the rabbit and dog as well. Nevertheless, in subsequent accounts by Watson himself and by other authors, these details were leveled out of the story.

A particularly interesting consequence of the processes of sharpening and leveling concerns our impressions of people we only know about secondhand.[12] Everyday experience seems to tell us that we often develop exaggerated or extreme impressions of people we have heard or read about but never met. The most telling evidence in this regard is that when we finally meet someone we have been led to believe is, say, unusually charismatic and compelling, or uncommonly wicked and detestable, we are often "disappointed." The person often seems less worthy of positive or negative regard than we had been led to expect. Sharpening and leveling can help explain this phenomenon.

When someone tells us about another person and his or her actions, the account we receive tends to be organized around the person rather than the context in which the actions took place. The person, after all, generally constitutes the core of the story. Information about the person and the action tends to be sharpened, whereas information about the surrounding context and various mitigating circumstances tends to be leveled. There are a couple of reasons for this disparity in emphasis. First, with all else being equal, people tend to think of actions and actors as going together: An actor's dispositions are considered to be more of a preeminent cause of behavior than the dictates of the surrounding context.[13] It may thus seem more natural, typically, to construct an account of a person's actions that makes greater reference to the type of person involved than to the nature of the existing circumstances. Second, it is probably *easier* to construct such accounts: People and their actions can often be described in the same terminology; situations and actions usually cannot.[14] There are compulsive people and compulsive actions, but there is really no such thing as a compulsive situation—although situations do vary in how much they call for compulsive behavior.

Because of this asymmetry in what is transmitted via secondhand accounts, our impressions of people we have heard about but never met may be relatively unaffected by how their actions may have been elicited or constrained by various situational determinants. Their behavior may thus seem to be more a product of underlying personal dispositions, leading us to form more extreme impressions of such people than we would have if we had witnessed their actions firsthand.

A series of recent studies provides support for these ideas.[15] In one set of experiments, a group of "first generation" subjects watched a videotape of a "target" person describing two events from his or her past. The subjects then rated the target person on a variety of trait dimensions, and provided a tape-recorded account of what they had seen. Subsequently, a group of "second generation" subjects listened to these secondhand accounts and then made the same trait ratings. As predicted, second generation subjects made more extreme ratings of the target than did their first generation counterparts. Furthermore, an analysis of the accounts provided by the first generation subjects indicated that they did indeed underemphasize the situational determinants of the target person's actions. An event that the target person regretted, for example, tended to be described as a bad deed rather than as a likely product of difficult circumstances. Aspects of the target person's dispositions were sharpened, whereas features of the surrounding context were leveled.

Further evidence of the relative extremity of secondhand impressions was provided by a very different experiment in which pairs of friends were asked to identify a third ("target") person whom one of them knew well, but the other had never met, and had only heard about from the first. The two friends then individually rated the target person on a set of trait scales chosen for their relevance to the target. As expected, more extreme ratings were made by the person who had only heard about the target from his or her friend.[16] This phenomenon frequently occurs in real life when college students meet their roommates' parents, siblings, or childhood friends for the first time. Those who come prepared to meet an impossible ogre or the very embodiment of charm, wit, and intelligence are usually relieved to meet someone much more normal and human.

The relatively simple processes of sharpening and leveling can thus distort much of what we "know" secondhand—from secondhand impressions of other people to the reported results of scientific experiments. As these accounts are continually retold, we get further away from the original source, and whatever distortions have been introduced stand little chance of ever being corrected. An innocuous and rather charming example of the permanence of misconceptions brought about by a different sort of sharpening and leveling involves the origins of the term "Pennsylvania Dutch." The Dutch never settled in Pennsylvania in great numbers, but the Germans did—giving rise to the term Pennsylvania Deutsch. Because of the difficulty many Americans have in pronouncing "Deutsch," it has gradually been sharpened over the years to the more accommodating "Dutch." As a result, large segments of the U.S. population currently believe that the ancestors of the Keystone state came from Holland. Indeed, a number of products marketed for the state's tourist trade have a windmill displayed on the packaging to certify that it is an authentic product of the Pennsylvania "Dutch" country.[17]

DISTORTIONS IN THE SERVICE
OF "INFORMATIVENESS" AND ENTERTAINMENT

The distortions discussed thus far stem in part from the speaker's attempt to meet the preconditions necessary for making the communication worthwhile for both speaker and listener. Most important, a good story should not burden the listener with too much minutia, and so, for example, many of the specific details about the objects to which Little Albert's fears generalized were leveled out of many subsequent accounts of the experimental results. Beyond meeting these preconditions, however, there are a number of other criteria that must be met to make a communication worthwhile. Foremost among them is making the communication informative or entertaining. If the listener comes away from the communication either informed or entertained, the interaction has been worthy of his or her time and attention, and the speaker has met one of his or her most basic requirements.

One way that a message can be made to be more entertaining or more seemingly-informative is to increase its immediacy. Something that happens to someone we know can be said to have happened to us. Something that supposedly happened to someone in my uncle's office can be described as having happened to my uncle. Often such alterations in the story are made for the speaker's self-aggrandizement—it places him or her closer to center stage. At other times, however, the alteration is completely innocent: Making a story less remote in this way can seem to make a story more entertaining or perhaps more informative by making it more vivid and concrete.

The net effect of this exaggerated immediacy is that it is difficult for the listener to accurately gauge the reliability of the message. Accounts presented as firsthand are in fact often secondhand; those believed to be secondhand are often third-, fourth-, or fifth-hand. Returning to the story of Little Albert for a moment, part of the reason that many textbooks presented so much misinformation about this classic study is that a number of the textbook authors never read the original research reports. This is a common problem of the academic world: What is implicitly presented as secondhand is often more remote. To be sure, people are generally aware that the more links there are in a communication chain, the more likely it is that some distortion has been introduced somewhere along the line. However, if they are misled about the true source of a story, it is difficult to put this realization into practice. It is hard to adjust for the remoteness of the message if one does not know how remote it actually is. The cautionary alarms that would normally be sounded remain silent.

Sometimes the adjustment that is cut short would have been a general one: Be skeptical in direct proportion to the remoteness of the message. Other times, however, the precluded adjustment is more specific. For example, I might accept a story at face value because I heard it from someone trustworthy. Unbeknownst to me, however, he or she heard it from someone who is less credible. By treating the story as secondhand and taking into account only the credibility of the most immediate source, we run the risk of uncritically accepting too many fabricated stories and bogus claims.

Presenting (and accepting) remote accounts as if they were secondhand can be particularly misleading when it comes to estimating the commonness of some phenomenon in the general population. If eight people tell us they know somebody whose teenage child became brain damaged from playing too much Nintendo, then we may be safe in concluding that Nintendo is indeed a potentially dangerous activity. If, on the other hand, the eight people who tell us this story have only *heard of* a teenager who suffered brain damage in this way (possibly the same teenager in each case), then the problem is probably less widespread.

An interesting real-life example involves the problem of sexuality in the era of AIDS. I have heard the following story at least four times. Each time the person telling the story introduced it as something that happened to "a friend of mine," "a friend of my brother," or "a guy at work." Many people I know have also heard it a similar number of times with a different cast of characters. Michael Fumento describes it as a widespread rumor in his book on heterosexual AIDS.[18] The story is as follows:

My friend (my brother's friend, this guy, etc.) began flirting with a particularly attractive woman at a bar in the city (on a Caribbean vacation). One thing led to another and they ended up sleeping together. The next morning when he woke up, the woman was gone. He saw a note on the bed (a message on the bathroom mirror): "Welcome to the world of AIDS."

It is possible that such a nightmare did in fact happen to someone, somewhere, at some time. However, it is also possible that it is an inauthentic but plausible tale that is designed to impart a moral lesson. It is certainly the case, however, that it did not happen as many times, to as many people, nor to so many who are so closely connected to each of us, as is implied by the pervasiveness of this story. There simply are not enough women in the U.S. who: a) have AIDS, b) know they have AIDS, c) are seeking revenge from innocent targets, and d) express their vengeance in precisely this way, for all of these accounts to be true. Nevertheless, after hearing one of these stories and believing that the event happened to someone "close to home," the danger can certainly seem to be acute.

Informativeness. Beyond this tendency to exaggerate the immediacy of some message, the need to entertain or inform can tempt a speaker to communicate something other than the complete truth as he or she knows it. We readily acknowledge this fact when it comes to entertainment: We recognize that people will sometimes take liberties with the truth to tell a more entertaining tale, and sometimes we correct for this tendency when we interpret what we hear. We may be less savvy, however, to distortions introduced by the need to be "informative." An audience may consider a message to be uninformative if it contains too many qualifications, and, as a result, a speaker may be inclined to omit them. This is often seen when scientific findings are reported in the news media: Promising developments are sometimes reported with important qualifications buried in remote parts of the text or omitted alto-gether. Press reports of studies indicating that a low-fat diet can reduce serum cholesterol, for example, almost always neglect to point out that a significant reduction in cholesterol is generally obtained only by individuals who reduce their dietary fat intake *and* take a cholesterol-inhibiting drug.[19]

The desire to be informative can also lead people to stretch the facts to make sure the audience gets the point. Public service cam-paigns often suffer from this problem. The "missing children" cam-paign, for example, performed a valuable public service by alerting parents to the dangers of leaving small children unattended in certain areas. However, it may have done so at the cost of generating more fear and over-protectiveness than was warranted, or at least misdirecting much of that fear. Most of the reports failed to mention that an overwhelming majority of the missing children were taken away by estranged husbands and wives, not by the strangers bent on mayhem that everyone most fears.[20] The old campaigns against marijuana—exaggerated to the point of farce in films such as *Reefer Madness*—and many of the current claims about the dangers of cocaine suffer from the same problem.[21] The "facts" about potency, addictiveness, and prevalence are stretched beyond recognition to make a more compelling story. (Note, however, that in these examples, the goal is not just to inform, but to motivate a particular course of action—or inaction.)

Sometimes such distortions are introduced when the person sim-ply has the story wrong and he or she sincerely believes in the literal truth of what is conveyed. Other times, however, people knowingly provide misinformation in the service of what they be-lieve to be "the greater truth." This happens at all levels. Parents tell their children, "Don't get into a car driven by a stranger. A little boy down the street did that and his parents never saw him again." There may never have been such an incident with the boy down the street, but getting into a car with a stranger is an unwise thing for children to do and if this story more effectively gets that point across, it's all for the better. Similarly, certain drugs may not be as addictive or harmful—or affect the lives of as many people—as some public service campaigns would have us believe. Nevertheless, drug use does entail some real risks and it has ruined the lives of many individuals. If a little sharpening and levelling is necessary to drive home this greater truth, some will conclude that that is exactly what should be done.

Entertainment. The possibility of inaccuracy obviously increases enormously when the worth of the message is measured by how well it entertains rather than how well it informs. Our appetite for entertainment is enormous, and it has a tremendous impact on the tales we tell and the stories we want to hear. The quest for entertainment is certainly one of the most significant sources of distortion and exaggeration in everyday communication. Unfortunately, psychology has not adequately come to grips with the difficult subject of entertainment (or with its opposite, boredom). Despite a few initial efforts in this regard,[22] the discipline has not developed an adequate conceptual framework for thinking productively about what people find entertaining, why they find it so, how—and how much—the desire for entertainment governs everyday life, etc. The absence of such a framework is a noteworthy failure in an era in which people spend so much time and effort in the pursuit of entertainment—in this society surely, more time than they do in the "struggle" for survival; and, for many, more time than they do in the existential search for meaning and purpose.

Fortunately, such a framework is not necessary to examine how the desire to entertain and be entertained can introduce distortion in everyday communication. For this purpose, the most important point could hardly be more simple: The desire to entertain often creates a conflict for the speaker between satisfying the goal of accuracy and the goal of entertainment. The desire to entertain can sometimes be the stronger of the two, putting the truth in jeopardy.

Often the speaker's desire to entertain is matched by a listener's desire to be entertained, and an implicit understanding develops whereby the speaker need not be constrained too heavily by having to tell the absolute truth as he or she knows it. In everyday social life, this can be seen in our willingness to grant other people "literary license." We generally have no quarrel with claims such as "I nearly died, I was laughing so hard," or "Those were the most awesome waves anyone has ever seen around here," as long as these claims make the account more entertaining, as long they are not too incredible, and as long as it is clear that we are "in on the game"—that permission to stretch the truth is mutually agreed upon. One of the clearest testimonials to the frequency with which people grant, and take, literary license is the fact that the word "literally" has lost its meaning in everyday use. Few seemed to mind, or even notice, for example, when Illinois Congressman Henry Hyde defended President Reagan during the 1987 "Iran-Contra" hearings by saying that "the President signed that bill with a gun *literally* pointed at his head."

Beyond the individual or personal level, moreover, we see a similar tacit agreement that the truth can be set aside on the part of certain periodicals and their readers. This is best exemplified by the existence and financial health of tabloids like the *Sun* and the *National Inquirer.* The readers of these tabloids for some reason find the usual brew of tall tales and unsubstantiated gossip mixed with a smattering of factual stories to be well worth their entertainment/education dollar. Apparently, stories that appear under such headlines as "I Was Bigfoot's Love Slave" or "Cannibals Shrink Alien's Head" are sufficiently entertaining that many people consider the "transaction" to be worthwhile. Publisher and reader have struck a deal: The stories need not stick to the truth as long as they entertain.

More ominously, the desire to entertain can also lead a speaker to take liberties with the facts without any tacit agreement on the part of the listener. The decision to stretch the truth is often made unilaterally, and the inaccuracies and distortions are foisted on what is frequently an unsuspecting audience. One of the most common sources of such inaccuracy is the dissemination of unfounded or fallacious claims by news and other media organizations that try to entice an audience by their ability to entertain. As NBC News anchorman Tom Brokaw admits, "It's tricky, trying to generate understanding and insight while not ignoring the entertainment factor."[23] Inaccuracies and fabrications propagated by the media are a particularly powerful cause of people's erroneous beliefs, in part because of the reputation much of the media have for objectivity and accuracy, a reputation that is not always deserved. The prescription that "you cannot believe everything you read" has unfortunately not been adequately incorporated into the public consciousness. It often seems overshadowed by the counter-slogan that "they couldn't say it if it wasn't true."

But much *is* said that is not true. Those who work in the mass media face tremendous pressure to put out a product—to meet a deadline, fill an hour, or generate advertising space. Often the demand for suitable material outstrips the supply of factual stories that are novel and interesting, and the temptation to stretch the truth or lower one's standards of objectivity and verification can be enormous. The demand for news is met by an artificial increase in supply. The public is then treated to misleading stories about psychic detectives, UFO's, the Shroud of Turin, and the like—stories that leave a permanent imprint on the beliefs of much of the public, even in those rare cases in which the critical response to the initial story is given coverage as well. One wonders, for example, what kind of rash decisions have been made because of the well-publicized, but subsequently discredited claim that an unmarried American woman over 40 is as likely to be killed by a terrorist as to experience matrimony.[24]

Because amazing feats are entertaining, the media often plays up amazing events for all (or more than) they are worth, distorts many not-so-amazing events to make them appear extraordinary, and sometimes even passes on complete fabrications from unreliable sources. As indicated previously, the most common subjects of such uncritical, sensationalistic coverage are examples of paranormal phenomena such as Bigfoot, UFO sightings, and the (positive) findings of ESP experiments. Also common are extraordinary applications of the ordinary processes of the human mind, like the use of mental imagery to cure cancer and other physical and social ailments. It may be helpful to examine in some detail one such example of media distortion in the pursuit of entertainment.

NBC-TV once ran several episodes of "Project UFO," a program dealing with reports of unidentified flying objects.[25] The show tried to garner legitimacy for its contents by stating that the series was inspired by a U.S. Air Force investigation of UFO's called "Project Blue Book." Although the official emblem of the U.S. Air Force was prominently displayed on the screen as an implicit seal-of-approval, much of what was depicted in the show was at variance with the conclusions of the Air Force investigation. Project Blue Book, for example, ended with this summary:

1. no unidentified flying object reported, investigated, and evaluated by the Air Force has ever given any indication of threat to our national security;
2. there has been no evidence submitted to or discovered by the Air Force that sightings categorized as UNIDENTIFIED represent technological developments or principles beyond the range of present-day scientific knowledge;
3. there has been no evidence indicating that sightings categorized as UNIDENTIFIED are extraterrestrial vehicles.

Project UFO, however, after depicting numerous flights of alien space ships throughout the program, ended by showing—for two and one-half seconds—the text of only the first of these conclusions. The implication conveyed to those who were quick enough to read this disclaimer was that there may have been some UFO's that were identified as extraterrestrial, but that were not dangerous. For all but the most sophisticated or skeptical viewers, Project UFO's treatment of this subject obviously made the claims of extra-terrestrial visitation seem much more substantial than they really are. The interests of entertainment won out over the responsibility to inform.

An experience of my Cornell colleague Daryl Bem is also informa-tive as to how the media's desire to provide its audience with tidy, interesting stories can deprive the public of an accurate per-spective on a flashy topic. Bem had been invited to participate on CBS's *Good Morning* program to share his expertise on the subject of graphology, or handwriting analysis. Bem was appearing as a skeptic, the main attraction being a gentleman who, for an impressive fee, performs handwriting analysis for large corpora-tions to help them with personnel selection. For each exciting claim made by the graphologist, Bem countered with a sobering statement from the research literature about the severe limitations on what a sample of a person's handwriting can really tell us.

Because of a late-breaking news story, Bem and his counterpart did not appear live, but their segment of the show was taped to be shown later that week. In the interim, however, the producers thought better of the idea. The program just was not sufficiently "interesting." All they had was a discussion in which one person made a number of exciting claims, only to have them shot down by the other. Bem has concluded that CBS would have had a much "better" show if he had not been invited—a show they would have been more inclined to air. Although one cannot be anything but pleased by CBS's original decision to include a skeptical per-spective, the cancellation tells us a great deal about the kind of presentation of such subjects that we are likely to receive from mainstream media. Flashy stories that promote the existence of special capacities tend to be well received by the general audience, and therefore are likely to be shown. More balanced accounts that take a hard look at these extraordinary claims are less likely to be aired.

DISTORTION IN THE SERVICE OF SELF-INTEREST

In addition to satisfying the requirement that a communication be worthy of the listener's attention, telling an entertaining story also accomplishes another common communicative goal: It promotes the speaker's narrow self-interest. To tell an entertaining story is to be an entertaining person. Doing so enhances the speaker's public image. But the desire to be seen as an entertaining person is only one kind of self-interest. People pursue a host of more selfish motives in the process of communication, pursuits that may lead them to distort their messages in systematic ways.

One such motive stems from the fact that people frequently have some ideological or theoretical ax to grind. People are often interested in getting others to believe a certain way, a goal that can lead to selective sharpening and leveling. The distorted accounts of the dangers of marijuana and cocaine that were discussed earlier are good examples. Because the powers-that-be assume that significant segments of the population are incapable of evaluating the true risks of these drugs, the risks are exaggerated in an attempt to turn potential users away. Again, a "greater truth" takes precedence over the literal truth. A number of people have argued that similar distortions underlie the efforts to portray the AIDS epidemic as a significant threat to the heterosexual population in the United States. The proponents of this view note that the oft-predicted "breakout" of AIDS into the heterosexual population has never materialized. Nor, it is said, was it ever likely to, given the sexual practices of most heterosexuals and the difficulty of transmitting the AIDS virus through penile-vaginal or penile-oral intercourse.*

Accentuating the risk to heterosexuals, however, served two political agendas. First, from the standpoint of the gay community, it prevented people from thinking of AIDS as "just a gay disease." This, in turn, would further the worthy goals of increasing society's willingness to spend money on AIDS research and preventing an increase in discrimination against gays. The second agenda served by heterosexualizing AIDS was that of moral conservatives who

---

*Estimates of the transmissibility of the AIDS virus vary enormously, but the estimate provided by the most visible proponent of the "myth" of heterosexual AIDS, Michael Fumento, is that there is a 1 in 500 chance of an infected person giving the virus to an uninfected partner through a single episode of penile-vaginal intercourse. The odds are considered to be somewhat less likely for penile-oral intercourse, and enormously higher for penile-anal intercourse.

wanted to rein in society's sexual habits and practices. It was their fervent hope that people would simply become too scared to engage in anything but monogamous sex in the context of marriage. AIDS could thus be used to instill "morality" in the same way that syphilis was used at the turn of the century. At that time, some of those with a moralizing bent did not want to see a cure for syphilis developed because one of their most potent weapons in the battle for sexual restraint would be lost. Said one, "I believe that if we could in an instant eradicate the diseases, we would also forget at once the moral side of the question, and would then, in one short generation, fall wholly under the domination of animal passions, becoming grossly and universally immoral."[26]

For the threat of AIDS to be an effective deterrent to sexual freedom, however, it could not be seen as a threat that was largely confined to gay or bisexual men, intravenous drug users, hemophiliacs, and the heterosexual partners of such individuals. As a consequence, apparent cases of heterosexual transmission were publicized with great fanfare, as were the rates of infection among heterosexuals in Africa and Haiti. Far less publicized were the facts that the overwhelming majority of heterosexual transmissions did in fact involve the partners of members of one of these high risk groups, and that the sexual practices and state of public health in Haiti and Africa are so different from those in the United States that their experiences may tell us little about what is likely to happen here.

Turning to a less grave example, the case of Little Albert also illustrates how distortions can be introduced through self-interest— theoretical self-interest in this case. Authors interested in promoting a purely behaviorist account of human learning tended to introduce distortions to the effect that Albert's fear generalized to other objects according to their similarity to the rat along a number of dimensions. Thus, Albert has been erroneously reported to have developed rather negative reactions to white objects, like a white glove, and to furry objects, like his mother's fur coat. Later on, however, when the advocates of "preparedness" theory argued that organisms are predisposed to learn certain associations and not others, Albert's fear was said to have generalized mainly along the dimension of furriness and animalness dictated by evolutionary considerations.[27] This revisionist account appears to capture more accurately what happened during Watson and Raynor's experiment, but it too has been shaped by the processes of sharpening and leveling. For instance, Albert is now said to have developed a phobic reaction to "rats, rabbits, and other furry objects" that did "not extinguish readily."[28] This is hard to reconcile with the fact that Albert was only tested with respect to a single rat and a single rabbit, and, as we have already seen, the evidence that any of his fears was long-lasting is extremely dubious.*

DISTORTIONS DUE TO PLAUSIBILITY

There are times when inaccurate or fictitious stories are told and retold because they just seem so plausible. When what we hear could so easily be true, we often let down our critical guard, accept what we are told, and pass it on as is. Our standards for what is plausible, furthermore, are not always so high: Sometimes all that is necessary is a sense of ironic plausibility. This is presumably what was responsible for the widely circulated rumor (circa 1988) that Bobby McFerrin, the creator of the song "Don't Worry, Be Happy," committed suicide. A similar sense of ironic plausibility (as well as the sense that somehow it *ought* to be true) no doubt underlies the continual reappearance, in print, of the claim that an official of the U.S. Patent Office once resigned his post because he thought there was nothing left to invent.[29] Although this tale has appeared numerous times over the past century, there never was any such official. Still, it seems like something someone, at some time, might do.

A less ironic, but similarly playful story that also owes its existence to its superficial plausibility involves an irrepressible tale of the verbosity of government bureaucrats. The most common version of the story, begun in the early 50s, runs as follows. "The Ten Commandments contain 297 words. The Declaration of Inde-

---

* The various distortions in the case of Little Albert are mentioned here *not* because they represent particularly egregious examples of either calculated or subconscious distortion. They do not. Rather, they may represent fairly typical examples of the tendency to do a little sharpening here, a little leveling there, in order to make a better story. Indeed, I must confess that I found it difficult to avoid sharpening a few points myself in order to make my own point more clearly. Telling a succinct, coherent story demands that one sharpen and level, and even when one tries to tell the story perfectly straight, doing so can be difficult.

pendence is stated in 300 [sic] words. Lincoln's Gettysburg Address contains 266 words. A recent directive by the Office of Price Stabilization to regulate the price of cabbage contains 26,911 words." In reality, never in its entire existence from January 1951 to April 1953 did the OPS ever regulate the price of cabbage. Nevertheless, repeated attempts by OPS officials to bring this to the public's attention were unsuccessful in squelching the story. Equally ineffective in halting its spread was the demise of OPS itself. The story was still appearing in newspapers in the mid-1960s, but with the attribution to the OPS changed to "a federal directive."[30]

The robust life of this fallacious story is no doubt partly traceable to its plausibility. Government officials are known to be long-winded, and government regulations are often impossibly complex. Why wouldn't there be such a detailed and verbose regulation? It fits people's sense of what easily could happen, and so it is readily passed on.

Thus far, all of the tales attributed to considerations of plausibility—the suicide of Bobby McFerrin, the limited vision of the patent official, and the incredible length of the cabbage regulation—are rather whimsical. This is fitting. The most common type of story that is accepted and spread because of its plausibility is one that is also entertaining and not particularly serious. The desire to entertain (and be entertained), and the sense that something is plausible, combine to foster the diffusion of a number of false rumors. Beliefs obviously vary in their importance and in the conviction with which they are held. Some have important consequences and are deeply held; others are less serious. For the latter, it is not so much that we *have* a belief, but that we *entertain* the belief and entertain ourselves with it. It is this kind of belief that is most easily spread through the rumor mill and for which its plausibility and entertainment value are nearly sufficient for its acceptance.

This is not to suggest, however, that a sense of plausibility does not foster the dissemination of false claims that have more serious consequences. It does. This is seen most clearly in the field of health, where bogus claims about the effectiveness of various practices in warding off ill health—claims that have the ring of plausibility—are frequently spread through the media and through everyday social exchange. These claims are discussed in detail in Chapter 8.

A VEXING PARADOX

Upon reading this chapter, the reader may feel in a bit of a bind. The implication of much of the earlier part of this book is that our habitual ways of evaluating evidence are subject to error, and that therefore we can be misled by the apparent lessons of everyday experience. Thus we should place a little less trust in what our personal experience tells us, and we should rely more heavily on hard evidence and objective facts—on information that comes from beyond our own personal experience. The data of our own experience are often biased and incomplete, and we cannot always be counted on to evaluate them fairly. Consequently, those who study human judgment and decision-making urge us to give less weight to our own impressions and to assign more weight to the "base rate," or general background statistics. For instance, in contemplating the odds that our own marriages might end in divorce, we should attach less significance to our present passion and current conviction that we have found the right person, and we should pay more attention to the overall divorce rate of approximately 50%. To be sure, we should not discount our current feelings and self-knowledge altogether; we just need to temper them a bit more with our knowledge of what happens to people in general. This is the consensus opinion of all scholars in the field. Because personal experience is not an infallible guide to the truth, we must augment it (augment it more than we apparently do) with relevant background statistics.

That is all well and good, but how do we get these background statistics? How do we know they are accurate? Indeed, what does the oft-cited 50% divorce rate mean anyway? Is it that 50% of all *marriages* end in divorce (in which case the total would increase for each and every one of the divorces filed by people like the Gabor sisters, making the odds of divorce seem worse than they are), or is it that 50% of all *people* get divorced at least once (so that no single person affects the total disproportionately)? It is hard to incorporate the overall divorce rate into one's personal assessment without knowing which it is.*

---

*The divorce rate is generally calculated by dividing the number of divorces by the number of marriages in a given year. For several years now, there has been one divorce for every two marriages, hence the phrase, "half of all marriages

More generally, the information presented in this chapter indicates that it can be extremely difficult to get a truly accurate estimate of the relevant base-rate. We generally do not collect the base-rate data ourselves; it must be obtained from secondhand sources. Moreover, few people have the wherewithal to look up (and decode) the relevant data in scientific journals, and so their exposure is limited to the summaries presented by various media outlets. But alas, as we have just seen, the summaries presented for mass consumption are often terribly distorted.

The portrayal of the heterosexual AIDS risk provides a good example. If you are an exclusively heterosexual, non-IV drug-using, middle-class person in the United States, how worried should you be about contracting the AIDS virus? Here are some of the things we have been told: "Research studies now project that one in five heterosexuals could be dead from AIDS at the end of the next three years. That's by 1990. One in five. It is no longer just a gay disease. Believe me." (Oprah Winfrey).[31] "By 1991, 1 in 10 Babies May Be AIDS Victims." (USA Today).[32] "The AIDS epidemic is the greatest threat to society, as we know it, ever faced by civilization—more serious than the plagues of past centuries." (A member of the President's AIDS commission).[33] Using information like this, the apparent base-rate is frightening indeed. One in five heterosexuals dead by 1990! One in ten babies with AIDS by 1991! To justify such predictions, the virus clearly must have been spreading wildly in the heterosexual population at the times these estimates were made. The risks to heterosexuals of a single sexual episode must have been enormous at that time. Anyone who followed the advice of decision theorists and gave considerable weight to the base-rate should have sworn off sex with anyone other than a long-time, faithful spouse.

---

end in divorce." Note, however, that this calculation includes multiple divorces, and thus exaggerates the likelihood of divorce for the average person. How much it does so is difficult to assess because of another problematic feature of this statistic: The overall divorce rate is the sum of the various age-specific divorce rates in a given year—the divorce rate of people in their 20s, 30s, 40s, etc. However, the cohort of people who are currently in their 50s and 60s may be less inclined to get divorced than today's younger cohort may be when they reach that age. As a result, estimates of the chances that a young married couple will get divorced at some time during their lives are very uncertain and should be interpreted with caution.

Fortunately for those who did not rein in their sexual habits, the base-rate implied by these alarmist accounts was way off the mark. It is now 1990 and nowhere near one in five heterosexuals are infected, let alone dead. It is still the case that the *overwhelming* majority of AIDS cases involve gay men, intravenous drug users, and the heterosexual partners of the latter. 1991 is close at hand, but there is not even the faintest hint of an upsurge in babies with AIDS that would justify an expectation of 1 in 10 in the next year. Anyone who looked to the media to try to establish a sensible base-rate was not well served.

In marked contrast, people's personal experience, fallible as it may sometimes be, would have given them a much more accurate estimate of the heterosexual AIDS threat. The vast majority of the U.S. population cannot think of a single person who has contracted AIDS through heterosexual intercourse, nor can they think of someone who knows someone who has. (The one-night-stand nightmare that was described earlier does not qualify because that story does not specify whether the "victim" actually contracts AIDS). By the light of personal experience, then, the heterosexual AIDS threat seems overblown. How overblown is hard to tell just yet, and the question is exceedingly controversial. The profile of the epidemic that is shaping up, however, indicates that the true threat is much closer to that intuited by personal experience ("It cannot be that pervasive, no one I know has it") than that implied by alarmist media accounts ("One in five heterosexuals could be dead in the next three years").

On what, then, should one's judgments and decisions be based? Personal experience, or what we are told are the base-rate statistics? What happens when the two conflict? Decision theorists have developed formal procedures for combining these two sources of information into one overall assessment. Applying these procedures can be problematic, however, when the base-rate information is prone to inaccuracy. When both personal experience and the relevant background statistics tell us the same message, things are easy and we can be quite confident that our understanding is correct. When they conflict, however, we should understand that our assessments are particularly prone to error. We must learn to distrust personal experience a bit when it conflicts with the base-rate; but when the base-rate comes from an uncertain secondhand source, we must also distrust it when it conflicts with personal experience. Conflict between these two important but imperfect sources of information should temper our judgments and beliefs. Sometimes this note of epistemological caution is all that can be said about integrating divergent sources of information. But even that can be helpful because distinguishing what we know well from what we only think is true is itself an important advance. Sometimes it is not "the things we don't know that get us into trouble; it's the things we know that just ain't so."

The issue of how to think about the evidence of everyday life so as to avoid erroneous beliefs will be addressed more extensively in the final chapter. For now, it may be most important to consider how one should evaluate secondhand claims reported in the media. How can we know whether to trust a given claim? How can we know whether to accept a reported base-rate? Fortunately, there are several helpful guidelines.

Consider the Source. One of the most important things to consider is something we all recognize in theory, but sometimes overlook in practice—the need to consider the source of the message. We all seem to honor this principle when we discount what we see in the *National Enquirer* and put more stock in what we read in *The New York Times.* But who or what is the source being cited by a reputable newspaper? With respect to the coverage of AIDS, we should know that we ought to give more credence to the words of epidemiologists than sex therapists, rock stars, or actors. Epidemiologists spend their working hours trying to understand and predict the spread of infectious diseases. No one is more equipped than they to issue projections about the spread of AIDS. Sex therapists are presumably quoted on this issue because of the connection between sex and AIDS. But however much a sex therapist might be helpful in overcoming sexual dysfunction or dealing with problematic sexual feelings, they are not expert in the complicated business of predicting the course of an epidemic. Throughout all of the massive, confusing, and often alarmist coverage of AIDS, it has been the epidemiologists who, on the whole, have issued statements most consistent with the facts as we now know them.

Attaching special significance to the words of the true experts, however, is not as easy as it might seem because reporters will often distort what an expert really said. A common way of doing so is to place an innocuous quote by a credible person next to an outlandish claim, and thus make it appear that the former endorsed the latter. For example: "One source claims that one in three teenagers could be addicted to cocaine within the next five years. Says Elliot Ness, a member of the President's commission on drug abuse, "There are no easy solutions in the drug war.' " Mr. Ness might indeed believe that there are no easy solutions to the drug war, but nonetheless want to have nothing to do with the "one in three" estimate. The proximity of the two statements in the same paragraph, however, makes it easy to think he is responsible for both. Look carefully at what is actually quoted and what is only implied.

Trust Facts, Distrust Projections. Predicting the future is risky business, even for those experts whose job it is to do exactly that. Just think of how often meteorologists are wrong about tomorrow's weather, or how frequently economic forecasters misread the leading economic indicators. This means that we should give more weight to statements of fact by experts, and less credence to their projections of the future. Although the projections of epidemiologists for the spread of AIDS are certainly worth noting, we should pay even closer attention to their reports of current facts, such as the number of current AIDS patients, the percentage of cases among homosexuals, heterosexuals, and IV drug users, or the rate of seropositivity in blood samples donated to blood drives. Again, the message is one of epistemological caution: Be wary of those who claim to know the future.

Be on the Lookout for Sharpening and Leveling. Scientists rarely make exact predictions. For instance, rather than stating that "54% of the electorate favors a tax on imported oil," they will say that "54% plus or minus four percent favor an oil import tax." Scientific predictions are almost always given as a range or "confidence interval." Thus, the Center for Disease Control might say that "we estimate that somewhere between 500,000 and 1,500,000 people are infected with the HIV virus in the United States." The larger number is obviously more newsworthy, however, and so news reports will often drop the range and report only the higher figure: "The CDC reports that as many as one and a half million people. . . ," We should be aware that any statement of the form "as many as" means that an extreme end of a confidence interval has been sharpened and presented for our attention. We must learn to scale such estimates down and put more faith in the downsized estimate.

Be Wary of Testimonials. Often the media tries to impress us with the seriousness of some problem by presenting a vivid testimonial of an individual who suffers from it. These accounts are enormously successful in getting us to imagine what it would be like to be in similar circumstances, and they make us much more sympathetic toward those who suffer some bad fate. And well they should! By themselves, however, there is no reason they should have much influence on our sense of the *prevalence* of some malady. Their impact on our compassion is perfectly justified; their influence on perceived commonness is not. Any testimonial, no matter how moving, represents the experience of only one person. Often there is little reason to believe that that person's experience is any more informative than one's own in estimating overall prevalence. We should not allow the depth of our feeling toward any one person to influence our assessment of how *many* such people there are. Be wary of testimonials that urge us to do just that.

Summary. Implicit in the discussion throughout this chapter is the idea that many of the inaccuracies that are part and parcel of secondhand information have an unfortunate impact on what people believe. It can hardly be otherwise. A person's conclusions can only be as solid as the information on which they are based. Thus, a person who is exposed to almost nothing but inaccurate information on a given subject almost inevitably develops an erroneous belief, a belief that can seem to be "an irresistible product" of the individual's (secondhand) experience.

7

The Imagined Agreement of Others

Exaggerated Impressions of Social Support

My opinion, my conviction, gains infinitely in strength and success, the moment a second mind has adopted it.

Novalis

What we believe is heavily influenced by what we think others believe. We favor or oppose experimentation with sex, drugs, and various other "lifestyle" practices in part because of what we think other people think, or do, about these matters. We consider a theater production to be worthy or unworthy of our attendance partly by the number of people who line up to see it. When asked at the office to donate money for a "going-away" gift for someone, we usually try to find out how much others have given and then decide our own contribution accordingly.

Within limits, this tendency to let the beliefs of others influence our own beliefs is perfectly justified. What other people think and how other people behave are important sources of information about what is correct, valid, or appropriate. Other things being equal, the greater the number of people who believe something, the more likely it is to be true; the more people who do something, the more we are well-advised to do the same.

Unfortunately, our ability to utilize effectively the opinions of others as an important source of indirect information about the wisdom of our actions, or the validity of our beliefs, is compromised by a systematic defect in our ability to estimate the beliefs and attitudes of others. We often exaggerate the extent to which other people hold the same beliefs that we do. Because our beliefs appear to enjoy more social support than is actually the case, they are more resistant to change than they would be otherwise. Thus, our difficulty in accurately estimating what other people think represents an important determinant of the maintenance of erroneous beliefs.*

SOCIAL PROJECTION AND THE FALSE CONSENSUS EFFECT

The idea that we project onto others our own beliefs, attitudes, and predispositions has a long history. Perhaps the most widely known treatment of this notion is Freud's analysis of the defense mechanism of projection.[1] Freud, of course, was concerned with the special case of people detecting characteristics in others that, because of their threatening nature, they are *unaware* of possessing themselves. A man who has yet to come to grips with his dissatisfaction with his wife might see evidence of marital discord in numerous relationships. Since Freud's time, however, there has also developed an extensive literature on the tendency of individuals to attribute to others characteristics that they know they themselves possess.[2] People who like loud music, fast cars, and late nights—and who are willing and able to say so—also tend to project their affinities onto others.

Most of the recent research on this topic has focused on what has come to be known as the "false consensus effect."[3] The false consensus effect refers to the tendency for people's own beliefs, values, and habits to bias their estimates of how widely such views and habits are shared by others. Francophiles think that more people

* The idea that we overestimate the extent to which others share our beliefs implies that this mechanism concerns beliefs that we already hold. This mechanism is thus most directly relevant to understanding the *maintenance*, rather than the *formation*, of erroneous beliefs. Because of this, and because this mechanism is so general that it serves to bolster almost *any* belief, it will receive less explicit discussion than the mechanisms discussed in earlier chapters when it comes to dealing with the specific beliefs addressed in chapters 8–10. Nevertheless, perceived consensus has such an important and pervasive impact on people's views that any analysis of the mechanisms underlying questionable and erroneous beliefs would be incomplete without a discussion of the sources of error in people's judgments of what other people think.

are fans of French culture and cuisine than do Francophobes; drinkers believe that more people like to imbibe than do teetotalers. The most widely-cited demonstration of this phenomenon is one in which university students were asked, as part of an experiment, whether they would be willing to walk around campus wearing a large sandwich-board sign bearing the message "REPENT." A substantial percentage agreed to wear the sign, and a substantial percentage refused. After agreeing or declining to wear the sign, the students were asked to estimate the percentage of their peers who would agree or decline. The students' estimates were slanted in the direction of their own choices: Those who agreed to wear the sign thought that 60% would do so, whereas those who refused thought that only 27% would agree to wear it.[4]

It is important to emphasize at the outset the *relative* nature of the false consensus effect. People do not always think that their own beliefs are shared by a majority of other people. Rather, the false consensus effect refers to a tendency for people's estimates of the commonness of a given belief to be positively correlated with their own beliefs. Religious fundamentalists do not necessarily believe that most people have a similar orientation, although their estimates of the percentage of religious fundamentalists in the general population can be counted on to exceed similar estimates made by their more secular peers.

Most of the recent research on the false consensus effect has been devoted to understanding why people unknowingly exaggerate the extent to which others share their beliefs. The authors of the seminal paper on the subject had argued that there is probably no single cause. They claimed that the false consensus effect was most likely a multiply-determined phenomenon, and they described a number of specific mechanisms that might be responsible for it.[5] Subsequent research has largely confirmed their initial speculations by documenting the mediating role of a host of cognitive and motivational variables.

There is evidence, for example, that the false consensus effect is partly a motivational phenomenon that stems from our desire to maintain a positive assessment of our own judgment—a desire that is bolstered by thinking that our beliefs lie in the mainstream. Consistent with this idea, people have been shown to be particularly likely to exaggerate the amount of perceived social support for their beliefs when they have an emotional investment in the belief,[6] and when their sense of self-esteem has been threatened by a previous failure experience.[7] Also consistent with this explanation are results indicating that people are particularly likely to exaggerate the extent to which attractive, respected, and well-liked people have beliefs similar to their own.[8]

Other explanations of the false consensus effect focus on the information to which we are generally exposed and the way we process that information. It is a fact of social life that we are selectively exposed to information that tends to support our beliefs.[9] Conservatives read conservative periodicals and thus receive support for a conservative political agenda; religious fundamentalists tend to read "creationist" literature rather than contemporary evolutionary biology and thus buttress their conviction that evolution is a mere theory, not a historical fact. Because we so often encounter arguments and evidence in support of our beliefs while generally staying clear of information that contradicts them, our beliefs appear to be more sensible and warranted—and therefore common—than they would if we were exposed to a less biased body of information. Furthermore, in addition to being exposed to a biased set of *arguments* relevant to a given belief, we are also exposed to a biased sample of *people* and their opinions. Liberals associate with fellow liberals; exercise enthusiasts affiliate with other athletes. Indeed, similarity of beliefs, values, and habits is one of the primary determinants of those with whom we associate. As a result, when trying to estimate the percentage of people who hold a particular belief, examples of people who believe as we do come to mind more readily than examples of people who believe differently. Our own beliefs thus appear to be quite common. The most direct evidence for the influence of this mechanism on the false consensus effect is the finding that people's estimates of the prevalence of smoking are positively correlated with the number of people they know who smoke.[10]

The false consensus effect is also partly a product of the type of causes people believe to be responsible for why they believe or act the way they do. When we think our beliefs or actions are the result of external elements like the situation or issues involved, we assume that those elements would have a similar influence on others and so we infer that other people would tend to think or act likewise. We believe, in other words, that what are powerful situational influences on our own behavior should govern the behavior of others as well. Alternatively, when our beliefs or actions seem to us to be more the product of personal dispositions or idiosyncratic past experiences that do not pertain to others, we have less reason to believe that others would think or act similarly. Overall, the false consensus effect should be quite pervasive because there is a well-documented tendency for people to be generally more inclined to explain their own behavior in terms of external, situational causes than in terms of internal, personal dispositions.[11]* Nevertheless, people do not *always* cite situational elements as the cause of their actions, and so the false consensus effect should vary in strength with the extent to which people do in fact identify such external factors as the cause of their beliefs, attitudes, or behavior.

Research that my colleagues Dennis and Susan Jennings and I conducted a number of years ago supports this analysis.[12] In one experiment, individuals who were induced to explain their preferences in terms of personal causes exhibited less of a false consensus effect than those who were led to explain them in terms of external factors. In another study, the size of the false consensus effect for a variety of different issues was related to the extent to which those issues typically prompt situational explanations for a person's responses. Items that tend to elicit external reasons for one's choice ("Would you rather buy stock in Exxon or General Motors?") yielded larger false consensus effects than items that elicit more personal reasons ("Would you rather name your son Jacob or Ian?").

Finally, there is yet another determinant of the false consensus effect, one that may be the most interesting and may have the most far-reaching consequences. This mechanism involves the resolution of ambiguities inherent in most issues, choices, or situations. Before we can decide what we think about some issue, we must first arrive at an exact definition or specification of its meaning. When deciding whether we prefer French or Italian films, for example, we must first determine exactly what the terms French and Italian films mean. The precise way that we interpret these two

---

* This tendency applies only to people's explanations of their *own* behavior. As discussed in the previous chapter, people tend to think of other people's behavior as the product of underlying personal traits and dispositions. For more information on this asymmetry in causal attribution, the reader should consult: E. E. Jones, & R. E. Nisbett (1971) The actor and the observer: divergent perceptions of the causes of behavior. In E. E. Jones, D. Kanouse, H. H. Kelley, et al. (Eds.), *Attribution: Perceiving the causes of behavior,* pp. 79–94. Morristown, NJ: General Learning Press, or D. Watson, (1982) The actor and the observer: How are their perceptions of causality divergent? *Psychological Bulletin, 92,* 682–700.

categories will not only decide our own preference, but will exert a parallel influence on our estimates of the preferences of others. If we think of *The Bicycle Thief* and *La Strada* when we think of Italian films, for instance, we may be more likely to prefer Italian films ourselves and to estimate that a larger percentage of the general population would have the same preference than if we construe Italian films to mean spaghetti Westerns.

Note that this interpretation of the false consensus effect rests on two assumptions: a) different people construe the same choices quite differently, and b) people generally fail to recognize this fact and thus fail to make adequate allowance for it when making consensus estimates. It seems that the process of interpretation is so reflexive and immediate that we often overlook it. This, combined with the widespread assumption that there is but one objective reality, is what may lead people to overlook the possibility that others may be responding to a very different situation.

The extent to which such differences in construal give rise to the false consensus effect has been amply demonstrated by empirical research.[13] What this research implies is that people are generally aware that others have different tastes, values, and orientations, and this awareness influences their judgments about the extent to which other people believe as they do. People are less aware, however, of another source of divergent beliefs—the fact that the same issue or situation is construed quite differently by different people, even people with the same tastes, values, and orientations. As social psychologist Solomon Asch noted many years ago, differences of opinion between people are not always linked to differences in their "judgment of the object," but often reflect differences in the very "object of judgment" itself.[14] To the extent that we are unaware of this hidden source of divergent opinion, we are likely to overestimate the extent to which others share our beliefs. With our beliefs thereby bolstered by unwarranted levels of perceived social support, we hold them with greater conviction and are less likely to abandon them in the face of logical or empirical challenges to their validity.

INADEQUATE FEEDBACK FROM OTHERS

It might be expected that most of our misconceptions, particularly our misconceptions about what other people think, would be corrected by feedback from others. People might be expected to let us know when our beliefs are out of line, or at least when our assumptions about *them* are out of line. This is no doubt true to some degree: Many of our most bizarre and erroneous beliefs do not survive our interactions and discussions with others. Nevertheless, I will argue in the balance of this chapter that such corrective feedback is not as common as one might think. To a certain extent this is due to the fact—discussed above—that we associate primarily with those who share our own beliefs, values, and habits. Even more important, however, is that even when we do cross paths with people whose beliefs and attitudes conflict with our own, we are rarely challenged. People are generally reluctant to openly question another person's beliefs.*

My own experience in writing this book is instructive in this regard. Over the last several months, numerous people have asked me about what I am writing, including many who hold the kind of beliefs about psychic powers and holistic health practices that I call into question in Chapters 8 and 10. One might expect, then, that a brief description of the book would produce spirited argument over our various points of disagreement. I am sad to say that this has rarely happened. Instead, my descriptions of the book are met with the kind of acquiescence and affirmative nods that generally connote agreement and approval. And I believe that my own experience in this regard is quite typical! Consider how often we hold back our own reservations and disbelief when the roles are reversed and it is we who disagree with what someone is saying. When colleagues confide that they are mistreated, unappreciated, and underpaid, for example, we often remain silent or nod in apparent approval even if we consider the colleague's complaints groundless. When someone tells us what they intend to name their newborn child, we generally give some bland indication of approval, although privately we may consider the name to be discordant or

---

* *Adults* are generally reluctant to do so, that is. Children tend to be more brutally honest with one another, and, as a result, it is in childhood that we receive some of the most informative feedback about how we affect others. If we believe that we have funny ears, cannot sing, or look awkward when we run, chances are that we were apprised of this fact by a childhood acquaintance. A telling comparison: It is not an uncommon experience for an adult to return from a social gathering and learn that his fly is open, she has broccoli in her teeth, or that one's nasal hairs have grown too long—and no one said a word! On the playground, however, children point out such offenses with great enthusiasm.

pretentious. The same is true when others ask us about the color they have just painted their house, or show us a piece of furniture or art they just bought. Even political and intellectual issues, presented in literature and film as sources of contentious debate at the dinner table, seem to produce less vocalized disagreement in real life than one might expect.

Evidence for this comes from several sources. First, people who live alone, elderly widows and widowers in particular, often worry that they will develop odd habits because there will be nobody around to point out their oddity or inappropriateness. They recognize that only our most intimate friends and relatives can be counted on to tell us when our beliefs are out of line or when our actions are inappropriate. More casual acquaintances generally try to sidestep the awkwardness of disagreement and thus leave us without essential corrective feedback.

A second source of evidence for people's reluctance to openly disagree with others can be found in etiquette manuals. As sociologist Erving Goffman notes, etiquette manuals represent a codification of society's norms and practices and thus can sometimes tell us a great deal about how people are expected to behave.[15] Most are very clear on this issue of whether we should air our disagreements with others. "Miss Manners," for instance, tells her readers that "One cannot go around correcting others."[16] Emily Post expresses the same sentiment when she says that "The tactful person keeps his prejudices to himself. . . ." and that "Certain subjects, even though you are very sure of the ground upon which you are standing, had best be shunned; such, for example, as the criticism of a religious creed or disagreement with another's political conviction."[17] The guardians of proper behavior, in other words, seem to agree with the poet Heinrich Heine that "God has given us speech in order that we may say pleasant things to our friends." The implication of their advice should be clear: To the extent that people routinely follow these prescriptions, we are unlikely to have our misguided beliefs and questionable habits reined in by explicit challenge from others.

Our reluctance to voice our disagreements has also been demonstrated in psychological research. Although there is not a large research literature on this issue, what evidence there is clearly supports the contention that people generally try to avoid potential conflict with others. In several experiments, individuals have been asked to discuss an issue or another person in front of an audience known to have a particular opinion about the subject in question. Sometimes the participants are asked to discuss their own opinion of the subject, and at other times they are merely required to summarize an assessment given to them by the experimenter. In either case, their comments are generally slanted to appear to be more in line with those of their audience than is actually the case.[18] We tend to discuss a person's good points with his or her friends, but focus more on flaws when talking to his or her adversaries. We tend to soften or intensify our expressed position about, say, bilingual education or tax reform in accord with what we think are the beliefs or preferences of our audience.

The reasons we act this way are hardly mysterious. Doing so allows us to avoid the unpleasant emotions produced by discordant interactions. Disagreement often spoils our social encounters, and it is understandable that people might want to feign agreement to head off conflict and disharmony. In addition, people are also intuitively aware of one of the most basic laws of social psychology—that we tend to like people who are similar to ourselves. Thus, people recognize that to express disagreement is to risk being disliked. We sometimes try to shield ourselves from such antipathy by claiming that we are "just playing devil's advocate" or that we are simply relaying the opinions of someone else. Such gambits are not always effective, however, because people tend to infer that a speaker's statements reflect his or her true opinions to some degree even when they know that the substance of the speaker's remarks were determined by someone else.[19] The tale of the messenger who was beheaded for reporting that the royal army had been defeated is relevant here: There are risks involved in being the "bearer of bad tidings" even when the bad tidings are not of one's own making.

Our relative inexperience with open conflict is partly responsible, I believe, for a peculiar pattern of behavior that is exhibited after faculty meetings in the Department of Psychology at Cornell University (and elsewhere, I assume). Even in harmonious departments, a faculty meeting can sometimes be a stressful affair in which solutions to difficult problems are sought by people who often have fundamentally different interests and orientations. As a result, it represents one of those relatively infrequent occasions in which we participate in open, competitive lobbying and, occasionally, in acrimonious debate. Of course, all of the conflict that comes out in such a meeting exists beforehand, but it remains mostly unspoken until then, as everyone talks primarily with his or her known allies, and most of the dialogue with the "other side" is circumspect.

What occurs after such meetings is a period of "decompression" in which everyone mills around the halls and, in small groups, replays what was said in an effort both to determine what it all means and, more important, to smooth over any bitterness that may have been created. At such times, the faculty resembles nothing so much as a collection of people in need of an encounter group session or two. It is hard to resist the conclusion that this reaction might be diminished if we encountered such open discussions of differences more often.

Our inexperience with open disagreement and conflict is also reflected in the phenomenon of gossip. Gossip can be seen as a vehicle through which we release the pent-up dissent we are unable to express directly. What cannot be said to the source of our dis-agreement or disbelief is conveyed to someone else (who, by the way, is expected to agree with us—or at least appear to agree). Furthermore, gossip is also a means for getting us closer to the truth through a process of "triangulation" in which our own imper-fect knowledge is combined with that held by others. Because we know that everyone tries to put an agreeable slant on things in our everyday interactions, we can never be sure whether we have heard the complete and honest truth from someone. "Did she really like my lecture?" "Do they honestly like him, or are they just saying that because they know I do?" By consulting other people's knowledge, we can see things from several angles, and can try to make adjustments for any biases in our own knowledge base. Inconsistencies in what people say to us and what they say to other people, for example, enables us to get a better idea of what their true feelings are likely to be. Previous accounts of gossip have discussed how it serves as a way for people to achieve a stable and shared definition of reality;[20] what these accounts have failed to emphasize, however, is that one of the reasons gossip is particularly well-suited to this task is that we do not always receive veridical feedback from others. Gossip helps fill the void.

Thus far, this discussion has focused on the reluctance to express disagreement in everyday social interaction. This is undoubtedly where the reluctance occurs most frequently. This does not imply, however, that the phenomenon exists only in such everyday circum-stances where the consequences of not speaking up can sometimes be rather negligible. Even members of Presidential advisory groups have been known to suppress their dissenting views when airing them would have promoted a more thorough and vigorous deliberation and a more effective policy. Sometimes doubts are withheld because of members' fear that their sentiments will not be well received and that their personal status and future political effectiveness will diminish as a result. Vice President Hubert Humphrey, for example, learned to swallow his doubts about the Johnson administration's Vietnam policy and "get back on the team" after his statement of his initial reservations had him banished from the inner circle for a number of months.[21] Even when an advisor is not concerned with his or her own status and power, doubts are sometimes suppressed in the interest of group harmony. As psychologist Irving Janis's work on "Groupthink" suggests, members of highly cohesive advisory groups who are under considerable pressure to devise effective courses of action can become overly concerned with maintaining apparent consensus within the group and will sometimes censor their personal reservations to accomplish it. Disastrous policies sometimes result. Janis cites the passage from Arthur Schlesinger's account of the Bay of Pigs fiasco in which he castigates himself "for having kept so silent during those crucial discussions in the Cabinet Room. . . . I can only explain my failure to do more than raise a few timid questions by reporting that one's impulse to blow the whistle on this nonsense was simply undone by the circumstances of the discussion."[22]

Inside accounts of Presidential advisory groups make it clear that the failure to express dissent can have direct, immediate, and severe consequences. More relevant to the purposes of this book, however, is the damage that stems from its less direct, less immediate, but more pervasive effects. Because so much disagreement remains hidden, our beliefs are not properly shaped by healthy scrutiny and debate. The absence of such argument also leads us to exaggerate the extent to which other people believe the way that we do. Bolstered by such a false sense of social support, our beliefs strike us as more warranted than is actually the case, and they become rather resistant to subsequent logical and empirical challenge.

PART THREE

Examples of Questionable and Erroneous Beliefs

8

Belief in Ineffective "Alternative" Health Practices

Next to the indeterminacy principle, I have learned in recent years to loathe most the term "holistic," a meaningless signifier empowering the muddle of all the useful distinctions human thought has labored at for two thousand years.

Roger Lambert, in John Updike's *Roger's Version*

No area has been more plagued by questionable, erroneous, and often harmful beliefs than the field of medicine and health. As recently as the nineteenth century, the acclaimed physician and signer of the Declaration of Independence Benjamin Rush treated victims of yellow fever, himself included, with vigorous bloodletting. Today, people afflicted with cancer flock in great numbers to worthless Laetrile clinics in Mexico, fraudulent psychic "surgeons" in the Philippines, and profiteering faith healers in the United States. Desperate AIDS patients seek help in all manner of worthless rituals and costly potions, including pounding themselves on the chest to stimulate the thymus gland, exposing their genitals to sunlight, rectally administering ozone gas, and injecting themselves with hydrogen peroxide.[1]

It is not just the uneducated or dull witted who are vulnerable to these beliefs. Francis Bacon believed that warts could be cured by rubbing them with pork rinds. George Washington thought that various bodily ills could be cured by passing two three-inch metal rods over the afflicted area. The British statesman William Gladstone thought that we would all be healthier if we chewed each bite of food precisely 32 times: Why else, he argued, did nature endow us with exactly 32 teeth?[2]

If the bloodletting of Benjamin Rush did not make this clear, it is also important to note that such beliefs are not just harmless sources of idle talk and speculation. They often exact a fierce price, a price paid in dollars, in physical health and emotional trauma, and in lives lost. It has been estimated that Americans spend ten billion dollars per year on quack remedies, including three billion on bogus cancer "cures" and one billion on worthless AIDS treatments.[3] In the more important currency of lives lost, John Miner of the Los Angeles County District Attorney's office goes so far as to claim that "quackery kills more people than those who die from all crimes of violence put together."[4]

Why do so many people subject themselves to such expensive and, in many cases, injurious treatment? Something must make these treatments seem effective, or potentially effective, even when they are not. What is it? What is there about such treatments, about the nature of disease and dysfunction, and about the way people think that makes so many people believe in the therapeutic value of demonstrably ineffective health practices?

THE WILL TO BELIEVE

Part of the reason that erroneous beliefs about health are so rampant is that what they offer is so tempting. Having an untreatable disease—or the possibility of contracting one—is so threatening that people desperately grasp at claims that the threat is not so severe or so completely beyond their control. Alternative medical practices offer hope when the limits of conventional medicine are exceeded. It is no accident that bogus remedies are most prevalent for those problems, such as arthritis, cancer, or aging, that orthodox medicine can do little or nothing about. The temptation to believe in such cases is so strong that we do not exercise our critical faculties to their fullest; sometimes we suspend them altogether.

The contrast between the cold truth of conventional medicine and the warm comfort of "fringe" practices can affect our thoughts and actions in several ways. Many individuals faced with a terminal illness that conventional medicine cannot cure will turn to various fringe practices out of desperation. "I have to try something," "I have nowhere else to turn," or simply "Why not?" are some of the sentiments expressed in such cases. Then, if a little positive thinking is considered necessary for the treatment to be effective, the person will no doubt do everything possible to muster the necessary optimism. The individual then acts as if he or she believed fully in the treatment's effectiveness. Upon doing so, it is not always easy to distinguish desperate actions from genuine belief—even to the person doing the acting. Just as our actions can convince others about what we believe, they can also convince us.[5]

Under such dire circumstances, a person can hardly be faulted for trying anything that has even the most remote chance of success. (Provided, of course, that the "remedy" in question does not do any actual harm, or does not do more harm than a more conventional treatment.) Desperate times call for desperate measures. And besides, why not?

But it is not these practices that serve as the subject of this chapter because in such cases, at least initially, there is no strong belief. Instead, the focus here is on those instances in which people genuinely believe in the practice's effectiveness—instances in which people insist their beliefs are warranted in light of experience, or in light of some underlying theory of the practice's soundness. Here too the will to believe has an impact. The comfort provided by believing that there are remedies for many of life's afflictions can affect how we evaluate information pertaining to a remedy's effectiveness. We may become kinder to information that supports our hopes and rather critical of information that is antagonistic to them (see Chapter 5).

Note, however, that this does not mean that people will simply believe whatever they want to believe. Usually there must be some evidence that a particular fringe practice may be effective. Granted, the evidence may seem compelling only when evaluated rather uncritically, but to the person holding the belief, it is evidence nonetheless. People rarely defend their beliefs in certain health practices by simply asserting, "I just prefer to believe it is true" (as they do when defending certain religious beliefs, in contrast). But what evidence is there? How can a demonstrably ineffective health practice nonetheless appear to be effective? To answer this question we must consider certain aspects of the nature of disease and dysfunction.

POST HOC ERGO PROPTER HOC

Many people do not appreciate how much healing is done, not by doctors, drugs, or surgery, but by our bodies themselves. Roughly

50% of all illnesses for which people seek medical help are "self limited"—i.e., they are cured by the body's own healing processes without assistance from medical science.[6] The body is a truly amazing machine with remarkable powers to set itself right. If this were not the case, it is entirely possible that the practice of medicine would not have survived the long formative period of its history when it offered a host of destructive interventions like bloodletting and trephining (i.e., drilling holes in the skull to allow evil agents to escape). Civilization might well have given up on the quest to treat disease and injury before the development of antisepsis, vaccination, antibiotics, and improved surgical procedures in the nineteenth and twentieth centuries. (Or at least it might have limited itself to interventions like rituals and prayers in which there is no bodily intrusion.)

With the body so effective in healing itself, many who seek medical assistance will experience a positive outcome even if the doctor does nothing beneficial. Thus, even a worthless treatment can appear effective when the base-rate of success is so high. When an intervention is followed by improvement, the intervention's effectiveness stands out as an irresistible product of the person's experience. As Sir Peter Medawar describes it: "If a person a) is poorly, b) receives treatment intended to make him better, and c) gets better, then no power of reasoning known to medical science can convince him that it may not have been the treatment that restored his health."[7]

This, then, is a particularly noteworthy example of the general problem of learning from experience discussed in Chapter 3. By trying one treatment, the person cannot learn what would have happened if another treatment (or no treatment at all) had been attempted. The current success dominates the person's experience, making it difficult to consider likely outcomes under other, hypothetical conditions. *Post hoc ergo propter hoc.*

Another source of misplaced faith in ineffective treatments stems from the precise course of ailments that are *not* self-limited. Even when the body cannot heal itself of certain afflictions, the ailments generally do not result in a steady, uniform deterioration. Rather, the problems unfold in fits and starts, with periods of deterioration mixed with episodes of improvement. It is these temporary periods of relief that give rise to erroneous perceptions of a treatment's effectiveness. When, after all, will a treatment most likely be applied? Generally, it will be administered when there is a marked deterioration in the person's condition. And, as with all trends characterized by considerable fluctuation in improvement and deterioration, such low points will tend to be followed by periods of improvement even if the treatment is completely ineffective. Statistical regression guarantees it. Thus, without a general appreciation of the phenomenon of regression, or without an awareness of the common fluctuations in the course of most diseases, any temporary improvement is likely to be attributed to the treatment. *Post hoc ergo propter hoc.*

In fact, when a "treatment" is introduced immediately after a flare-up in a person's symptomatology, almost any outcome can appear to support its effectiveness. If the treatment is followed by improvement, it will be deemed a success as just described. The treatment might also be considered successful if the person merely stays the same: After all, the treatment was able to arrest the person's slide and successfully stabilize his or her condition. Furthermore, if one's initial confidence in the treatment is sufficiently strong, all may not be lost even if the person deteriorates or dies. Even such dramatic failures can sometimes be accounted for in ways that leave one's faith in the treatment intact. Perhaps the dosage was insufficient. Maybe the patient waited too long before seeking help. Because such rationalizations do so much to sustain people's beliefs in ineffective health practices, it is important to examine them in some detail.

SNATCHING SUCCESS FROM THE JAWS OF FAILURE

Although a high rate of spontaneous remission can provide apparent support for the effectiveness of even a completely worthless treatment, it still leaves a number of unambiguous failures that need to be accounted for in some way. Often the failures are simply discounted, as in the examples above. Faith healers employ a particularly convenient form of this defense by attributing any setbacks to the sufferer's lack of spiritual purity or the vagaries of God's will. The faith healer J. J. Rogers, a.k.a. Prophet Johnson, is remarkably clear on this matter: "If I can't heal them, there's something wrong with their souls."[8] The more widely-known Kathryn Kuhlman employs the same tactic when she professes that "I don't heal; the Holy Spirit heals through me."[9]

The field of holistic health, with its emphasis on mental control over physical states and the importance of mind/body/spirit integration, has spawned similar explanations for its failures. Consider one of the holistic health movement's most popular credos: "It is much more important to know what sort of patient has the disease than what sort of disease the patient has."[10] Apparently, those whose physical symptoms do not abate are simply not the right "sort of patient." Perhaps they have not meditated sufficiently, have not achieved the proper integration of mind, body, and spirit, or have not abstracted the proper "meaning" from their illness. Failures are not the fault of the underlying theory, but stem from the patient's inability to apply it effectively.

Belief in the effectiveness of an intervention or an overarching philosophy of health can also be bolstered by attributing failure to the inadequacies of the *practitioner* as well as the patient. The treatment is still thought to be generally effective, it just was not administered correctly. One holistic health advocate goes so far as to state that most of the failures of holistic interventions stem from the practitioner's failure to adequately understand or administer the proper holistic techniques.[11]

To be fair, it is important to note that such rationalizations plague conventional medicine as well—witness the old standby of the surgical profession that "the operation was successful but the patient died." Such justifications, however, are more common and are taken more seriously in the field of fringe medicine because it is a field that relies so heavily on anecdotal evidence. In fact, many advocates of alternative health practices completely reject controlled experimentation as a valid means for arriving at the truth. "Real life" experience is considered the only informative guide to whether a treatment is beneficial. But everyday experience, as we have just seen, can sometimes make even worthless remedies seem effective. Conventional practitioners might initially defend their pet treatments by explaining away their failures, but most at least acknowledge the supremacy of scientific investigation. Under such scrutiny, a treatment's weaknesses will eventually come to light, as it has with bloodletting, laetrile, and the porta-caval shunt (see Chapter 10).

This tendency to blame the patient for a treatment's deficiencies is often adopted, not only by practitioners, but, sadly, by the patients themselves. Most individuals who seek out Kathryn Kuhlman for a miraculous cure for their afflictions do not blame her when improvement is not forthcoming. Many conclude that it was their own fault—they had not lived a sufficiently holy life. Others assume that their getting well was just not a part of God's plan.[12] Likewise, many of those who do not benefit from various holistic health regimens engage in similar self-blame to protect their belief in the treatment's general effectiveness. Carl and Stephanie Simonton, pioneering advocates of the use of mental imagery as a tool for treating cancer, provide a telling example of how far this can go:

> Some of our early patients felt we had given them the key to certain recovery, and thought, "Yes! I can do it!"—and then, as we discovered later, felt guilty if they failed to recover. . . . Eventually, their families brought us . . . [the patients'] . . . last words: "Tell Carl and Stephanie that the method still works," or "Tell them it isn't their fault."[13]

Explaining away obvious failures is really just part of a broader tendency to evaluate treatment outcomes in a biased manner. Evidence indicating that a favored practice might be effective is considered decisive; information to the contrary is critically scrutinized and explained away. While even unambiguous failures can sometimes be discounted (as in the examples above), it is obviously easier to maintain belief in an ineffective intervention when the outcomes are less clear-cut. Thus it is easier to believe that a treatment is effective in bringing about vague improvements in symptomatology than in effecting a genuine cure. Consider the results of a recent survey of cancer patients receiving unorthodox treatment for their illness (e.g., metabolic therapy, diet therapy, faith healing, etc.) either in concert with or instead of more conventional treatments like chemotherapy, radiation, or surgery. In line with the results presented thus far in this chapter, the patients were generally pleased with their decision to undergo an unconventional treatment. However, they were more likely to believe that the treatment had some vague positive effect on their general health than to believe that it had an actual impact on their cancer. Less than half of the respondents felt that the treatment had affected their cancer, whereas two-thirds thought that it had brought about an improvement in their general health.[14] The more ambiguous the criterion, the easier it is to detect evidence of success.

It is for precisely this reason that many alternative health practices do not offer precise remedies for specific disabilities. They promise instead to bring about "wellness," "higher functioning," or "better integration"—ambiguous benefits that may be hard to refute. Faith healers take full advantage of ambiguous criteria and studiously avoid pinning themselves down to verifiable predictions. When Kathryn Kuhlman announces that "I see someone up there [in the audience] being cured of their arthritis; I rebuke that disease," the risk of being disproven is slight indeed. In the enthusiasm of the moment it is almost certain that at least one person will experience some alleviation of symptoms and will stand up to "claim a cure." Who can tell whether the cure is genuine? Note that Ms. Kuhlman does not proclaim that "someone with skin disease has just been cured; I rebuke that disease." Such a claim would be manifestly false to those assembled. Instead, she sticks mainly to cures for relatively invisible or ambiguous maladies like bursitis, migraines, cancer, or hearing loss.[15] In a similar vein, an insightful Frenchman once remarked after visiting Lourdes, where there is an abundant supply of discarded eyeglasses, hearing aids, canes, etc., "What? No artificial limbs?"

I do not mean to imply that Kathryn Kuhlman deliberately hides behind ambiguous criteria to dupe individuals with terrible illnesses. Although some faith healers cynically play upon the public's hopes in search of profit, others sincerely and fervently believe in what they offer. I do not wish to speculate as to which camp any particular healer belongs. The important point is that although ambiguous criteria can be deliberately exploited by someone wishing to pass off a bogus therapy as effective, they can also impede our genuine efforts to understand whether or not a given treatment works. Without a precise specification of what constitutes success and failure, our hopes and expectations can lead us to detect more support for a given treatment than is actually warranted. A brief anecdote illustrates, perhaps, that even two-time Nobel Prize winners can be misled by the juggling of ambiguous criteria. Linus Pauling, a long-time proponent of vitamin C as an antidote to the common cold and other physical ailments, was once asked whether it was true that he and his wife (who, of course, make sure they consume the requisite amount of the vitamin) no longer suffer from colds. "It is true," he said, "We don't get colds at all." Then he added, "Just sniffles."[16]

THE AURA OF PLAUSIBILITY

We believe certain things because they ought to be true. We believe that handwriting analysis or various projective tests yield deep insights into a person's personality because the underlying logic seems plausible. People *ought* to leave traces of themselves in their overt responses, especially their responses to ambiguous stimuli (such as an inkblot or a blank sheet of paper). Similarly, most people are convinced that eating beef contributes to heart disease, in part because the fat on the side of a steak or on the bottom of a skillet looks ideally (and diabolically) suited to clog coronary arteries. What is gummy and coagulated outside the body, the thinking goes, ought to be gummy and coagulated on the inside as well. Of course, things that ought to be true often are. But many times our sense of what ought to be true obscures our vision of what is actually the case, particularly when the underlying theories that generate this sense of plausibility are rather superficial.

This tendency to rely heavily on what seems plausible has contributed to a number of questionable beliefs about health. Misguided general theories about nature or about the way the body works have made certain notions seem plausible, and this in turn has led to the adoption of various ill-advised practices. One such general theory (so general, in fact, it is perhaps best considered a metatheory) is the representativeness heuristic discussed in Chapter 2. According to this overarching belief, effects should resemble their causes, instances should resemble the categories of which they are members, and, more generally, like belongs with like. In the realm of health, this results in the belief that the symptoms of a disease ought to resemble or in some way suggest its cause. Similarly, the symptoms of a disease ought to resemble or in some way suggest its *cure.*

These beliefs are revealed most clearly in certain primitive medical practices, according to which substances that cause or cure a particular condition tend to share various external features of the condition itself. In ancient Chinese medicine, for example, people with vision problems were fed ground bat in the mistaken belief that bats had particularly keen vision and that some of this ability would be transferred to the recipient. Similarly, primitive tribes have forcibly fed liver (thought to be the locus of mercy) to the mean-spirited, early Western physicians prescribed the meat of the fox (known for its endurance) for asthmatics, and even today a number of alternative medical practitioners recommend raw brain concentrate for people with psychological problems.[17]

This belief that like goes with like finds one of its most interesting and consequential expressions in the field of homeopathic medicine developed by Samuel Hahneman in the late eighteenth century and still advocated today by many holistic health practitioners. Hahneman believed that every disease could be cured by administering to the sick individual whatever substance *produced* similar symptoms in a healthy person. Thus, the cure is suggested by the cause—like goes with like. He called this the "law of similia." Hahneman carried out systematic "provings" in which he administered various herbs, minerals, and other substances to healthy individuals and noted any symptoms that developed. The results were compiled in reference books, his *materia medica*, that are still consulted by homeopaths today. Although this simple connection between cause and cure might give homeopathic medicine some intuitive appeal, research studies have shown it to be ineffective.

Perhaps the other founding principle of homeopathy will more clearly lay bare its lack of value. This is Hahneman's "law of infinitesimals," which also follows a crude sort of logic. Hahneman noticed that the less of a substance he administered to a healthy person, the less severe were the resulting symptoms. He then concluded that the less concentrated were the remedies administered to the sick, the *more* they would help alleviate the sick person's symptomatology. As a consequence, books on homeopathic medicine describe in great length how to create extremely diluted concentrations of various medicines. In some cases, the recommended dilutions are as high as one part active ingredient per decillion parts water. At such concentrations, it is unlikely that what is given to the person actually contains any of the supposedly active ingredient. Nevertheless, homeopaths insist that their interventions are effective, and that they are more effective at lower concentrations. Once again, research shows otherwise.[18]

The influence of representativeness is also present in people's intuitive beliefs about nutrition, according to which whatever simple properties are present in certain foods will be directly transferred to the person who eats them. Like promotes like. Of course, this belief that "you are what you eat" is sometimes valid: We can gain weight by eating a lot of fat or develop an orange tint to our skin by ingesting a lot of carotene—a compound found in carrots and tomatoes. Many times, however, this belief is taken to almost magical extremes. Psychologist Paul Rozin asked groups of college students to speculate about the personalities and physical attributes of members of (hypothetical) primitive cultures. For example, one group was given a description of a tribe that ate wild boar and hunted sea turtles for their shells; another was told of a tribe that ate sea turtles and hunted boars for their tusks. The students' responses indicated that the tribe members' physical and personality traits were assumed to match the characteristics of the food they ate. Members of the turtle-eating tribe were considered to be better swimmers and more generous; the boar eaters were thought to be more aggressive and more likely to have beards. What we consume is believed to influence, in the most detailed ways, who we are.[19]

Various dietary "remedies" for arthritis are similarly based on the assumption that the external properties of food will be maintained after digestion, and that these properties will have the same effect inside the body as they do outside. Dr. Dan Dale Alexander, author of *Arthritis and Common Sense*, argues that you can fight arthritis by essentially oiling your joints. He recommends that arthritis sufferers ingest liberal amounts of oil, and that they not drink water during meals that contain oil (they don't mix, he argues, so water might destroy the lubricating properties of oil). Utilizing analogous logic, Dr. DeForest Jarvis, author of the phenomenally-popular *Folk Medicine: A Vermont Doctor's Guide to Good Health*, states that in searching for an arthritis remedy he ". . . studied methods used by plumbers in freeing the inside of the furnace water compartment from deposited calcium."[20] Whatever breaks down calcium outside the body is supposed to do the same to recalcitrant compounds on the inside. Because plumbers use an acid compound to solve their problem, Dr. Jarvis recommends vinegar—a mild acid—to relieve the stiffness of arthritis.

These remedies ignore the fact that the body transforms most ingested substances, and therefore whatever properties they have outside the body can be radically altered or completely absent inside. Vinegar, for example, is transformed after metabolic breakdown from a mild acid to an alkaline residue. Without this understanding, unfortunately, people continue to try worthless treatments because they seem to make some intuitive sense. Many diet fads suffer from the same problem. Dr. Jarvis again: "Oil and vinegar don't mix. Maybe vinegar and fat wouldn't either, and vinegar might win out."[21] His logic apparently has some surface appeal because his diet prescription was widely followed.

Simple theorizing has also contributed to the widespread belief that we should periodically "cleanse" the insides of our bodies. Just as we periodically clean our car engines or our videocassette recorders to make them function more effectively, so it is believed that our alimentary canals could benefit from an occasional house-cleaning as well. Some people do so by fasting, others by administering enemas, drinking large quantities of water, or eating yogurt. Perhaps the most extreme manifestation of this belief was the surgical procedure known as "Lane's kink." The British physician Arbuthnot Lane was concerned, along with many of his colleagues, about the deleterious consequences of "auto-intoxication," or the build-up of waste products in the body. Dr. Lane believed that he had spotted a location in the colon in which the flow of waste slowed down, and so he developed a surgical procedure to cut it out and speed up elimination, a procedure he performed on hundreds unfortunate enough to seek out his services.

Dr. Lane's practice aside, many of these techniques seem to make some intuitive sense, but their appeal is more metaphoric than logical. People say that they "give the body a rest" by periodic fasting. They "wash away" toxins with an occasional enema. Although these metaphors of rest and rinse may seem compelling, our bodies do not necessarily work so simply. Although the build-up of toxins in the body is certainly something to be avoided, the body has evolved to handle this job extremely well. Our simplistic tinkerings can hinder this process as much as help it.

What all of this boils down to is that we need to question whether our beliefs (about health or anything else) stem mainly from a sense of surface plausibility. The naturalness with which we base judgments on representativeness should lead us to be particularly concerned with beliefs that conform to the principle of "like goes with like." It has been argued, for example, that this guiding assumption was partly responsible for people's initial resistance to the germ theory of disease. It just did not seem plausible that a "big" effect like death and disability could stem from such a "little" cause as microscopic organisms. Causes often do resemble their effects, of course, but there are more than enough exceptions to warrant a little caution and a little healthy skepticism.

HOLISTIC HEALTH PRACTICES IN THE "NEW AGE"

During the past twenty-five years, increasing numbers of people have sought alternatives or complements to conventional medical practice, alternatives that are often labelled "holistic" or "New Age." These increasingly popular treatments merit special discussion for two reasons. First, in part because some holistic ideas are promoted by sober scientists and others by pop enthusiasts, it is often unclear what "holistic medicine" encompasses and what these alternative health practices offer. Second, because of this ambiguity as to exactly what constitutes the field of holistic health, it can be difficult to assess the merit of this growing trend. Are there benefits to be derived from these New Age ideas? Alternatively, does the very ambiguity of these approaches make any assessment of their effectiveness particularly vulnerable to the kind of errors and illusions discussed above?

What is holistic medicine? Most broadly, it is an orientation toward health and medicine that rejects or deemphasizes what is considered to be a materialistic and reductionistic bias on the part of conventional "Western" medicine. Orthodox medicine most often seeks to find the organic cause of a disease or dysfunction, and tries to alleviate it with some physical intervention like antibiotics or surgery. The emphasis is on the specific, local cause of the malady and how to fix it. Holists, on the other hand, are more inclined to consider psychological and even spiritual factors as either the cause or the remedy for a given condition. They emphasize the "whole person" rather than the local cause of the dysfunction, and many problems are thought to stem from a lack of "balance" among mind, body, and spirit. The *Journal of Holistic Medicine*, for example, states that its mission emphasizes "personal efforts to achieve balance."

How then does one achieve physical, psychological, and spiritual balance? At its simplest, holistic medicine consists of a set of relatively uncontroversial preventive health practices such as maintaining a proper diet and getting sufficient exercise. The individual is urged to take responsibility for his or her own health, both in terms of adopting lifestyle practices designed to promote "wellness" and in the sense of making informed choices about the treatment of any illness. More directly relevant to the goal of achieving balance, many holists also promote the practice of meditation, yoga, biofeedback, and positive mental imagery. In addition to their purported ability to bring about harmony of mind, body, and spirit, these practices are also thought to reduce stress and thus lower one's susceptibility to diseases considered to be psychological, social, or environmental in origin. The effectiveness of these techniques in meeting either goal, however, has been the subject of considerable controversy. Finally, the most questionable aspects of the field of holistic health are a set of bizarre practices, both ancient and new age, that are linked only through their rejection of and by conventional medicine. Included here are such practices as psychic diagnosis and psychic healing, palmistry, colonic irrigation, faith healing, and iridology (i.e., diagnosing disease anywhere on the body by examining spots on the iris of the eye). These practices are either based on principles that conflict with established knowledge, or have been shown by empirical research to be of absolutely no value (or both).

The "Up" Side of Holistic Medicine. If we ignore these latter, demonstrably bogus interventions, there is surely some merit to both the underlying philosophy and many of the specific practices of holistic medicine. The emphasis on taking responsibility for the direction of one's own treatment, for example, is certainly wise. No matter how concerned and compassionate a doctor might be (and not all of them excel at this part of their job), they cannot be as concerned as the patients themselves. Thus, it is very much in the patient's interest to be well informed about the nature of an illness, and to take an active role in determining the course of treatment. Doctors make mistakes, sometimes very costly ones. They should be viewed, not as infallible miracle workers, but as knowledgeable consultants who assist the patient in doing battle with a particular illness.

Another positive feature of holistic medicine is its emphasis on prevention. Although both preventive medicine and direct intervention can be effective in thwarting disease, prevention is generally less aversive and less expensive. It can also be more effective. Many people are surprised to learn that relatively little of the improvement in health and longevity during the last two hundred years is due to drug and surgical treatment of sick individuals. Most of the gain is attributable to various preventive measures such as improved sewage disposal, water purification, the pasteurization of milk, and improved diets. In fact, our greater longevity is mainly due to our increased chances of surviving childhood, chances increased by these very preventive measures and by the introduction of vaccines for the infectious diseases of youth. The life expectancy of those who make it to adulthood has not changed much during the last hundred years. The life expectancy of a 45-year-old man in the nineteenth century was roughly 70 years, a figure not much different from that of today.

Another way in which the field of holistic health is often beneficial is by helping people to cope with their illness, their disability, or their pain. This is particularly important in today's world where very few of the advances in medicine are of the "magic bullet" variety that completely cure or eradicate a given health problem. Progress in the war on cancer, for example, is slow and incremental. Prognoses are improving and patients are being kept alive longer, but often under a trying regimen of nauseating drugs and disfiguring surgery. The net effect of many of today's medical advances is that people are able to live with their illnesses longer. Various holistic health practices such as meditation, deep muscle relaxation, and positive mental imagery can make doing so easier and more gratifying. Even if such practices did nothing at all about the underlying organic causes of illness, they nevertheless help people to manage their symptoms, and they give people a sense of control over their illness—a sense of control that might be tremendously beneficial even if it turns out to be illusory.

The Unknown Side of Holistic Medicine. Holistic practitioners make a number of claims about how the mind can influence the body that cannot be evaluated adequately at the present time. Sober scientists claim that a person's moods and personality can influence the functioning of the immune system. Pop enthusiasts assert that spiritual harmony and moral integrity have similar effects. Holists from both groups argue that mental imagery might prevent or arrest organic disease.

These claims touch on one of the most exciting areas of research in all of science, the field of psychoimmunology. Researchers in this area are concerned with mapping out the biochemical pathways that connect the brain and the immune system, and thus with how mental states might influence a person's health. Although a number of exciting discoveries have been made, the field is not sufficiently advanced to permit a definitive critique of various claims like those mentioned above. (Incidentally, the very existence of this active field of research within "mainstream" biomedicine contradicts a claim often made by holistic health advocates—that research on the interaction between the mind and body is actively discouraged and even suppressed by the medical "establishment.")

Although it may be too early for definitive answers to many of these questions, a few tentative assessments and predictions might still be warranted. My own view is that the most extreme hopes and predictions about this area of research ultimately will prove to be unfounded. For instance, I am skeptical that mental imagery, however beneficial it might be psychologically, will ever constitute an effective technique for arresting or eliminating organic disease. In part this skepticism stems from a simple "regressive" prediction (see Chapter 2): Very few of the most extreme predictions of *any* emerging field turn out to be true. The "smart money" generally lies on the more modest claims.

Beyond such abstract considerations, however, there are various features of the research findings themselves that warrant some caution about the scope of eventual practical application. One source of potential skepticism, one that is sure to sound paradoxical to some people, is the very abundance of findings that have already been reported in the literature. Sometimes it seems that virtually any psychological variable that might influence the immune system has in fact been shown to have an effect. There are studies indicating that taking an examination, suppressing anger, wanting to exercise power over others, or feeling socially isolated all serve to inhibit certain indices of immune function; whereas relaxation, mental imagery, and watching a comedy film all serve to enhance them.[22]

Together, these findings make it abundantly clear that mental states can exert some influence over the immune system. This by itself is not surprising because it has been known for years that stress can lead to illness. But when we add together all of these more recent findings, they seem to imply the existence of a world very different from the one we inhabit. They suggest a world in which it is mainly the unhappy, the asocial, and repressed who become ill, and one in which our mere thoughts can mitigate the ravages of disease. This jars with our experience of a world in which illness strikes blindly and progresses inexorably in the face of the individual's conscious efforts and desires to stay healthy.

How can we reconcile this optimistic body of research with the grim face of everyday life? One solution is to suggest that although it is relatively easy to demonstrate effects of mental states on certain aspects of immune function, the resulting changes in the immune system may have less of an effect on a person's health than one might initially suspect. Indeed, a number of immunologists have questioned whether specific changes in immune function such as those described above have any effect on an individual's susceptibility to illness. There is no single, valid measure of immunocompetence, only a host of indices related in complex ways to a person's overall ability to resist disease. Thus, temporary deficiencies in specific immune functions may not be terribly significant because they are generally followed by quick recovery and can be compensated for by changes in alternative areas of the immune system.[23] Other investigators argue that while mental states might exert some influence on the initiation of disease, they are likely to be powerless to affect advanced organic pathology.[24]

It may be helpful to examine this issue from a historical perspective. Until very recently, it was widely believed that the immune system operated independently of the central nervous system and thus functioned completely beyond our control. Such a belief was not only consistent with existing knowledge of physiology, but it also made sense from the standpoint of adaptive evolutionary design. Biological functions as important to survival as the immune system might work best if they operate autonomously and are not subject to the vicissitudes of conscious thought. Just as we want our muscular reflexes to be automatic and encapsulated from mental states, we might want our immune system to be equally impenetrable. Because sadness, anxiety, and anger are such common emotions, individuals whose immune functions are dampened by such states are at risk. An advantage in the evolutionary battle for survival would seem to belong to those whose immune functions remain unaffected.*

Advances in our knowledge of physiology have dispelled the idea that the nervous system and the immune system are completely independent. Nerve fibers have been detected in the thymus, spleen, lymph nodes, and bone marrow (regions that produce our most

---

* Some people may be tempted to argue that the advantage would belong to those whose mental states could *enhance* immune function, but not depress it. True, but one cannot have it both ways. If one opens the door to the influence of transient moods and thoughts on the immune system, one must accept the good (enhancement) with the bad (suppression). In point of fact, the relevant literature seems to indicate that it is every bit as easy to show immune suppression due to negative mental states as it is to show immune enhancement due to positive states.

important immune cells), and chemical receptors for various neuro-transmitters have been found on immune cells themselves. This does not mean, however, that the argument of adaptive design no longer has any force. We may still be better off with an immune system that is at least semi-autonomous. An immune system that is easily influenced by various mental states might provide certain benefits such as the ability to lessen the symptoms of disease by mental imagery. But there would also be severe costs to such a system. It is at least as easy to imagine bad things happening as it is to imagine good; it is at least as easy to picture disease as it is to picture health. Thus, if our health were as susceptible to the products of our imaginations as some of the pop advocates of mental imagery would have us believe, it is not clear that it would be much of a blessing. Indeed, if such were the case, it is not clear how medical students would survive (literally) their first year of medical school: Upon learning about a new disease, many students imagine (*vividly*) either that they have it or that they might get it. Perhaps they are better off with an immune system that ignores their conscious thoughts.

Indeed, the idea of an immune system that is so responsive to the products of one's mental and emotional life has its troubling aspects. It may be preferable to have a system that hums along just as efficiently regardless of one's mood. It may be preferable to have a system that does not put one at risk after seeing a sad film, delivering a speech in front of a critical audience, or learning that one's dog has died. Personally, I find it more comforting to believe that whatever crosses my mind will *not* affect my health. Indeed, if you are like me, then the very thought that the products of our imaginations might influence our state of health produces a flood of images of hair loss, cardiac arrhythmia, and advanced carcinomas that, according to many holists, should have dire conse-quences. The phenomenon is analogous to the results of a simple thought experiment: When asked to imagine that someone can "read your thoughts" or listen in on your internal dialogue, many people report that they cannot avoid thinking of their most humiliat-ing impulses. Similarly, if it were ever conclusively demonstrated that our health conforms to the pictures we have in our minds, I suspect that most of us would have difficulty suppressing images of pathology and decrepitude.

What all of this speculation amounts to is that while we await the results of further research in the field of psychoimmunology, we should bear in mind two ideas. First, the most extreme claims made about the extent of mental control over immune function (claims generally made by holistic health advocates who are not themselves a part of this field) are likely to turn out to be unfounded. Second, upon closer inspection, the world implied by these more extreme claims may be not be a very desirable one after all.

The Down Side of Holistic Medicine. The holistic emphasis on personal responsibility for one's state of health has many meanings and, as a result, has a number of costs and benefits. On one hand, as I noted earlier, it simply means that the individual, and not the individual's doctor, is in the best position to look after his or her health. This can encourage people to adopt healthier lifestyle practices and to become more informed "consumers" of medical services. Alternatively, the holistic emphasis on personal responsibility can refer to the conviction that the proper thoughts and feelings can promote health. The down side, however, is the obvious implication that if the appropriate thoughts and feelings promote health, then a failure to adopt the right attitude looms as a plausible cause of sickness. The sick and disabled are subject to blame, by themselves and others, for their misfortune.

The ease with which the holistic philosophy can lead to blaming the victim is apparent in numerous comments made by representatives of the field. Recall the oft-quoted holistic credo that "it is much more important to know what sort of patient has the disease than what sort of disease the patient has." Consider also the claim made by the author of an influential textbook on holistic nursing who states that "Illness occurs when people don't grow and develop their potentials."[25] Similarly, New Age faith healer Elizabeth Stratton argues that "disease is merely a symptom of a deep psychological problem that the person probably isn't even aware of. . . . What I look for is why they created the illness and why they're hanging on to it."[26] Finally, Eileen Gardner, who served for a brief period in the Reagan administration as an aide to Education Secretary William Bennett, once wrote that handicapped individuals ". . . falsely assume that the lottery of life has penalized them at random. This is not so. Nothing comes to an individual that he has not, at some point in his development, summoned." She also claimed that, "As unfair as it may seem, a person's external circumstances do fit his level of inner spiritual development."[27] This is not exactly the philosophy that one would want in the upper reaches of the Department of Education, the department that is responsible for overseeing educational opportunities for the handicapped.

To be sure, there are many responsible advocates of a holistic approach to medicine who are aware of the potential for blaming the victim and who try to combat it. However, it is not clear whether their efforts can ever be successful. If one assigns a large role to psychological and spiritual factors in maintaining health, then logically one must suspect the absence of these factors in the etiology of disease. It is almost impossible for the victim of a disease or disability not to ask "why?" or "why me?" Often there are no real answers to these questions, and any salient cause can seem compelling, including the psychological and spiritual factors trumpeted by proponents of holistic medicine. A letter to the editors of *New Age* magazine is informative in this regard:

> I am physically disabled by a chronic inflammatory disease. I have not healed myself. I have visualized until I can hardly stand to do it anymore; I have been on countless diets and fasts. I have worked courageously and consistently in every possible area that might be an avenue. Last winter I finally understood that I was hurting rather than helping myself with my fanatic, stress-filled desire to heal. Everyone was telling me that what was preventing me from healing was that I was doing something wrong. I believed them. It has been very hurtful to me to have everyone around me blame me for my illness.[28]

Sadly, this is not an isolated occurrence. Interviews with cancer patients indicate that many view their disease as partly the result of their own personal inadequacies.[29] The tragedy of the disease itself is compounded by the anguish of believing that it stems from one's own mental and spiritual shortcomings. What can be more cruel than adding self-recrimination to a victim's misfortune?

I am reminded here of the central element of William Styron's powerful novel *Sophie's Choice*. Sophie is presented as someone running from a traumatic past, and only gradually does the reader learn of the grotesque cruelty of a choice she was once forced to make: Disembarking from the train that brought her to Auschwitz, she is told by an SS officer that only one of her two children may live—the other is to be sent to the gas chambers. She must decide who will be sacrificed so that the other may live. If she cannot decide, both will die. As doubtless any parent would do, she refuses to make the choice. Refuses, that is, until the SS officer motions for both her son and daughter to be taken away. Then, in instinctive response made with instant self-recrimination, she yells, "Take my little girl!"

Is it possible to imagine a more cruel fate, or a trauma from which one is less likely to recover? Sophie can never get past her nightmare as some Holocaust survivors have done, because she cannot fully externalize her misfortune or her anger. She cannot simply blame her fate on the malevolence of someone else and move on with her life because she played too large and too active a role. The SS officer made her an accomplice to her own victimization.

Victims of disease and disability face the same problem in a world in which their misfortune is thought to reflect "uptightness," unresolved conflict, moral transgression, and arrested spiritual development. They are seen as accomplices to their victimization as well. Victims are not free to curse the fates for their affliction; instead they are left to torment themselves by wondering what they did to bring it about. Victims cannot turn to others for compassion without wondering what suspicions the others harbor or what inferences they have made. Susan Sontag argues in *Illness as Metaphor* that the belief that diseases are caused by mental states and can be cured by the exercise of will is "an index of how much is not understood about the physical terrain of a disease."[30] Until the terrain is understood, furthermore, those who suffer from the disease are blamed for having it—as those who suffered from tuberculosis were blamed for their affliction before the discovery of the tubercle bacillus.

Our knowledge of the terrain surrounding the relationship between mental states and illness is nothing if not uncertain. While this uncertainty lasts, perhaps we should err on the side of caution and assume that those who are ill did nothing to contribute psychologically or spiritually to their disease. Their burden is heavy enough already.

9

Belief in the Effectiveness of Questionable Interpersonal Strategies

And oftentimes excusing of a fault
Doth make the fault the worse by the excuse.

William Shakespeare, King John

There are many wonderful things about teaching at Cornell University, one of the best being the faculty tennis courts. The courts are located at the bottom of a gorge on the edge of campus and they offer the faculty tennis player visual splendor, shelter from annoying winds, and a soft clay surface that slows the pace, extends rallies, and generally creates the illusion of having more skill than one actually possesses. I was playing on these courts recently when I overheard something like the following conversation between two nationally-known scholars and locally-known tennis enthusiasts.

PLAYER 1: "This ought to be interesting; I haven't had a chance to get on the court in a couple of weeks."

PLAYER 2: "I like having a layoff now and then. I feel fresh when I come back, and I feel like I can concentrate better."
(Players 1 & 2 exchange further small talk)

PLAYER 2: "My knee is really bothering me. I twisted it while playing last week and haven't had the same mobility since. Maybe I should see an orthopedic guy."

PLAYER 1: "Umm."
(Players 1 & 2 engage in further small talk, and then, after the first game. . .)

PLAYER 1: "I'm not happy with the way they strung my racket. I can't seem to get the same pace on the ball. Where do you get yours strung?"
(Player 2 returns to the baseline, seemingly not having heard the question.)

As a social psychologist, this dialogue was unusually interesting to me because it nicely illustrates a phenomenon I describe in some of my courses, a phenomenon known as "self-handicapping." Self-handicapping refers to our attempts to manage how others perceive us by controlling the attributions they make for our performance. By drawing attention to those elements that inhibit performance, the self-handicapper tries to induce the other person to discount a potential failure. Under such trying circumstances, it is implied, anyone would have failed. And things are even better if we succeed: Logically, the other person should augment his or her impressions of our ability. Anyone capable of overcoming such obstacles must be gifted indeed.

There really are two classes of self-handicapping strategies, real and feigned. "Real" self-handicapping involves placing visible obstacles to success in one's own path. The obstacles make one less likely to succeed, but they provide a ready excuse for failure. The student who neglects to study before an exam or the aspiring actor who drinks before an audition are good examples. Sometimes failure is all but guaranteed, but at least one will not be thought to be lacking in the relevant ability (or so it is hoped).

"Feigned" self-handicapping, on the other hand, is in certain respects a less risky strategy, one in which the person merely *claims* that there were difficult obstacles in the path to success. This kind of self-handicapping consists simply of making excuses for possible bad performance, either before or after the fact. Although it is surely employed in all walks of life, this strategy is probably most common in areas such as sports and (undergraduate) academics in which outcomes are often unambiguous and performance can be precisely quantified. With respect to the world of sports, I trust that the dialogue that began this chapter is familiar to all. With respect to academic performance, students at many universities seem almost to be in competition for who can study the least—or claim to—and still get high grades. Indeed, there is a term, "sneaky bookers," which refers to students who study only in the strictest privacy so that they can pretend to devote minimal effort to their courses.

The phenomenon of self-handicapping raises several interesting questions. Real self-handicapping makes one wonder about people's preferences for how they wish to be perceived. Is it really better to be thought of as a talented drunk than as a moderately gifted person who has at least actualized his or her potential? How did wasting four years of college by not studying develop such cachet? I am reminded of a recent interview of tennis star John McEnroe on CBS's *60 Minutes*. When asked to comment on his relative decline on the tennis circuit and the simultaneous rise of Ivan Lendl, McEnroe boasted that he was still the superior talent, but that Lendl was higher ranked "merely" because he worked harder at his craft. A curious form of self-presentation! Are we supposed to think less of Lendl because he has applied himself, and more of McEnroe because he has not? It speaks to how far perseverance and hard work have fallen in value in the current culture that such strategies of self-presentation are so commonly employed. It also makes one wonder about the future of a society that more visibly rewards beauty, glibness, and athletic prowess over determination and sustained effort.*

Another issue raised by the phenomenon of self-handicapping is the question of who the self-handicapper is trying to fool. Artists who drink to excess might do so to prevent others from concluding that they lack sufficient talent, or they might do so to shield *themselves* from a similar inference. Students who do not study (or pretend not to) do not want others to think of them as dull, nor do they want to think that of themselves. At whom, then, are the attempts at self-handicapping directed? This question has been the subject of much of the research in the self-handicapping litera-

---

* The explanation for much of this curious preference in self-presentation is that it is not acceptable in certain domains to be merely "good" (i.e., above average); one must be—or be seen to be—"exceptional" (say, in the top percentile). Unfortunately, often one cannot be exceptional on effort alone; one must have unusual ability as well. Thus, if a person cannot actually perform at a level equal to the top percentile, he or she can at least try to create the impression that that level would have been reached if not for some handicap. This form of self-handicapping, then, may be a strategy in which a person willingly sacrifices a probable moderate outcome (i.e., being perceived as "good") for a chance at a much more positive one (i.e., being perceived as having exceptional potential, but at the risk—if the ploy is unconvincing—of being seen as a posturer).

ture, and thus far a definitive answer has been elusive. Many self-handicapping attempts have been shown to be clearly directed at managing the impressions of others; in contrast, definitive instances in which such strategies have been employed to fool the self have yet to be documented.[1] This does not mean, of course, that such instances do not exist, but rather that a conclusive answer to the question of why people self-handicap—to influence their own or other people's impressions—must await the outcome of further research.

There is yet another "why" question that is raised by the phenomenon of self-handicapping, particularly by the phenomenon of feigned self-handicaps. This question does not involve "why" in the sense of to whom the strategy is directed, but "why" in the sense of how it is that people believe such strategies to be effective, or why people continue to employ them if they are ineffective. Our excuses sometimes "work" because it can be difficult for a person to determine whether they are genuine. However, most self-handicaps seem to meet with much less success and do not have the intended effect on how one is perceived. Instead, counterfeit excuses are generally seen through and given little weight. The two tennis players discussed earlier were clearly unimpressed by the hardships that supposedly confronted the other. College students are hardly in awe of the average peer who gets good grades but professes not to study—witness the aforementioned term "sneaky bookers." Indeed, my colleagues and I have recently conducted several studies that demonstrate that feigned self-handicaps are generally ineffective. For example, we asked samples of students to think of people they know who claim to rarely study and yet do very well in school. When asked their opinions of these people, our respondents indicated that they believed very few of the claims, and instead considered them to be poorly disguised self-presentational ploys.[2]

THE PERSEVERANCE OF INEFFECTIVE STRATEGIES

Self-handicapping is just one example of a class of social strategies people employ to boost their status or achieve some goal, but that in fact often backfire. Name-dropping, boasting, and "coming on strong" are other examples of social strategies that are generally ineffective but are frequently employed. "Showing off" and "holding forth" by dominating conversation sometimes fall in this class as well. Why do people continue to employ such strategies if they are so ineffective? Why don't people learn that these techniques more often hurt their cause rather than help it? When individuals name-drop by alluding to their connections to the rich and famous (e.g., "Francis did not have the artistic freedom he needs in that picture," or "Although publicly she indicated otherwise, Brooke gave me the impression that she was never really comfortable here at Princeton"), we often turn away and roll our eyes in disbelief and disgust. When people directly boast about their accomplishments and associations (e.g., "I went backstage at the Stones concert and Mick and I shared a beer," or "My dad was the guy who gave Wozniak and Jobs the main idea for the Apple II"), we secretly get angry and wonder just how gullible they think we are.

The central concern of this chapter is how it is that phenomena like boasting, self-handicapping, and name-dropping survive despite the fact that they so frequently fail. At first glance, it might seem that flattery or ingratiation belongs in this group. Indeed, there are times when an attempt at ingratiation is so blatant that it is perceived as manipulative and actually backfires ("I just wanted to tell you how much I have been enjoying your course. About my midterm. . .").[3] However, I suspect that such failures are not the norm because the warm glow of being flattered often overcomes the cold realization that it might be strategic. Also, we can be won over by transparent ingratiation because we are impressed that the flatterer at least has the good taste to consider us worthy of flattery! ("Surely she does not flatter everybody.") Flattery, then, is like the other strategies discussed above in that it *should* be ineffective; unlike the others, however, it usually works. As Milan Kundera points out, "How defenseless we are in the face of flattery!"[4] An argument could even be made that flattery is a strategy that is actually underutilized.

Flattery aside then, what can we say about why these other, generally ineffective, social strategies are nevertheless employed? First, it is important to be clear at the outset that sometimes these strategies are used with no illusions about their effectiveness. It is not possible to tell, from the mere fact that a person *employs* a given strategy, whether he or she necessarily *believes* it to be effective. We have all had the experience of returning from a social gathering and thinking "There I go again!" or "Am I ever going to stop doing that?" Such counter-productive actions that we carry out in spite of ourselves are not at issue here. Nor is this chapter concerned with those instances in which a person consciously acts in ways that he or she knows will entail some cost (such as alienating others) in order to achieve some compensatory gain. People are sometimes willing to sacrifice successful self-presentation for other benefits. For example, a person might provide a bogus excuse for failure that he or she expects nobody to believe just to avoid having to talk about the outcome—and its real implications—any further.

What this chapter *is* concerned with is the persistence of counterproductive strategies that the people who employ them truly believe to be effective. A great many name-droppers, bores, boasters, and self-handicappers walk away from social encounters convinced that they have skillfully managed the interaction and made a favorable impression—while their interaction partners walk away shaking their heads and muttering under their breath. It is this mismatch between presumed and actual effectiveness that is at issue here. How can it be explained?

Dysfunctional Persistence as Inaccurate Covariation Detection. A little thought reveals that this issue is really a special case of the problem of assessing relationships that was discussed in chapter 3. In this case, it involves people's ability to assess the relationship between their own strategies and various social outcomes. As we saw in chapter 3, people sometimes have difficulty estimating relationships because of common limitations in the evidence available to them, and because of various imperfections in the way they evaluate that evidence. Both play an important role in making ineffective social strategies seem effective.

The commonly available evidence is limited in two ways: a) information regarding the chosen strategy's effectiveness is often biased, and b) information about the effectiveness of alternative strategies is often difficult or impossible to obtain. Information about how well a given strategy has fared is often biased because of people's reluctance (discussed in Chapter 7) to convey to others their negative reactions. As alluded to above, when someone boasts, drops names, or self-handicaps, we usually turn away and roll our eyes or mutter under our breath. We may subsequently express our disgust to someone else (usually a sympathetic fellow-victim), but we rarely confront the offender directly. Thus, the inveterate name-dropper or self-handicapper rarely receives the feedback necessary to lay bare the futility of his or her efforts. The person can therefore only learn that the strategy is ineffective by taking note of what did *not* happen, such as the absence of a deepening bond or the failure to achieve greater warmth in the relationship. Drawing appropriate inferences from such non-occurrences is notoriously difficult.[5] As a result, the person observes that nothing really bad happens, and so assumes that the other person has "bought" the excuse, the bogus affiliation with someone of prestige, or the fabricated account of previous exploits.

A friend of mine has an absolutely delightful father who has one unfortunate fault—whenever more than one other person is around, he will not let anyone talk but himself. My friend has complained about her father's habit for years, but she has never had the heart to tell him and urge him to change. Because no one else has told him either, he can be forgiven for talking away, blissfully unaware of his audience's discomfort. Recently, however, an opportunity presented itself. Her father returned from a dinner party in even better spirits than usual and told his daughter how he had regaled everyone with an array of insights, witticisms, and anecdotes. She then tentatively interrupted, "You know, Dad, sometimes people would enjoy the evening more if they were encouraged to participate more in the conversation themselves." He protested: "I asked several times whether I was going on too long and everyone said 'No, no, please continue'." This shows just how hard it can be to get accurate information about one's effect on others: When even explicit requests for feedback elicit disingenuous support and praise, is it any wonder that people sometimes stick with alienating interpersonal strategies?

Although the biased feedback we receive from others no doubt contributes a great deal to people's dysfunctional adherance to ineffective social strategies, it does point to one important question that remains unanswered: If people are so disgusted by the name-dropping and boasting of others, why do they attempt it themselves? Why do people fail to generalize from their own silent reactions to such strategies, and thus learn that the silence of others does not indicate approval but disapproval?

The problem of receiving biased feedback about a given strategy's effectiveness is compounded by an inability to adequately evaluate alternative strategies. Because a given strategy is initially thought to be effective, *only* that strategy is ever employed. The person never learns what would have happened if a different tack had been taken, and thus cannot assess the true effectiveness of his or her efforts. Consider the common belief among some segments of the population that "the only way to get anywhere with the opposite sex is to come on strong." Someone who holds such a belief will consistently come on strong and, at some point, will succeed in meeting his or her objective. The occasional success, however rare, will then be attributed to the choice of tactics, and its effectiveness will seem to be an unassailable fact of the person's own experience. Because no single failure serves to disconfirm the strategy's effectiveness (after all, nothing works all the time), the only way it can be shown to be ineffective is by discovering that the rate of success is lower with this strategy than with others. Given that alternative techniques are rarely if ever employed, the person is in no danger of having his or her favorite theories disabused.

In cases such as these, a belief in the effectiveness of a given strategy can also be aided and abetted by a self-fulfilling prophecy. Psychologist Robyn Dawes provides the example of people who believe that "the only way to get anywhere in this world is to push, push, push."[6] Like someone who thinks it's necessary to come on strong with women, such a person will consistently push for what he wants. The occasional success will "prove" the wisdom of the chosen course of action, and the individual will never learn how effective he might have been had a different strategy been employed. In addition, the person's aggressiveness may very well foster resistance in other people, and thus unintentionally create a hostile world in which it really is true that the only way to get anywhere is to push, push, push.

Thus far, the persistence of dysfunctional social strategies has been largely attributed to the imperfect nature of the evidence available to us. Some of the blame, however, must be assigned to the way we evaluate the evidence we receive. As discussed in chapters 3 & 4, we tend to attach too much significance to those occasions when the strategy proves to be effective, and too little to those times when it fails. This is partly a testimonial to the seductive power of partial reinforcement. However ineffective in general, the dysfunctional strategies discussed here do occasionally work. The relevant question, bear in mind, is not why people continue to employ strategies that are *never* effective (few people ever do), but why they engage in actions that so rarely accomplish their intended goal. Even the most far-out excuses are sometimes taken at face value and even the most outrageous boasts do not always arouse suspicion. Reinforced by occasional success, the name dropper or self-handicapper becomes deluded about the prospects for future attempts and employs the strategy too often.

This tendency to focus too heavily on the occasional success is helped along by an asymmetry in the way we evaluate success and failure. A single success generally does more to confirm a strategy's effectiveness than a single failure does to disconfirm it. Indeed, successes tend to be taken as prima facie evidence that the strategy is effective. If coming on strong with someone leads to success, the value of assertiveness seems apparent. If it leads to failure, in contrast, it could easily be due to other factors ("s/he's just a cold fish," "Nobody could have gotten anywhere"). Successes, in other words, are generally seen as confirmations of one's underlying strategy, whereas failures tend to be thought of only as failures of outcome, not as failures of strategy.

Such biases result from a seemingly compelling logic: To achieve a desired outcome, every step in a causal chain must turn out correctly; any break in the chain will lead to failure. A given failure thus does not mean that one's strategy was ineffective, because the failure could be due to a break in any of the other links in the causal chain. Success, on the other hand, implies that the chosen strategy and all other links in the chain functioned smoothly. Otherwise things would not have worked.

This logic suffers from two flaws. First, a given success could have been produced by an entirely different causal chain. A triumph can occur in spite of, rather than because of, one's efforts. Second, although a given failure *can* be due to some other link in the chain, it does not follow that it *is* produced by such an extraneous element. We are often too quick to externalize our failures in this way.

At first glance, the class of erroneous beliefs that serves as the focus of this chapter might not seem to be terribly consequential. Indeed, a questionable social strategy that leads one person to alienate another may, in some real sense, be less harmful than a misguided belief that causes the deterioration of a person's physical health. Nevertheless, the impact of dysfunctional social strategies should not be underestimated. One of the primary human struggles in today's world is the effort to achieve meaningful and gratifying personal relationships. At a time when less of a human connection is guaranteed by family relations or by membership in close, stable communities, we must form, indeed earn, our social relations through our own efforts and the strength of our personal and social attributes. To the person who seeks more gratifying relationships but cannot achieve them, to the person whose misguided attempts to get closer to others only serve to drive them away, the questionable beliefs discussed in this chapter are surely consequential enough.

10

Belief in ESP

Two elderly women are at a Catskills mountain resort and one of them says, "Boy, the food at this place is really terrible." The other one says, "I know, and such small portions."
Woody Allen, *Annie Hall*

In the mid-1940s, a surgical procedure known as the portacaval shunt was developed to treat esophogal hemorrhaging, and its use was later expanded to treat a variety of ailments of the intestinal cavity. Studies of the effectiveness of this procedure were carried out in numerous hospitals, and, twenty years after the development of the surgery, the literature on this subject was reviewed.[1]

Table 10.1 presents the results of this review. Each study was categorized along two dimensions: the methodological quality of the study (i.e., degree of experimental control) and the amount of enthusiasm the investigators expressed about the procedure as a result of their study. As Table 10.1 makes clear, the investigators' enthusiasm for the procedure was negatively correlated with the quality of the study. Uncontrolled and poorly-controlled studies produced considerable enthusiasm for the shunt; well-controlled studies generated virtually none.

This investigation teaches several important lessons. First, most research in this area (and in many others as well) is of poor quality. Only 4 of the 51 studies employed the absolutely essential procedure of randomly assigning participants to treatment conditions. The quality of research has undoubtedly improved since the time these studies were carried out, but badly-flawed research has by no means disappeared. Second, as already mentioned, the conclusions drawn often depend on the quality of the research performed.

Table 10.1 Degree of Experimental Control versus Degree of
Investigator Enthusiasm for the Portacaval Shunt
Degree of Enthusiasm

Degree of Control*	Marked	Moderate	None	Totals
Uncontrolled	24	7	1	32
Poorly-controlled	10	3	2	15
Well-controlled	0	1	3	4
Total	34	11	6	51

* "Well controlled" studies were those in which subjects were randomly assigned
to the treatment and control conditions. In "Poorly controlled" studies, a selected
group of patients was compared to an unselected control group. "Uncontrolled"
studies had no control group.
FROM: D. Freedman, R. Pisani, & R. Purves. *Statistics.* New York: W. W. Norton,
1978.

Faulty research designs can obscure phenomena that are really
there, or lead us to believe in phenomena that are not. Finally,
and most importantly for present purposes, the existence of a large
number of studies does not by itself compensate for their lack of
quality. Adding together a set of similarly-flawed investigations
does not produce an accurate assessment of reality. As statisticians
like to say, sample size does not overcome sample bias.

This last lesson is sometimes hard for people to accept. Somehow
it just seems that if one conducts enough studies, the flaws should
cancel each other out and allow "the truth" to shine through. Like
Woody Allen's Catskills vacationer, people tend to think that sufficient quantity can compensate for a lack of quality. There are domains in life in which it does, but as the example of the portacaval
shunt makes clear, empirical research is not one of them.*

This lesson is important to keep in mind when trying to determine
why so many people believe in the existence of extra-sensory per-

* It could be argued that few experiments with absolutely no flaws are ever performed, and that scientists nearly always draw conclusions from a pattern of
data obtained from variously flawed studies. It is important to point out, however,
that scientists only feel comfortable basing conclusions on the results of a series
of flawed studies if the flaws are *varied* and *compensatory*. Indeed, successive
studies are explicitly designed to rule out the problems with earlier experiments,
and in so doing they often eliminate one shortcoming and create another. The
successive studies, then, are not all subject to one or more of a small number of
flaws. This is not true of the research on the portacaval shunt, in which the
flawed studies all suffered from the lack of random assignment of patients to
treatment conditions.

ception (ESP). One could argue that the single most important reason is simply that there seems—to the average person—to be so much apparent evidence for it. Everyday life brings its share of support as friends tell us about premonitions that have come true, and we experience extraordinary coincidences ourselves. Press reports provide us with even more apparent evidence: Scientists at "Stanford" test Uri Geller under controlled conditions and conclude that his psychic powers are genuine.* Reports from the Soviet Union suggest that the Russians are ahead of us in psychic espionage and warfare. Psychics routinely predict upcoming events and help the police solve criminal cases. Celebrities tell of their prophetic dreams or their memories of "past lives." The list goes on and on. As we shall see, none of this apparent evidence provides truly solid support for the existence of ESP, but the examples do pile up.

Some people accept these examples at face value and conclude that ESP is a fact of life. Others may question these claims, or may be vaguely aware that some of them have been scientifically challenged, but nevertheless decide that "there must be something there." Much of the evidence may be fraudulent or faulty, but there is so much of it. Can't we conclude that "where there's smoke, there must be fire?" We cannot, of course, as the example of the portacaval shunt makes clear. But this reasoning is seductive nonetheless. Indeed, it is not just the average person who falls prey to this fallacy. Well-trained scientists have been known to make the same argument. Stanford professor William Tiller, for example, has argued that even though the evidence from ESP experiments is shaky, it should be taken seriously because there is so much of it.[2] Similarly, parapsychologist John Beloff has stated:

> It is not my contention that any of the aforegoing experiments were perfect . . . or beyond criticism. . . . Moreover, unless a much higher level of repeatability becomes possible, the skeptical option, that the results can be attributed to carelessness or to conscious or unconscious cheating on the part of one or more of the experimenters, remains open and valid. Nevertheless, it

---

*This research, for which the controls were in fact less than adequate, was conducted at Stanford Research Institute. The institute is not affiliated with Stanford University. A summary of the methodological flaws of this research can be found in J. Randi (1986) *Flim-Flam*. Buffalo, NY: Prometheus Books.

is my personal opinion that these . . . investigations represent an overwhelming case for accepting the reality of psi phenomena.[3]

Sure the food is terrible, but such large portions! It seems clear from all of this that one of the most powerful determinants of people's dubious belief in ESP is simply the availability of so much apparent evidence of its existence—evidence from both everyday life and the laboratory. What does this evidence really show?

THE CASE AGAINST ESP

Is it fair to characterize belief in ESP as dubious? Perhaps some readers will feel that I have jumped the gun by making such a, well, dubious statement. Is ESP as questionable as I seem to imply? To address this question requires a brief critique of the laboratory evidence offered in support of ESP.* First, however, it is important to clarify the precise meaning of the concepts and phenomena under discussion. Extrasensory perception is defined by those who study it (known as parapsychologists) as the "experience of, or response to, a target object, state, event or influence without sensory contact."[4] Several types of ESP are thought to exist. *Telepathy* refers to the direct transfer of thoughts from one mind to another; *clairvoyance* corresponds to the ability to sense or "see" events and objects that are absent from one's visual field; and *precognition* represents the perception of future events. A fourth ability, *psychokinesis (PK)*, or the ability to move, alter, or influence objects without any known material contact, is also generally considered to be a component of ESP because it too represents influence at a distance. However, because psychokinesis does not involve "perception" in any sense, parapsychologists now generally include it with the other abilities under the more general term "psi."

It may be best to begin an examination of whether these phenom-

---

*This is not meant to be an exhaustive review of the history of research on ESP. I attempt only to provide an overview of some of the most well-known and widely-cited studies in the field, and to discuss the problems associated with those studies. For the reader interested in obtaining a more complete review, an useful introduction may be obtained by reading the exchange between believers and skeptics in *Behavioral and Brain Sciences*, 1987, vol. 10, pp. 539–643.

ena are likely to exist by looking at a sample of opinion from people with strong ties to this field. A scientific panel commissioned by the National Research Council to study this area concluded that ". . . despite a 130-year record of scientific research on such matters, our committee could find no scientific justification for the existence of phenomena such as extrasensory perception, mental telepathy, or 'mind over matter' exercises. . . . Evaluation of a large body of the best available evidence simply does not support the contention that these phenomena exist."[5] Ray Hyman, a psychologist who has devoted much of his career to evaluating claims of paranormal phenomena, similarly states that ". . . there is no scientifically acceptable basis, as of today, for accepting the reality of psi."[6] Even many of those who fervently believe in the reality of psi can sound a similar theme. Stanley Krippner, a firm believer in psi and an articulate advocate for parapsychology, nevertheless states that "since Charles Richet first applied statistics to psychical research data nearly 100 years ago, no experimental procedure has emerged which would invariably produce the same results no matter who followed it. Furthermore, no mechanism underlying psi has been discovered . . . Finally, no practical use of ESP or PK has been validated by laboratory research."[7]

Hardly a ringing endorsement. In part, this gloomy assessment of the status of ESP stems from a disturbing pattern that has repeated itself over the past 130 years. First, the believers and skeptics stake out their positions, the believers by citing anecdotes of unexplained phenomena in everyday life, and the skeptics by noting the inherent implausibility of psi (e.g., its existence would violate a number of physical laws such as the inverse square law and the second law of thermodynamics). While the debate rages on, the parapsychologists energetically conduct experiments on psi, and, at some point, produce supposedly "definitive" evidence. At first blush, the evidence can seem rather convincing and the initial skeptical response can sound rather weak and even petty. Convinced that they hold the upper hand, the believers then chide the skeptics for their closed-mindedness. The skeptics are likened to the medieval clerics who refused to look through Galileo's telescope and persecuted those who espoused the heliocentric view of the solar system. They are castigated as representatives of a scientific "establishment" who stand in the way of unprecedented progress in our understanding of our world and ourselves.

The believers' euphoria does not last long, however. As soon as enough time has elapsed to allow sufficient scrutiny of the evidence, it generally becomes clear that it is hardly definitive. Rather, it is often shown to be the result of deliberate fraud or critical methodological shortcomings. What is once offered as the very best evidence for ESP becomes an embarassment to the field. Consider a few examples from the history of parapsychological research during the past 130 years.

J. B. Rhine. J. B. Rhine is generally credited with initiating the investigation of psi under laboratory conditions. Before Rhine, research on psychic phenomena, carried out under the auspices of the Society for Psychical Research in Great Britain and the American Society for Psychical Research in the U.S., focused mainly on the investigation of spontaneous experiences of psi and on the study of spiritual mediums who claimed to be able to contact the souls of the dead. (Note that the niche occupied by the mediums of the early twentieth century is now filled by modern-day "channelers.") At his Parapsychology Laboratory at Duke University in the 1930s, Rhine developed an experimental procedure in which subjects were asked to identify which of five symbols (circle, cross, rectangle, star, or wavy lines) were on the concealed sides of a deck of cards. The number of correct responses was then compared to the number to be expected if the subject was simply guessing. This procedure can be used as a test of telepathy (a "sender" looks at each card while the "percipient" tries to discern its identity), clairvoyance (the card is set face down on the table without anyone having seen it), or precognition (the percipient guesses the sequence of cards from top to bottom, and *then* they are shuffled and compared to the percipient's responses).

In 1934 Rhine published the results of several years of research involving nearly 100,000 guesses made by a large number of subjects. Rhine concluded that he had obtained overwhelming evidence for the existence of ESP. His subjects averaged 7.1 correct identifications per deck of 25 cards compared to the 5 expected by chance. Although the magnitude of the results may be fairly small (i.e., only two extra successes per deck), the odds of such a result happening by chance over such a huge number of trials are virtually zero.[8]

Rhine's results quickly reached a wide popular and scientific audience. Because the research had the veneer of carefully-controlled scientific research, the skeptical community initially was at a loss about what to think. Gifted subjects performed undeniably better than one could do by chance. However, as more details about the exact procedures employed became known, the data began to lose their lustre. Most observers became convinced that the results were due to methodological artifact rather than genuine ESP. Some of Rhine's subjects, for example, were allowed to shuffle and handle the cards, a procedure that would permit a conjurer to use trickery to discern their identity. One of Rhine's most gifted subjects, Hubert Pearce, was consistently able to obtain positive results under such conditions—except when persons other than the experimenter were present.[9] Skeptics find this pattern—of successful performance when cheating is relatively easy, and unsuccessful performance when it is difficult—to be extremely suspicious. Believers, in contrast, attribute it to an "experimenter" or "shyness" effect whereby a person's psi powers disappear in a skeptical atmosphere. Psychics, like temperamental Rock stars, often do not perform in the presence of bad vibes.

An additional problem with Rhine's results was that the cards themselves were not manufactured with the strictest quality control, permitting an observant subject to identify the cards by certain irregularities like warped edges, spots on the backs, or design imperfections. The symbols on some cards reportedly could even be read through their backs under certain lighting conditions.[10]

Questions about how well ordinary shuffling succeeds in truly randomizing a deck of cards also clouded Rhine's findings. Without a randomly-ordered set of cards, the statistical analyses that are the centerpiece of Rhine's research are meaningless: The beyond-chance results could stem from a pattern inherent in the cards being matched by a response bias on the part of the subjects. The seriousness of this problem is demonstrated by experiments in which results comparable to Rhine's have been produced by simply shuffling two decks and comparing them to one another! Beyond-chance matching has been found in several such comparisons of "random" sequences, with the sequences produced either by card shuffling[11] or by comparing columns from published tables of random numbers.[12] These simulation experiments have also yielded various supplementary findings common to the field of parapsychology, such as *psi-missing* (significantly *fewer* guesses than chance expectation) and the *decline effect* (initial impressive success that trails off and eventually disappears over trials).

How much stock can be placed in Rhine's data if strong results emerge when controls are lax but disappear when they are tightened? Can we infer the existence of psi from beyond-chance scoring when similarly impressive deviations from chance results can be obtained—without the intervention of a mind—by simply comparing seemingly random lists? The net result of these and other questions about Rhine's research is that his work is rarely cited by parapsychologists these days as among the best evidence for the existence of psi.

The Soal-Goldney Experiments. With the doubts surrounding Rhine's findings, the burden of representing the definitive evidence for psi was passed to a set of similar experiments conducted by the British mathematician G. S. Soal and his assistant K. M. Goldney. Their procedure was as follows: An experimenter sat in one room with the "agent," while the "percipient" was in an adjoining room. The experimenter, after consulting a randomized target list of the digits 1–5, would hold up the target number through a hole in a partition that separated the agent and experimenter. The agent would then pick up the one picture from a group of five that corresponded to the target digit. By concentrating on the selected picture, the agent would try to "send" the image to the percipient. The percipient would write down his or her guess, and the list of guesses was subsequently compared to the target sequence.

These procedures were conducted under much tighter experimental control than that which existed in the early days at Rhine's laboratory. Independent witnesses were allowed into both rooms. Special precautions were taken to ensure that neither the agent nor the percipient knew the contents of the target sequence. Sophisticated tests of randomness were applied to check the target sequences, and copies of all records were sent after each session to a Cambridge University professor of philosophy, C. D. Broad.

Soal conducted these experiments during a four-year period beginning in 1935, during which time he examined the performance of 160 subjects on over 128,000 trials. The results of his efforts were tremendously disappointing: Absolutely no evidence for telepathy was obtained. Upon hearing these results, the parapsychological community was obviously disheartened.

Shortly afterwards, however, a colleague suggested that Soal check his results for "displacement" effects. Perhaps subjects' guesses correlate significantly, not with the target cards, but with the cards that immediately preceded or followed the target cards. Beyond-chance matches to the subsequent cards might reflect precognition, for example. Soal initially considered this suggestion to represent somewhat questionable science and he was reluctant to try it. Eventually relenting, Soal discovered significant displacement effects for two of his subjects, Basil Shackleton and Gloria Stewart.

Recognizing the limitations of such a post-hoc analysis, Soal retested his two potentially-gifted percipients. Basil Shackleton was subsequently tested from 1941 to 1943 in over 400 sittings in which he made more than 11,000 guesses. As before, his responses were at chance level when compared to the target cards, but showed an excess of hits when compared to the card immediately following the target (2,890 hits compared to a chance expectation of 2,308; the odds of this happening by chance were estimated to be 10^{35} to 1). Gloria Stewart also provided additional tests. She made over 37,000 guesses in 130 separate sittings, and her responses—unlike Shackleton's or her own earlier performance—were found to correlate significantly with the target cards, not those immediately following or preceding (9,410 hits compared to a chance expectation of 7,420; the odds of this happening by chance were estimated to be 10^{79} to 1).

Not surprisingly, these data were soon hailed as conclusive evidence for the existence of psi. Here were significant results produced under rigorous experimental control by an investigator whose integrity, by virtue of his earlier failures, was obviously beyond question. Parapsychologist R. A. McConnell stated that ". . . if scientists will read [Soal's report] carefully, the 'ESP controversy' will be ended."[13] Similarly, Whately Carington said that:

> If I had to choose one single investigation on which to pin my whole faith in the reality of paranormal phenomena, or with which to convince a hardened skeptic (if this be not a contradiction in terms), I should unhesitatingly choose this series of experiments, which is the most cast-iron piece of work I know, as well as having yielded the most remarkable results.[14]

The Soal-Goldney experiments stood as the cornerstone of the evidential foundation of ESP for the next twenty years. Skeptics were reduced to rather weak speculations about how Soal *might* have cheated.[15] Gradually, however, more substantial reservations about this work emerged, and today it seems clear that Soal faked his data.

Suspicions began to form when an agent in several of the Shackleton experiments, Gretl Albert, informed Mrs. Goldney that she had seen Soal altering the records during one of the sessions. Mrs. Goldney checked the score sheets soon afterwards, but she could find no evidence to support the accusations. Nor could a colleague that Mrs. Goldney had asked to do the same. When Mrs. Goldney brought the accusation to the attention of Soal, he apparently became indignant and insisted that Mrs. Albert not be allowed to participate in further experiments. Soal also persuaded Mrs. Goldney that they should not mention Mrs. Albert's accusation in their reports of their work. In fact, Mrs. Albert's charges were publicly acknowledged by Soal only when, more than fifteen years later, Christopher Scott pressured him to do so with the threat of publishing the accusations himself. Further suspicion was generated by Soal's claim that he had lost the original score sheets in 1946, but that hand-made copies were available.

By themselves, these facts are mere curiosities. Scientists do occasionally misplace data, and the tampering that Mrs. Albert witnessed may have been a fastidious experimenter's innocent efforts to tidy up the record. More damaging evidence eventually followed, however. To make his experiments as rigorous as possible, Soal had published detailed descriptions of how he had obtained the random numbers used to generate his target lists. However, computer analyses of the target lists provided by Soal indicate beyond any doubt that he either altered the lists or did not obtain his random numbers the way he said he did.[16] Thus, if fraud had been perpetrated, the most likely means would have been an alteration of the target list to match the percipient's responses. This suspicion was bolstered when Mrs. Albert provided additional information about her initial suspicions of Soal. She claimed to have seen Soal changing 1's into 4's and 5's on the target list. Guided by this claim, subsequent analyses of the full record confirmed that there were: a) an excess of hits when the target was a 4 or a 5, and b) a shortage of 1's on those trials in which the guess was a 4 or 5. It thus seems that Soal began with target lists that contained an excess of 1's, and that he subsequently changed some of the 1's into 4's and 5's to create more hits.[17]

The most conclusive evidence for this contention was obtained in a follow-up attempt to match Soal's target lists with sequences contained in the tables from which he claimed to have selected them. Like the previous computer search, this attempt did not find any exact matches in the two sources. However, there were numerous close approximations—target sequences that matched those in the random number tables with only a few exceptions, ". . . as though digits had been inserted into one of the pairs of sequences (or omitted from the other)."[18] Predictably, these extra digits almost always corresponded to hits.

With this final bit of damaging evidence, what was once the strongest evidence for the existence of psi is now an embarassment to the field of parapsychology.

Remote Viewing. Since Soal's time there have been other examples of deliberate fraud in parapsychological research. Most notable in this regard were the actions of Walter Levy, J. B. Rhine's top assistant and heir apparent, who was caught by staff members altering computer records of experimental results. Since Soal's time as well, other research findings have been put forward as the definitive proof of the existence of psi. The "remote viewing" experiments conducted at SRI International were briefly thought of in such terms.

Remote viewing experiments were devised by two physicists, Harold Puthoff and Russell Targ. In these experiments, a percipient is seated in the laboratory while another subject proceeds to a nearby site that has been randomly selected from a small set of possible locations. While at the target site, the subject looks carefully at the surroundings and tries to send impressions of the locale back to the percipient. At a prearranged time, the percipient is asked to describe any impressions he or she has "received" by drawing a picture, writing a description, or both. This procedure is repeated over several days until all target locations have been visited.

Performance in these experiments is assessed by having a group of judges travel to each site, giving them the percipient's pictures and descriptions (hereafter simply called "transcripts"), and having them rank the set of transcripts according to how well they describe each location. Are the rankings of the transcripts that correspond to each location higher than we can expect by chance?

The success rates claimed by Targ and Puthoff for their remote viewing experiments are among the most impressive ever reported in the field of parapsychology. For some of their more gifted subjects, the matching of transcripts to targets was almost without error. Moreover, Targ and Puthoff claimed that nearly everyone they tested was able to manifest this ability. Psi is not the exclusive property of the Uri Gellers of the world, but can be harnessed by anyone off the street. For some people, the publication of these results in the prestigious science journal *Nature*, rather than the usual parapsychology outlets, lent further weight to the evidence.

How well do these results stand up under close scrutiny? Careful examination of this work by New Zealand psychologists David Marks and Richard Kammann indicate that, like its predecessors as the bedrock support for psi, these experiments do not pass muster.[19] The problem in this case lies in the nature of the transcripts provided to the judges. Most of the material in the transcripts consists of the honest attempts by the percipients to describe their impressions. However, the transcripts also contained considerable extraneous material that could aid a judge in matching them to the correct targets. In particular, there were numerous references to dates, times, and sites previously visited that would enable the judge to place the transcripts in proper sequence. For instance, a comment such as "I've been trying to picture where you went yesterday on the nature walk" informs the judge that: 1) the correct target must not be the nature preserve; 2) this target, whatever it was, was not the first in the series; and 3) this target, whatever it was, came after the nature preserve. Knowing the target is not the nature walk obviously simplifies the judge's task regardless of what additional information he or she has. However, information about where the transcript fits in the sequence of target sites is only helpful if the judge is aware of the target order. Astonishingly, the judges in the Targ-Puthoff experiments were given a list of target sites in the exact order in which they were used in the tests!

To determine whether it was these extraneous cues rather than remote viewing that produced the remarkable accuracy of the judges' rankings, Marks and Kammann conducted a control assessment they call "remote judging." In remote judging, the judges are given a set of transcripts containing *only* the extraneous cues and none of the legitimate descriptive material. Then, *without visiting a single location*, they are given a list of the target sites in the proper order and asked to match transcripts to targets. They did so as accurately as the judges in the Targ-Puthoff experiments! As an additional control procedure, Marks and Kammann edited the transcripts from the Targ-Puthoff experiments so that they no longer contained these extraneous cues, and then asked a group of judges to match them to the targets. Without the help of the extraneous information, the judges were not able to do so with any accuracy. So much for remote viewing.

The Search for Replicability. The history of parapsychological research contains numerous examples in which the degree of deliberate fraud or methodological flaw is greater than that described in the cases above. On the other hand, there have also been other research efforts for which the methodological questions that have been raised are more subtle, and for which the question of dishonesty has yet to be raised explicitly. But regardless of what the rest of the field has to offer, the historical examples discussed above are important because they serve to remind us of what we should know all along—that no single experiment, or no set of experiments carried out in one laboratory, can ever stand as definitive evidence. Science requires that a phenomenon be reliably produced in different laboratories for it to be accepted as genuine. Whoever claims to have discovered a phenomenon must describe in sufficient detail how it was produced so that other investigators, following similar steps, can reproduce it themselves. This requirement of replicability applies to all fields of science. However, if it is possible to say that it should apply to some areas more than others, then surely it applies most to a field like parapsychology that has been plagued by an uncommon amount of fraud and deception.

Ultimately, it is the inability to produce a replicable experimental demonstration of psi that is most damaging to the contention that it exists. Psychic phenomena appear in one laboratory only to disappear in another. Occasionally, findings are announced that can seemingly be replicated by sympathetic believers, but not by skeptics or neutral scientists. Such is the case for the two research paradigms currently considered by parapsychologists to offer the best evidence for the existence of psi—the "ganzfeld" experiments of Charles Honorton and the studies of psychokinesis by Helmut Schmidt in Houston and Robert Jahn at Princeton.* Most parapsy-

---

*In the typical ganzfeld experiment, the percipient is put into a state of mild sensory deprivation (halved ping-pong balls are placed over the eyes and "white noise" is heard through a set of earphones). He or she then tries to report on the images being "sent" by someone in another room. In the typical psychokinetic study, a machine randomly selects which of a set of four lamps is lit on a given trial. The participant's task is to try to mentally influence the randomizing device to produce one particular outcome. As mentioned above, these two research paradigms are considered by many investigators to be the most promising in the field of parapsychology. Skeptics remain unconvinced, however, and they cite a number of procedural and statistical artifacts that could account for the results.

chologists themselves acknowledge this critical problem of a lack of replicability. Consider the following confessions of various members of the field:[20]

From D. J. West:

. . . [ESP experiments] fall short of the requirements for usual scientific conviction for several reasons, the chief one being that they are more in the nature of demonstrations than repeatable experiments. . . . No demonstration, however well done, can take the place of an experiment that can be repeated by anyone who cares to make the effort.

From John Beloff:

Rhine succeeded in giving parapsychology everything it needed to become an accredited experimental science except the one essential: the know-how to produce positive results when and where required. Without that the rest could never amount to more than trappings of a science.

From Adrian Parker:

The present crisis in parapsychology is that there appear to be few if any findings which are independent of the experimenter.

From Irving Child:

On the question of the reality of psi phenomena, no demonstration has been devised that is dependably repeatable.

A review of the evidence for ESP, then, provides little justification for the belief in psi. This does not "prove" that psi does not exist, only that 130 years of concerted effort has failed to document it. An examination of the evidence does make clear, however, that psi is currently a very dubious phenomenon, and it raises the important question—the one that is the central concern of this chapter—of why so many people nevertheless believe in its existence.

_____

[See R. Hyman, (1985). The ganzfeld/psi experiment: A critical appraisal. *Journal of Parapsychology, 49,* 3–49; R. Hyman & C. Honorton (1986). A joint communique: The psi ganzfeld controversy. *Journal of Parapsychology, 50,* 351–64; R. Hyman (1981). Further comments on Schmidt's PK experiments. *Skeptical Inquirer, 5,* 34–40.] None of these artifacts seem as definitive on the surface as those associated with the efforts of Rhine, Soal, or Targ and Puthoff, making the lack of replicability by independent investigators their most serious current shortcoming.

THE EXTENT OF BELIEF IN ESP

One thing that can be said about ESP is that it compels our attention regardless of whether or not it exists. If, despite current evidence to the contrary, we should someday discover the reality of psi, then both science and everyday life would change more dramatically than even the most creative science-fiction writers have imagined. On the other hand, if ESP really is nothing but the illusion that it currently appears to be, we are left with the fascinating question of why so many people are convinced of its existence. And the belief in ESP is truly widespread.

Many surveys of people's beliefs in paranormal phenomena have been conducted and, inevitably, the percentage of believers varies from sample to sample. In all samples, however, credulity is high. The most favorable attitudes toward ESP were found in a survey of Canadian college students, of whom 80% reported a belief in psi.[21] National surveys of the U.S. population have found that roughly 50% of the population are believers, including 67% of those who are college educated.[22] Perhaps most intriguing of all is the finding that two-thirds of a national sample of U.S. adults report having experienced ESP themselves.[23] Clearly, ESP is more credible to the average person than an even-handed appraisal of the objective evidence would warrant. Why?

WHY WE BELIEVE

Returning to the idea with which this chapter began, it seems that the most powerful determinant of the belief in ESP is all the apparent evidence of its existence, however unreliable such evidence may be, that one sees or hears about in everyday life. Psychics help the police solve a murder case. Apollo astronauts conduct a successful test of telepathy from outer space. The Pentagon spends millions to close the psi-gap with the Soviets.[24]

Can we really expect a healthy skepticism to flourish in this kind of soil? Even if each of these claims of the paranormal were disseminated with an accompanying skeptical response, we could still expect many individuals to commit the "where there's smoke, there's fire" fallacy and conclude that "there's probably something there." But such an even-handed treatment of these claims is simply not to be found. Rather, apparent demonstrations of ESP or any other paranormal phenomenon are considered newsworthy items to which substantial coverage is devoted. The critical appraisal of these claims, in contrast, is just not "news."

The magician James Randi cites the appalling news coverage of a "prediction" made by Duke University student Lee Fried.[25] Mr. Fried had deposited an envelope at the office of the president of Duke that supposedly contained a prophecy of an upcoming important event. When opened one week later, it contained a description of an incident that had in fact happened during the intervening week—the awful collision of two 747 jets that claimed the lives of 583 people. During interviews after his prediction was announced, Mr. Fried made it clear that he was a magician and that his apparent act of precognition was the result of a conjuring trick rather than psi. Nevertheless, of the seventeen newspapers Randi could find that covered this event, only one bothered to mention Mr. Fried's disclaimer!

Spectacular claims of paranormal powers are inherently splashy and arresting and thus can be counted on to sell more books, magazines, and advertising space than any critical analysis or rebuttal of these claims. Time-Life Books has for the past several years aggressively advertised its series "Mysteries of the Unknown" by inviting its audience to "discover the facts that have been uncovered and why, even after hundreds of years, the mysteries are still unexplained." Most of the events described in the promotional campaign, however, such as the Bermuda triangle, the lost continent of Atlantis, or the Shroud of Turin, are not really mysteries at all, but have been perfectly well explained for some time. But mysteries unsolved are more alluring than mysteries discredited, and so the resolution of these purportedly strange events is downplayed or ignored. Because the average reader is unaware that there simply is no Bermuda triangle "problem" or "mystery" to be explained, he or she can be taken in by the implication of these ads and the prestige of Time-Life Books and end up concluding that there must be something to the frequent reports of paranormal powers.

Those responsible for deciding how to present the paranormal in the popular media can be quite explicit about their interest in downplaying the skeptical position. As one example, a number of publishing houses declined to publish the excellent skeptical book, *The Psychology of the Psychic,* that, among other things, forcefully debunked the remote viewing experiments discussed earlier and the claims made by "superpsychic" Uri Geller. The authors report that the most common reason given for rejecting their manuscript was that "a pro-ESP book was already on their lists or in the pipeline, and they didn't think [our manuscript] and the 'pro' book would make very friendly neighbors."[26]

The net effect of the media's one-sided treatment is that the average person is many times more likely to encounter apparent support for the paranormal than any evidence that challenges its validity. A simple exercise supports this contention: The next time you are on vacation (and, for academics, no longer in a university town), take a trip to the local bookstore and examine the offerings in the general science section. In most cases, this section is almost comically small. Small in absolute terms; small compared to the science fiction section; small compared to the paranormal section; small compared to almost any reasonable category one might name. Published claims of the paranormal abound. With this as the data base confronting the average person, there is little wonder that belief in ESP is so widespread.

THE WILL TO BELIEVE

Some readers might question my claim that favorable media coverage is the preeminent cause of the belief in ESP, and accuse me of putting the cart before the horse. The media, after all, merely try to boost circulation, and doing so requires adhering to the beliefs and preferences of the audience. Paranormal claims would not sell, the argument goes, if they did not tap some pre-existing belief, or will to believe, in the general population. Is it not this will to believe that is ultimately responsible for the widespread acceptance of ESP?

There is truth to this claim. With respect to ESP, the media and the beliefs of the public clearly feed off one another. Belief, or the desire to believe, creates a market for the coverage of the paranormal, and this coverage in turn creates or reinforces belief. To many people, published claims about the existence of paranormal phenomena constitute sufficient grounds for belief because of the conviction that "they couldn't say it if it wasn't true."

The source of this "will to believe" is not hard to fathom. For many people, the existence of ESP implies several comforting corollaries. Most important, it suggests a greater reality which we have yet to fully understand. This can be an extremely seductive "transcendental temptation"[27] because it opens up several inviting possibilities, such as the potential for some part of us to survive death. One of the best known parapsychologists, Charles Tart, is quite forthcoming about such a basis of belief: "I happened upon a partial resolution of my personal (and my culture's) conflict between science and religion. Parapsychology validated the existence of basic phenomena that could partially account for, and fit in with, some of the spiritual views of the universe."[28] It is a rare person who does not want a ticket to immortality, or a piece of the transcendental. Most of us are prepared to believe such a doctrine if only the evidence could make it seem plausible.

Another seductive aspect of ESP is the implication that we all possess powers we have yet to develop. Perhaps we can more accurately predict the future through precognition, more efficiently communicate with others through telepathy, and more effectively control our physical health through something akin to psychokinesis. Perhaps many of the things we accomplish already through hard work and the application of our intelligence can be achieved more effortlessly through these special powers. May "The Force" be with us. It is worth noting that those who want psychic phenomena and parapsychological research to be more widely accepted in the general public often play upon this desire by emphasizing that psi is an undeveloped potential in everyone. For example, Targ and Puthoff say of their remote viewing research that:

> our laboratory experiments suggest that anyone who feels comfortable with the idea of having paranormal ability can have it. . . . In our experiments, we have never found anyone who could not learn to perceive scenes, including buildings, roads, and people, even those at great distances and blocked from ordinary perception. . . . So far, we cannot identify a single individual who has not suceeded in a remote viewing task to his own satisfaction.[29]

Although these appealing possibilities make many of us *want* to believe in ESP, the impact of such a desire may be less strong— or less direct—than is commonly thought. After all, nearly everyone is subject to the transcendental temptation, and yet only one-half to two-thirds of the population believes in ESP. More important, there are many things we would *like* to believe, but reality gets in the way. Personally, there are times—during a particularly difficult paragraph, let's say—when I would like to believe that I could take a leave of absence, join the Boston Celtics, and provide them with some much-needed scoring off the bench during the playoffs ("Professor Expels Lakers!"). But I, like nearly everyone else, am responsive to data. As we saw in chapter 5, people do not willy-nilly believe what they want to believe. Instead, people's preferences generally have their influence through the way they guide the evaluation of the pertinent evidence. The wish may be father to the belief, but like all fathers it requires a mate—some supporting evidence in this case.

Thus, if we are to fully understand the sources of people's belief in ESP, we must look elsewhere to discover how this general will to believe is satisfied. We must look at how people interpret everyday experience, and how that experience seems to support the existence of ESP. People would not endorse ESP if it did not resonate with their experience in everyday life.

THE DATA OF EVERYDAY EXPERIENCE

Numerous surveys have asked people to explain the origin of their belief in the paranormal, and all of them point to the importance of personal experience. Forty-one percent of the believers in a sample of Canadian undergraduates cited personal experience, or that of their friends and relatives, as the most important determinant of their belief,[30] as did 51% of the believers in a sample of readers of the British journal *New Scientist*.[31] Personal experience was also cited as the primary cause of belief by 71% of a sample of members of the Parapsychological Association.[32]

Clearly, personal experience plays an important role in people's views of ESP. What type of personal experience do people have in mind, and how is it construed, or misconstrued, as evidence of psi?

Mundane Psychokinesis. Given the widespread use of various randomizing devices in many gambling and board games, I am convinced that one of the most common (and for many people the earliest) apparent experiences of psi involves attempts to influence such random processes. Nearly everyone has played Monopoly, and who hasn't tried to "will" the dice to produce whatever numbers are needed to avoid the double hotels lurking ominously on Boardwalk? Occasionally, of course, whatever numbers one attempts to produce do come up. The question is how these successes are interpreted. Is there any reason to expect that they will be construed not as the occasional hits one can expect by chance, but as the product of paranormal powers?

First of all, because psychic powers and the ability to harness them are considered so mysterious, the door is open to selective encoding of success and failure. A hit may be thought to reflect the operation of one's psychic influence, whereas a miss may be considered nothing but one's inability to summon one's influence at that moment. This is reminiscent of the water witcher who only counted his hits in his success rate because "obviously, when I fail, the powers aren't working at that time, and, after all, I'm counting percentage on the cases where I'm divining, not when I'm just guessing."[33]

In addition, there are surprisingly many occasions when, just by chance, a random process produces numerous heads, sixes, or face cards in succession. As we saw in Chapter 2, people have a difficult time accepting the randomness of such streaks. They may thus walk away from the experience of these runs convinced that they have witnessed the operation of some special power.

Everyday Coincidence. Another phenomenon which tempts many people to speculate about a transcendent force is the experience of a remarkable coincidence. Two friends who have not seen each other in years sit in adjacent seats in a theatre in a foreign town. A man dials a wrong number in a distant city, and the recipient turns out to be his college roommate. A woman is thinking about an event she has not thought of in years and intends to discuss it with her spouse; miraculously, he brings it up first. These events seem so improbable, and often produce such powerful emotion, that they strike many people as more than just coincidence.

But how improbable are such events? Many coincidences that seem extraordinary are in reality quite common. The "birthday problem" discussed in many statistics courses is a good example. When asked to consider the probability that at least two people in a group of a particular size were born on the same day of the year, most people are shocked to learn that the odds are roughly 50–50 when the group is as small as 23. More shocking still is that the probability of a matching birthday is 85% when the group size is only 35. Thus, many people will be surprised by an outcome (a pair of matching birthdays) that is not unusual at all.

To the skeptic, all seemingly bizarre coincidences are not terribly amazing when considered from the appropriate statistical perspective. This may be what Aristotle had in mind when he said that "the improbable is extremely probable." Unlike the birthday problem, however, the exact probability of many coincidental events cannot always be determined. Rough approximations can nevertheless be attempted. A telling example is provided by physicist and Nobel laureate Luis Alvarez, who was struck by a remarkable coincidence in his own life. After reading a brief passage in a newspaper, Alvarez began a series of associations that led him to think of a long-forgotten acquaintance from his college years. Turning the pages of the paper, he was amazed to see an obituary of that very same individual!

Could Alvarez somehow have learned of this person's death through some non-sensory channel? Or might his recollection of this long-forgotten acquaintance been produced by a precognitive awareness of the obituary itself? Believing such paranormal explanations implausible, Alvarez proceeded to compute an approximate probability of such a coincidence by estimating the number of people the average person knows and how often the average person has such recollections. After making what appear to be reasonably conservative assumptions, Alvarez calculated that the probability of thinking of an acquaintance roughly five minutes before learning of that person's death is roughly 3×10^{-5} per year. Thus, with the population of the United States as it is, we can expect there to be over 3,000 of these events every year, or almost 10 every day.[34]

Although Alvarez's figures are not definitive, they nevertheless fit nicely with the results of the birthday problem, and they remind us that many coincidental events are far less remarkable than they seem. Our misguided intuitions about the true likelihood of such events appear to stem from two sources—a failure to appreciate how often we "sample" from the population of all events, and a reluctance to consider how many *different* events we would consider to be coincidental.

Given the vastness of our experience (how many thoughts we have, how many people we come in contact with, etc.) numerous coincidental events are bound to happen in a lifetime. As Stephen Jay Gould has said, ". . . time converts the improbable to the inevitable—give me a million years and I'll flip a hundred heads in a row more than once."[35] People fail to appreciate how many chances they have to experience something coincidental. Perhaps the key to this shortcoming of human intuition is that, unlike coin flipping, the repeated sampling is not obvious because it is not the *same distribution* being repeatedly sampled. By meeting a person here, thinking of someone there, receiving a phone call somewhere else, we are sampling from *different* distributions, and it is this difference that masks the repetitive element of the sampling process. Furthermore, people may be reluctant to think of their own experience, with all its attendant emotions, as a sample from a population of all possible experiences.

Our intuitions about coincidental events also suffer from the problem of "multiple endpoints" discussed in Chapter 4. While the odds of a *particular* coincidence may indeed be vanishingly low, the odds of any of a set of equally remarkable coincidences is generally much higher. Suppose an amateur thespian takes in the theatre while visiting London and runs into his high school drama teacher. An amazing coincidence to be sure. But would it be any less amazing if it had been his high school co-star? Or his understudy? And suppose it wasn't London, but Athens, Paris, or Rome? Or what if the encounter had taken place, not in the theatre, but at the opera house, a museum, or even a pub?

By pulling back a bit like this, we quickly see that although the probability of any one coincidence is indeed quite low, the probability of the *union* of all such coincidental events can be quite high. Our sense of astonishment when confronted by coincidence can thus be traced to our intuitive tendency to assess the likelihood of the *intersection* of the specific events that did occur, rather than the union of all similar outcomes that might have occurred. The birthday problem is instructive in this regard. Many people approach the problem with a fairly accurate sense of the long odds against a *particular* pair of people having the same birthdate (approximately 1/365), but they fail to appreciate how many different pairs of people there are (253) in a group of 23.

Finally, people may be inclined to see some sort of guiding hand behind many coincidental events because of the powerful emotions these experiences often produce. Because "big" events are thought to require "big" causes (see ch. 2), purely-random coincidence is considered by many to be an unacceptable explanation of such a compelling and evocative occurrence.

Everyday Premonitions. Premonitions tend to elicit paranormal explanations as much or more as a startling coincidence. In fact, premonitions are really a special class of coincidence—a coincidence between a person's thoughts and events in the outside world. Someone dreams about a plane crash and then hears about precisely that event on the evening news. Someone reminisces about an old acquaintance, and the acquaintance suddenly walks in the room.

Premonitions strike people as compelling for the same reason that underlies the impact of coincidence—they seem too improbable to occur by chance. But given how often an active mind thinks of people, places, and events, the briefest reflection informs us that a person is almost certain to experience quite a few premonitions in a full lifetime. Death, for example, is a very frequent topic of dreams, and so it is hardly surprising if one such dream should happen to correspond to a real-world fatality. That does not make a person's premonitions of death terribly meaningful or informative, however. One is reminded here of economist Paul Samuelson's crack that the stock market has accurately predicted nine of the last five recessions.

Premonitions are also precisely the kind of "one-sided" events (chapter 4) for which the successes stand out and the failures go unrecognized. People daydream about long-lost friends all the time, but little of the specific content of such reveries can generally be recalled—unless they should happen to be followed by an unexpected visit by that very same person. Against this background of selective recall, any one premonition looms as a much more impressive event than it really is. Francis Bacon noted this long ago when he said that ". . . all superstition is much the same whether it be that of astrology, dreams, omens, retributive judgment, or the like, . . . [in that] the deluded believers observe events which are fulfilled, but neglect or pass over their failure, though it be much more common."[36]

Another curious feature of premonitions that makes them more likely to happen is that they often occur after the fact. A man has a vague, unpleasant dream about riding in a plane that is out of control (or was it a boat?), and the morning paper carries the story of a fiery plane crash. This can be a striking experience to be sure, but how much of the recollection of the dream was shaped by the details of the next day's news? Dreams are particularly suspect in this regard because their multi-faceted, kaleidoscopic nature makes them something of a "one size fits all" premonition that is easy to fulfill. Psychologist James Alcock cites intriguing evidence of the retrospective nature of many prophetic dreams: Those who claim to have such experiences report that their prophetic quality disappears after he has them record their dreams![37]

Retrospective prophecies, if you will excuse the oxymoron, are so successful because they capitalize on multiple endpoints, a problem that plagues not only dream prophecies but those produced by conscious minds as well. Some prophecies are so vague that they can be "fulfilled" by almost any outcome. Those offered by that resurgent seer Nostradamus are a case in point. Although not quite as vacuous as those in Woody Allen's spoof of the sixteenth-century astrologer-physician ("Two countries will go to war, but only one will win"),[38] his prophecies are so vague and difficult to interpret that it is hard to imagine how they could be disconfirmed. His popularity is thus truly baffling, particularly when one learns that he essentially made this admission about his predictions himself! He stated that he phrased his prohecies in such a way that ". . . they could not possibly be understood till they were interpreted after the event and by it."[39]

People can also be unduly impressed by premonitions by failing to identify the operation of subtle causal factors that produced them. Suppose that after visiting a relative you depart with a vague sense of unease: Your relative looks "different" in a way that you cannot quite identify. This unease leads to anxious dreams about the person, perhaps one in which he or she is harmed. Suppose, in addition, that two days later you learn that this same relative has been hospitalized with a serious ailment. Under these circumstances, it is hard to resist the conclusion that you have forseen this bad turn of events—you have. But what is the cause of the premonition? Unfortunately, many people leap to a paranormal explanation, and miss completely how their initial unease was both a cause of their dream and a reflection of the ill health that led to the relative's hospitalization.

Telephone calls that occur "out of the blue" by the target of one's ruminations also have this quality. A rumination about a particular person may be triggered by some external event with which he or she is associated. That same external event, of course, can lead that same person to think about you and thus prompt a phone call. Because these associations can occur at a less than fully conscious level, there may be no obvious cause of the call, making one's thoughts appear to be truly psychic.

Extraordinary Premonitions. Putting aside all of these elements that make many astonishing premonitions much less than that in reality, there nevertheless are occasions in which people experience clear, precise foreshadowings of significant events that do in fact occur exactly as forseen. Here again, though, the important question is whether they occur more frequently than one would expect by chance. The notion that it is just coincidence may be difficult to accept for anyone who has had such a premonition and experienced all the powerful emotion and sense of awe they inspire. Intuitively, such awesome events demand more than mundane causes—certainly more than the implication that there is no cause at all. Furthermore, because these kinds of premonitions involve events like illness and death that we associate with the transcendent, it is only a small cognitive step to a transcendent explanation like ESP.

THE TENACITY OF PARANORMAL BELIEFS

Belief in ESP has been remarkably unaffected by the consensus of the scientific community that there is no "scientific justification for the existence of [such] phenomena."[40] Are there any factors other than the misconstrual of everyday experience, the will to believe, and exposure to pro-ESP media accounts, that can help explain the robustness of these beliefs? Here it may be important to focus particularly on the beliefs of that abstract entity, the "intelligent layperson," who is likely to be at least vaguely aware of the scientific skepticism about ESP and yet is not as psychologically invested in this issue as, say, a parapsychologist.

People generally believe the scientific community, even when it makes claims that seem bizarre or that conflict with the apparent lessons of everyday experience. Few quarrel with the claim that the earth is round or that it revolves around the sun, despite immediate experience that seems to suggest otherwise. People also readily accept the existence of quarks, black holes, and gaps in the ozone layer—entities that can be difficult to fathom. Why is the word of science accepted in these cases, but not with respect to ESP?

Part of the answer lies in the nature of the skeptical perspective on ESP. To say that ESP does not exist is to take something away from a person. Exciting phenomena either have one of several mundane explanations or they simply do not exist. Thus, the skeptic asks that what seems to be a unified—although not terribly deep—explanation of a host of phenomena (i.e., that psychic powers exist) be replaced by a patchwork of explanations or no explanation at all. The skeptical perspective, therefore, may sometimes be rejected because it can appear to lack elegance: A single explanation (ESP in this case), by the sheer force of its diversity, generally appears more plausible than a set of disjoint accounts. People act much like professional scientists who are willing to tolerate troublesome data in allegiance to a unifying theory—until a more elegant and unified theory is discovered.[41] The skeptical perspective on ESP, although driven by the pertinent data, does not provide such unity or elegance.

Note that people's discomfort with the absence of a unified theory can serve to subtly shift the burden of proof about ESP to where it does not belong—to the skeptic. Logicians and philosophers are in virtual unanimous agreement that the burden of proof on any question lies not with the skeptic, but with the person making the positive assertion. The tables are often turned in discussions of ESP, however. Because psi serves as the default explanation of seemingly paranormal events, the skeptic is often asked to specify "if it wasn't ESP, what was it?" How, in other words, can a particular anomaly be explained without ESP? But to claim that "if not this, it must be that" is to commit a logical fallacy. The failure to supply a convincing "natural" explanation for an anomalous event may be more a reflection of the limits of our knowledge than an argument for psi.

The Tenacious Beliefs of Parapsychologists. The debate about ESP is generally framed as a question of how likely it is that psi exists, given the evidence of everyday life and the parapsychology laboratory. Skeptics and parapsychologists obviously differ in their assessments of this likelihood. Another way to frame the debate, however, is to ask, "if psi existed, and a research program were conducted to examine it, what would we expect to discover?" Although this may seem like a mere semantic trifle, it focuses attention on some potentially informative questions. For instance, what would those who started the scientific investigation of psi have expected to result from 130 years of research? The answer is of course impossible to know with certainty, but it is hard to resist the conclusion that they would have been disappointed with what has been obtained thus far. After all, what regular phenomena has this research uncovered? There is the "experimenter effect," whereby positive results are obtained by sympathetic investigators and inhibited by skeptics. There is the "decline effect," whereby the psi powers of even the most gifted subjects decline and generally disappear over time. And there is "psi-missing," whereby gifted subjects sometimes reveal their powers of apprehending concealed targets by making significantly *fewer* correct responses than expected by chance.

If psi existed, is it likely that this is what we would have to show for 130 years of continuous investigation? To be fair, others might quarrel with my characterization of what are the consistent findings of parapsychological research, and they may want to include additional results. But even with a more generous inclusion of a few additional findings, the overall assessment remains much the same. When the debate is framed in this way, in other words, it becomes clear that the acceptance of ESP represents a classic case of people's beliefs surviving the challenge of disconfirmation at the hands of the relevant evidence.

—

FOUR

Where Do We Go from Here?

11

Challenging Dubious Beliefs
The Role of Social Science

The real purpose of [the] scientific method is to make sure Nature hasn't misled you into thinking you know something you actually don't know.

R. Pirsig, *Zen and the Art of Motorcycle Maintenance*

Many treatment strategies and training efforts are designed to eliminate the source of the existing problem. When someone has an infection, for example, the underlying cause can be treated by administering antibiotics. When someone first learns to drive a car with a manual transmission, problems often arise from the predisposition to let out the clutch prematurely. With practice, however, the person gradually learns to let it out at the appropriate rate and the initial tendency to rush things simply disappears.

There are other times, however, when the source of the problem cannot be eliminated, and so it must be counteracted. We do not cure nearsightedness; we prescribe corrective lenses. We do not eliminate the urge to eat in people who are overweight; we prescribe diet and exercise regimens to achieve a balance between caloric intake and output. When we teach ethics to our children, we are unlikely to eradicate fully their basic self-centeredness; instead, we counteract it by instilling compensatory moral principles—"Do unto others as you would have them do unto you," "What goes around, comes around," or "What would happen if everyone were to do what you did?"

When we turn to the question of what can be done to improve everyday reasoning and to spare us from the kinds of questionable and erroneous beliefs discussed in this book, it should be clear that it is the latter, compensatory strategy that is required. The underlying causes of faulty reasoning and erroneous beliefs will never be eliminated. People will always prefer black-and-white over shades of grey, and so there will always be the temptation to hold overly-simplified beliefs and to hold them with excessive confidence. People will always be tempted by the idea that everything that happens to them is controllable. Likewise, the tendency to impute structure and coherence to purely random patterns is wired deep into our cognitive machinery, and it is unlikely to ever be completely eliminated. The tendency to be more impressed by what *has* happened than by what has *failed* to happen, and the temptation to draw conclusions from what has occurred under present circumstances without comparing it to what would have occurred under alternative circumstances, seem to be similarly ingrained.

These underlying causes of erroneous beliefs will never simply disappear. They must, then, be held in check by compensatory mental habits that promote more sound reasoning. To avoid erroneous beliefs, in other words, it is necessary that we develop certain habits of mind that can shore up various deficiencies in our everyday inferential abilities.

Fortunately, there is reason to believe that these corrective habits of mind are not difficult to develop. Students who are familiar with the recent work on the errors and biases of human judgment seem able to apply the lessons of this research to their everyday lives. I have occasionally overheard my own students remark to their peers, "Yeah, but what do the other three cells look like?", "But we all know that people will see order in almost anything—isn't this just like the hot hand?", or "Remember, though, we've only heard about this secondhand." The necessary principles appear to be easy to understand and to learn; the critical task is to get them so firmly entrenched that they are readily applied to everyday life.

What are these essential habits of mind, and how can we develop them? To a large extent, they have already been discussed implicitly in earlier chapters. To specify the mechanisms that give rise to erroneous beliefs is to tacitly identify what is necessary to prevent them. Any analysis of a specific type of faulty reasoning implies a strategy for improvement. Given the contents of earlier chapters, then, here it is perhaps best if we only briefly consider some of the habits of mind that are most important to cultivate.[*]

Perhaps the most general and most important mental habit to instill is an appreciation of the folly of trying to draw conclusions from incomplete and unrepresentative evidence. An essential corrollary of this appreciation should be an awareness of how often our everyday experience presents us with biased samples of information. Rather than being overly impressed with the evidence immediately before us, we need to step back and ask, like the perspicacious graduate student mentioned above, "What do the other three cells look like?" Theists, for example, note the number of times their prayers have been answered and conclude that there is a benevolent god; atheists cite the occasions that their prayers have gone unanswered and conclude that we are on our own. Both need to develop the habit of thinking more broadly. Both must consider the number of times their hopes have been realized when they have prayed and when they have not, as well the number of times their hopes have been dashed when they have prayed and when they have not.

As we have seen many times throughout this book, not all of these four types of information are equally likely to come to one's attention, and so it is important to be particularly energetic in trying to dig up the most elusive information. We need to be aware, for example, of how often our role, status, or position in a social network can cut us off from certain classes of informative data. Clinicians should temper their conclusions about the prognosis and essential treatment of certain pathologies by considering how people who are not in therapy deal with the condition in question. Admissions officials should modulate their assessments of their ability to discriminate between qualified and unqualified applicants

---

[*] Another reason for brevity here is to avoid redundancy with several other recent books that, although not concerned with erroneous beliefs per se, nevertheless deal with the shortcomings of everyday reasoning that contribute so much to the formation of dubious beliefs. For the interested reader, some of the best to consider are R. Nisbett & L. Ross (1980) *Human inference: Strategies and shortcomings of social judgment.* Englewood Cliffs, NJ: Prentice-Hall; R. M. Dawes (1988) *Rational choice in an uncertain world.* San Diego, CA: Harcourt, Brace, Jovanovich; D. Kahneman, P. Slovic, & A. Tversky (1982) *Judgment under uncertainty: Heuristics and biases.* Cambridge: Cambridge University Press; and J. Baron (1988) *Thinking and deciding.* Cambridge: Cambridge University Press.

by considering how well the people they turned down would have performed had they been accepted. Before drawing firm conclusions, in other words, we need to ask ourselves whether there are any "invisible" data we may be overlooking.

A set of important mental habits we also need to develop are those that can help to overcome the drawbacks associated with one of our most remarkable skills—the facility with which we can explain a vast range of outcomes in terms of our pre-existing theories and beliefs. Because of our talent for *ad hoc* explanation, even quite unexpected and damaging outcomes can be seen to be consistent with our original convictions. Our beliefs thus appear to receive too much support from equivocal evidence, and they are too seldom discredited by truly antagonistic results. To compensate, we need to develop the habit of employing one of several "consider the opposite" strategies. We can learn to ask ourselves, for example, "Suppose the exact opposite had occurred. Would I consider *that* outcome to be supportive of my belief as well?" Alternatively, we can ask, "How would someone who does not believe the way I do explain this result?", or, more generally, "What alternative theory could account for it?" By asking these questions, we become aware that the link between evidence and belief is not so tight as it might first appear. These strategies thus help to guard against premature acceptance of doubtful propositions, and they encourage us to figure out (and try to obtain) the evidence necessary to truly test a belief's validity.

There are a number of other, less general habits of mind that are helpful in warding off many of the sources of erroneous beliefs discussed in earlier chapters. Guidelines for dealing with the uncertainties and distortions of secondhand information were offered in Chapter 6. To these it is important to add that we would be well advised to consider the possibility that information that comes to us from others may be more remote than it first appears. That which is described as secondhand is often thirdhand, that which is passed off as thirdhand is often even more distant, and so on. Events described to us by a trustworthy source may nonetheless have originated with someone less credible. We therefore should be more skeptical than we seem to be about evidence presented to us secondhand. We should become accustomed to asking ourselves where the information originated, and how much distortion—deliberate or otherwise—is likely to have been introduced along the way.

Chapter 7 suggests that we should question whether our beliefs are really as widely shared as they appear. The absence of explicit disagreement should not automatically be taken as evidence of agreement. Chapter 2 calls for an awareness of the human tendency to impute order to any complex set of stimuli and an understanding of when and where statistical regression is likely to occur. An appreciation of both phenomena should encourage us to consider the "just chance" hypothesis and to be less prone to rush to judgment and intervention.

THE VALUE OF SCIENCE EDUCATION

Many of these essential habits of mind, particularly the most general ones for dealing with incomplete and unrepresentative evidence, were originally developed as part of the scientific enterprise. For instance, the idea that what one observes under one set of conditions can only be evaluated with reference to what would have happened under slightly different circumstances is embodied in the scientist's use of the control group. Procedures for distinguishing random from ordered phenomena were developed not long ago in the field of statistics. Statistical regression was discovered through the study of genetic inheritance. And so on.

It stands to reason, then, that greater familiarity with the scientific enterprise should help to promote the habits of mind necessary to think clearly about evidence and to steer clear of dubious beliefs. Involvement in the process and concepts of science not only teaches these habits of mind directly, it also provides experience with problems, phenomena, and strategies from which they can sometimes be intuited, or at least more deeply understood. Also, one who participates in the scientific enterprise receives valuable exposure to uncertainty and doubt. Because science tries to stretch the limits of what is known, the scientist is constantly thrust against a barrier of ignorance. The more science one learns, the more one becomes aware of what is *not* known, and the provisional nature of much of what is. All of this contributes to a healthy skepticism toward claims about how things are or should be. This general intellectual outlook, this awareness of how hard it can be to really know something with certainty, while humbling, is an important side benefit of participating in the scientific enterprise.

A number of authors have recently written about the woeful

state of science and mathematics education in the United States and its role in producing a citizenry that is not at all critically minded. Sometimes the concern is with whether the voting public will be able to develop well-informed opinions about the increasingly complex issues that are part of our technological world; at other times the concern is about the state of our more abstract abilities to reason effectively. One can only agree with the general argument that generating more interest in the scientific enterprise would be helpful in these regards.

There is an intriguing twist to this general contention, however. A set of recent studies suggests—albeit only tentatively at this point—that a particular kind of science education may be especially effective in developing the habits of mind necessary for thinking clearly about the evidence of everyday experience. The logic that motivated these studies was quite simple: Exposure to the "probabilistic" sciences may be more effective than experience with the "deterministic" sciences in teaching people how to evaluate adequately the kind of messy, probabilistic phenomena that are often encountered in everyday life. Probabilistic sciences are those such as psychology and economics that deal mainly with phenomena that are not perfectly predictable, and with causes that are generally neither necessary nor sufficient. The death of a spouse, for instance, is associated with a deterioration of health in the bereaved, but not for all widows and widowers, and ill health often descends for other reasons. Thus, bereavement is neither a necessary nor sufficient cause of ill health. Likewise, attractive people are generally responded to more favorably than the unattractive, but not all beautiful people are well liked, and good looks are not a requirement for winning another person's esteem or affection.

Deterministic sciences, on the other hand, are those such as chemistry and many branches of physics that typically deal with much tidier phenomena for which the causal connections are more often necessary and sufficient. To increase the gravitational attraction of two objects of given mass, it is both necessary and sufficient to move them closer together. It is with respect to the uncertain phenomena studied by the probabilistic sciences that ideas like statistical regression, sample bias, and the importance of control groups are particularly germane. Familiarity with these fields, then, should best facilitate the habits of mind necessary to evaluate properly the evidence of everyday experience.

To test this idea, a group of psychologists administered a test of statistical and methodological reasoning to students receiving graduate training in psychology, chemistry, medicine, and law.[1] As a control procedure to assess any differences in general learning across the four disciplines, the students were also administered the verbal reasoning subtest of the Graduate Record Examination (GRE). The design of this study was both cross-sectional and longitudinal: First- and third-year graduate students in each field were compared to one another to assess the effects of their graduate training, and the first-year students were reassessed two years later, with their later performance compared to their original.

Two forms of the test were developed to permit retesting in the longitudinal component of the study. The questions were designed to assess the sophistication of the students' statistical and methodological reasoning in both scientific and everyday-life contexts. For example, in one of the scientific questions, the subjects were told about a hypothetical teaching experiment and were asked what could be expected to happen to students in the control condition of that experiment who had initially received relatively high or low grades. The question was meant to elicit whether the respondents would exhibit any recognition of the regression principle by stating that students with high initial grades could be expected to receive somewhat lower grades subsequently, and those with low initial grades could be expected to receive somewhat higher grades. In an everyday-life problem, the subjects were told about a mayor who boasted of the 12% reduction in crime that had taken place during his administration. They were then asked about the kinds of evidence they thought would be necessary to evaluate the validity and import of the mayor's claim. This question was concerned with whether they would recognize the importance of control-group data by, say, wanting to examine crime rates during the same period in cities of similar size and close geographical location.

The results for both cross-sectional and longitudinal assessments were clear-cut and pointed to the relative effectiveness of social science training in teaching statistical and methodological reasoning. There were no initial differences in test scores across the four disciplines. However, two years of training in psychology led to a 70% increase in test scores, whereas a similar period of training in chemistry or law produced no improvement whatsoever. Medical training also improved statistical and methodological reasoning, with two years of medical school producing a 25% improvement in test scores. Graduate education in the four different disciplines did not produce any reliable differences in improvement on the verbal reasoning sub-test of the GRE (gains ranged from 4% to 17%). The investigators concluded:

> It appears that the probabilistic sciences of psychology and medicine teach their students to apply statistical and methodological rules to both scientific and everyday-life problems, whereas the nonprobabilistic science of chemistry and the nonscientific discipline of the law do not affect their students in these respects (p. 438) . . . . the luxury of not being confronted with messy problems that contain substantial uncertainty and a tangled web of causes means that chemistry does not teach some rules that are relevant to everyday life (p. 441).

It seems, then, that social scientists may have a special opportunity to impart some wisdom about how to properly evaluate the evidence of everyday experience. The authors of the study just described argue that there are certain formal properties of the subject matter of social science (e.g., considerable irregularity and uncertainty, the relative lack of necessary and sufficient causal relations) that make it particularly effective for teaching some important principles of sound reasoning. There are also a number of pragmatic characteristics of social science that add to its effectiveness in this regard. Part of the popularity of college courses in such areas as personality and social psychology derives from the fact that they deal with phenomena that students have encountered and thought about in their everyday lives. Some of the material conflicts with students' pre-existing beliefs and thus provides much more than the usual incentive to engage in critical analysis, to suggest alternative explanations, and to consider the adequacy of both existing data and other potentially informative evidence. The student is thus encouraged to engage his or her analytic faculties with unusual intensity because the very nature of the material invites it. The complexity of the phenomena, the difficulty of untangling correlated variables, and the relative scarcity of truly decisive experiments compel all but the most disengaged students to dig deeper and think harder. The general principles of scientific inference are straightforward and easy to teach. What is difficult is to teach how and when to apply them. In this respect many branches of the social sciences have an advantage. Many of these fields are concerned with the highly visible processes and phenomena of everyday life in which nearly everyone can take an interest—the best ways to influence other people, the causes of people's attraction to one another, or the causes and correlates of happiness and well-being. Thus by their very nature, many of the social sciences provide helpful practice in thinking clearly and rigorously about the phenomena of everyday life.

THE SOCIAL SCIENTIST'S OBLIGATION

Social scientists suffer from physics envy. From the beginning, they have felt like poor relations among the sciences, unable to match the natural scientists' cumulative achievements, explanatory power, and predictive precision. There is indeed much to admire about the progress made in the "hard" sciences—progress that the social sciences will likely never match. Nevertheless, it is important to acknowledge that there is a special benefit from studying the messy, complex phenomena that constitute the subject matter of the social sciences. Dealing with such irregular, uncertain phenomena has led to a number of methodological innovations. Social scientists are generally more familiar than those in other fields with how easy it is to be misled by the evidence of everyday experience, and they are more aware of the methodological controls that are necessary before one can draw firm conclusions from a set of data. This may be one reason why fewer psychologists believe in the existence of ESP than their colleagues in the natural sciences or the humanities.[2]

As a consequence, what social scientists might best offer both their students and the general public is their methodological sophistication, their way of looking at the world, the habits of mind that they promote—process more than content. In fits and starts, social science has advanced human knowledge a great deal over the years. Nevertheless, much of what we think we have learned will certainly change over the next 50 or 100 years. How we go about our business, on the other hand, and the methods we employ to advance our knowledge, will be largely the same. An awareness of how and when to question and a recognition of what it takes to truly know something are among the most important elements of what constitutes an educated person. Social scientists, I believe, may be in the best position to instill them.

Some of what I have said about social science applies equally well to this book. Much that we currently know about what is or isn't so will surely change in subsequent years. What is most important, then, is not dispelling particular erroneous beliefs (although there is surely some merit in that), but creating an understanding of how we form erroneous beliefs. To truly appreciate the complexities of the world and the intricacies of human experience, it is essential to understand how we can be misled by the apparent evidence of everyday experience. This, in turn, requires that we think clearly about our experience, question our assumptions, and challenge what we think we know.

Notes

Chapter 1. Introduction

1. E. J. Lamb (1979) Does adoption affect subsequent fertility? *American Journal of Obstetrics and Gynecology, 134,* 138–44.

2. R. M. Dawes (1979) The robust beauty of improper linear models. *American Psychologist, 34,* 571–82.

3. G. O. Abell & B. Greenspan (1979) Human births and the phase of the moon. *New England Journal of Medicine, 300,* 96.

4. Gallup Opinion Index (1978) Political, social, and economic trends. June, pp. 1–5; A. Greeley (1987) From here to the hereafter. *San Jose Mercury News,* January 17, p. C1; "Gallup Poll of Beliefs" (1989) *Skeptical Inquirer, 13,* 244–45; "Scientific Literacy" (1989) *Skeptical Inquirer, 13,* 343–45.

5. J. A. Wheeler (1979) Paper presented to the American Association for the Advancement of Science. Houston, TX.

6. R. Nisbett & L. Ross (1980) *Human inference: Strategies and shortcomings of social judgment.* Englewood Cliffs, NJ: Prentice-Hall, p. 14.

7. R. K. Merton (1948) The self-fulfilling prophecy. *Antioch Review, 8,* 193–210.

8. E. B. Martin (1981) The conspicuous consumption of rhinos. *Animal Kingdom, 84,* 20–29.

9. M. Elkins (1989) Division of Law Enforcement, U.S. Fish and Wildlife Service. Personal communication.

10. R. M. Deutsch (1977) *The new nuts among the berries: How nutrition nonsense captured America.* Palo Alto, CA: Bull.

11. S. J. Gould (1987) *An urchin in the storm: Essays about books and ideas.* New York: W.W. Norton, p. 245.

Chapter 2. Something Out of Nothing

1. J. R. Vokey & J. D. Read (1985) Subliminal messages: Between the devil and the media. *American Psychologist, 40,* 1231–39.

2. J. W. Connor (1984) Misperception, folk belief, and the occult: A cognitive guide to understanding. *Skeptical Inquirer, 8,* 344–54.

3. T. Gilovich, R. Vallone, & A. Tversky (1985) The hot hand in basketball: On the misperception of random sequences. *Cognitive Psychology, 17,* 295–314.

4. T. Gilovich (1983) Biased evaluation and persistence in gambling. *Journal of Personality and Social Psychology, 44,* 1110–26.

5. R. Falk (1981) The perception of randomness. In *Proceedings, Fifth International Conference for the Psychology of Mathematics Education* Grenoble, France; Wagenaar, W. A. (1972) Generation of random sequences by human subjects: A critical survey of literature. *Psychological Bulletin, 77,* 65–72.

6. A. Tversky & D. Kahneman (1974) Judgment under uncertainty: Heuristics and biases. *Science, 185,* 1124–31.

7. Taken from R. Thaler (1983) Illusions and mirages in public policy. *The Public Interest, 73,* 60–74.

8. D. Kahneman & A. Tversky (1971) Subjective probability: A judgment of representativeness. *Cognitive psychology, 3,* 430–54; D. Kahneman & A. Tversky (1973) On the psychology of prediction. *Psychological Review, 80,* 237–51; A. Tversky & D. Kahneman (1971) Belief in the law of small numbers. *Psychological Bulletin, 76,* 105–110; A. Tversky & D. Kahneman (1974) Judgment under uncertainty: Heuristics and biases. *Science, 185,* 1124–31.

9. R. D. Clarke (1946) An application of the poisson distribution. *Journal of the Institute of Actuaries (London), 72,* p. 72; D. Johnson (1981) *V-1, V-2: Hitler's vengeance on London.* New York: Stein & Day.

10. R. D. Clarke (1946) An application of the poisson distribution. *Journal of the Institute of Actuaries (London), 72,* p. 72; W. Feller (1968) *An introduction to probability theory and its applications.* New York: Wiley.

11. D. Johnson (1981) *V–1, V–2: Hitler's vengeance on London.* New York: Stein & Day, p. 144–45.

12. L. Ross, M. R. Lepper, & M. Hubbard (1975) Perseverance in self-perception and social perception: Biased attributional processes in the debriefing paradigm. *Journal of Personality and Social Psychology, 32,* 880–92.

13. L. Ross, M. R. Lepper, F. Strack, & J. L. Steinmetz (1977) Social explana-

tion and social expectation: The effects of real and hypothetical explanations upon subjective likelihood. *Journal of Personality and Social Psychology, 35,* 817–29.

14. M. Gazzaniga (1985) *The social brain: Discovering the networks of the mind.* New York: Basic Books.

15. See also R. E. Nisbett & T. D. Wilson (1977). Telling more than we can know: Verbal reports on mental processes. *Psychological Review, 84,* 231–59.

16. D. Kahneman & A. Tversky (1973). On the psychology of prediction. *Psychological Review, 80,* 237–51.

17. "Letter from the publisher." (1979) *Sports Illustrated,* August 13, pp. 6–7.

18. O. H. Mowrer (1968) The law of effect, conditioning, and the problem of punishment. In E. E. Boe & R. M. Church (Eds.) *Punishment: Issues and experiments.* New York: Appleton-Century-Crofts.

19. B. F. Skinner (1953) *Science and human behavior.* New York: Free Press.

20. P. Aries (1962) *Centuries of childhood: A social history of family life.* New York: Vintage Books.

21. D. Kahneman & A. Tversky (1973) On the psychology of prediction. *Psychological Review, 80,* 237–51; A. Tversky & D. Kahneman (1974) Judgment under uncertainty: Heuristics and biases. *Science, 185,* 1124–31.

22. P. E. Schaffner (1985) Specious learning about reward and punishment. *Journal of Personality and Social Psychology, 48,* 1377–86.

23. "Women barred from funerals." *Jerusalem Post,* February 3, 1987; "No halachic basis for ban on women attending funerals." *Jerusalem Post,* February 4, 1987.

Chapter 3. Too Much from Too Little

1. H. J. Einhorn & R. M. Hogarth (1977) Confidence in judgment: Persistence of the illusion of validity. *Psychological Review, 85,* 395–416.

2. L. Allen & H. Jenkins (1980) The judgment of contingency and the nature of response alternatives. *Canadian Journal of Psychology, 34,* 1–11; R. Beyth-Marom (1982) Perception of correlation reexamined. *Memory & Cognition, 10,* 511–19; J. Crocker (1981) Judgment of covariation by social perceivers. *Psychological Bulletin, 90,* 272–92; J. Crocker (1982) Biased questions in judgment of covari-

ation studies. *Personality and Social Psychology Bulletin, 8,* 214–20; H. M. Jenkins & W. C. Ward (1965) Judgments of contingency between responses and outcomes. *Psychological Monographs: General and Applied, 79,* (1, Whole No 594); J. Smedslund (1963) The concept of correlation in adults. *Scandinavian Journal of Psychology, 4,* 165–73; W. D. Ward & H. M. Jenkins (1965) The display of information and the judgment of contingency. *Canadian Journal of Psychology, 19,* 231–41.

3. J. Crocker (1982) Biased questions in judgment of covariation studies. *Personality and Social Psychology Bulletin, 8,* 214–20.

4. R. H. Fazio, S. J. Sherman, & P. M. Herr (1982) The feature-positive effect in the self-perception process: Does not doing matter as much as doing? *Journal of Personality and Social Psychology, 42,* 404–11; H. M. Jenkins & R. S. Sainsbury (1970) Discrimination learning with the distinctive feature on positive or negative trials. In D. Mostofsky (Ed.), *Attention: Contemporary theory and analysis.* New York: Appleton-Century-Crofts; J. Newman, W. T. Wolff, & E. Hearst (1980) The feature-positive effect in adult human subjects. *Journal of Experimental Psychology: Human Learning; and Memory, 6,* 630–50; R. Nisbett & L. Ross (1980) *Human inference: Strategies and shortcomings of social judgment.* New Jersey: Prentice Hall; P. C. Wason & P. N. Johnson-Laird (1965) *Psychology of reasoning: Structure and content.* London: Batsford.

5. F. Bacon (1960/1620) *The new organon and related writings.* New York: Liberal Arts Press.

6. P. C. Wason (1966) Reasoning. In B. M. Foss (Ed.), *New horizons in psychology.* Harmondsworth: Penguin.

7. M. Bassok & Y. Trope (1984) People's strategies for testing hypotheses about another's personality: Confirmatory or diagnostic? *Social Cognition, 2,* 199–216; R. B. Skov & S. J. Sherman (1986) Information-gathering processes: Diagnosticity, hypothesis-confirmatory strategies, and perceived hypothesis confirmation. *Journal of Experimental Social Psychology, 22,* 93–121; M. Snyder (1981) Seek, and ye shall find: Testing hypotheses about other people. In E. T. Higgins, D. C. Herman, & M. P. Zanna (Eds.), *Social cognition: The Ontario symposium on personality and social psychology.* Hilsdale, N.J.: Lawrence Erlbaum; M. Snyder & W. B. Swann (1978) Hypothesis-testing processes in social interaction. *Journal of Personality and Social Psychology, 36,* 1202–1212; Y. Trope & M. Bassok (1982) Confirmatory and diagnosing strategies in social information gathering. *Journal of Personality and Social Psychology, 43,* 22–34;

Y. Trope & M. Bassok (1983) Information gathering strategies in hypothesis testing. *Journal of Experimental Social Psychology, 19,* 560–76.

8. M. Bassok & Y. Trope (1984) People's strategies for testing hypotheses about another's personality: Confirmatory or diagnostic? *Social Cognition, 2,* 199–216; Y. Trope & M. Bassok (1982) Confirmatory and diagnosing strategies in social information gathering. *Journal of Personality and Social Psychology, 43,* 22–34; Y. Trope & M. Bassok (1983) Information gathering strategies in hypothesis testing. *Journal of Experimental Social Psychology, 19,* 560–76.

9. M. Bassok & Y. Trope (1984) People's strategies for testing hypotheses about another's personality: Confirmatory or diagnostic? *Social Cognition, 2,* 199–216; R. B. Skov & S. J. Sherman (1986) Information-gathering processes: Diagnosticity, hypothesis-confirmatory strategies, and perceived hypothesis confirmation. *Journal of Experimental Social Psychology, 22,* 93–121; M. Snyder (1981) Seek, and ye shall find: Testing hypotheses about other people. In E. T. Higgins, D. C. Herman, & M. P. Zanna (Eds.), *Social cognition: The Ontario symposium on personality and social psychology.* Hilsdale, N.J.: Erlbaum; M. Snyder & W. B. Swann (1978) Hypothesis-testing processes in social interaction. *Journal of Personality and Social Psychology, 36,* 1202–1212.

10. M. Snyder & W. B. Swann (1978) Hypothesis-testing processes in social interaction. *Journal of Personality and Social Psychology, 36,* 1202–1212.

11. M. Snyder & N. Cantor (1979) Testing hypotheses about other people: The use of historical knowledge. *Journal of Experimental Social Psychology, 15,* 330–42.

12. A. Tversky & I. Gati (1978) Studies of similarity. In E. Rosch & B. Lloyd (Eds.), *Cognition and categorization.* Hillsdale, N.J.: Erlbaum.

13. For a more formal treatment of this issue, see H. J. Einhorn & R. M. Hogarth (1977) Confidence in judgment: Persistence of the illusion of validity. *Psychological Review, 85,* 395–416.

14. T. Gilovich (1987) Real world accuracy in human judgment: Baseball fans evaluate the front office. Unpublished manuscript; P. Hirsch (1972) Processing fads and fashions: An organization-set analysis of cultural industry systems. *American Journal of Sociology, 77,* 639–59.

15. R. M. Kaplan (1982) Nader's raid on the testing industry: Is it in the best interest of the consumer? *American Psychologist, 37* 15–23.

16. R. K. Merton (1948) The self-fulfilling prophecy. *Antioch Review, 8,* 193–210.

17. R. M. Dawes (1988) *Rational choice in an uncertain world.* San Diego: Harcourt-Brace-Jovanovich.

18. H. H. Kelley & A. J. Stahelski (1970) Social interaction basis of cooperators' and competitors' beliefs about others. *Journal of Personality and Social Psychology, 16,* 66–91.

19. M. Snyder & W. B. Swann (1978) Hypothesis-testing processes in social interaction. *Journal of Personality and Social Psychology, 36,* 1202–1212.

20. R. E. Nisbett & M. Smith (1989) Predicting interpersonal attraction from small samples: A reanalysis of Newcomb's acquaintance study. *Social Cognition, 7,* 67–73.

Chapter 4. Seeing What We Expect to See

1. A. Montagu (1961) Neonatal and infant immaturity in man. *Journal of the American Medical Association, 178,* 56–57; R. E. Passingham (1975) Changes in the size and organization of the brain in man and his ancestors. *Brain, Behavior and Evolution, 11,* 73–90.

2. G. Cooper (1987) *"Red tape holds up new bridge" and more flubs from the nation's press.* New York: Perigee.

3. R. C. Schank (1984) *The cognitive computer: On language, learning, and artificial intelligence.* Reading, MA: Addison-Wesley.

4. J. S. Bruner (1957) Going beyond the information given. In H. Gulber et al. (Eds.), *Contemporary approaches to cognition.* Cambridge, MA: Harvard University Press.

5. M. G. Frank & T. Gilovich (1988) The dark side of self and social perception: Black uniforms and aggression in professional sports. *Journal of Personality and Social Psychology, 54,* 74–85.

6. C. G. Lord, L. Ross, & M. R. Lepper (1979) Biased assimilation and attitude polarization: The effects of prior theories on subsequently considered evidence. *Journal of Personality and Social Psychology, 37,* 2098–2109.

7. T. Gilovich (1983) Biased evaluation and persistence in gambling. *Journal of Personality and Social Psychology, 44,* 1110–1126; T. Gilovich & C. Douglas (1986) Biased evaluations of randomly determined gambling outcomes. *Journal of Experimental Social Psychology, 22,* 228–41.

8. For evidence supporting this prediction, see A. F. Glixman (1949) Recall of completed and incompleted activities under varying degrees of stress. *Journal of Experimental Psychology, 39,* 281–95; A. G. Greenwald (1980) The totalitarian ego: Fabrication and revi-

sion of personal history. *American Psychologist, 35,* 603–18; S. Rosenzweig (1943) An experimental study of 'repression' with special reference to need-persistive and ego-defensive reactions to frustration. *Journal of Experimental Psychology, 32,* 64–74. But for evidence for the opposing point of view, see B. Zeigarnik (1967) On finished and unfinished tasks. In W. D. Ellis (Ed.), *A source book of Gestalt psychology.* New York: Humanities Press.

9. M. J. Mahoney (1977) Publication prejudices: An experimental study of confirmatory bias in the peer review system. *Cognitive Therapy and Research, 1,* 161–75.

10. S. J. Gould (1981) *The mismeasure of man.* New York: W. W. Norton, p. 89.

11. Ibid., p. 126.

12. P. B. Medawar (1984) *The limits of science.* New York: Harper & Row.

13. M. Gazzaniga (1985) *The social brain.* New York: Basic Books; R. E. Nisbett & T. D. Wilson (1977) Telling more than we can know: Verbal reports on mental process. *Psychological Review, 84,* 231–59.

14. P. Diaconis (1978) Statistical problems in ESP research. *Science, 201,* 131–36.

15. B. R. Forer (1949) The fallacy of personal validation: A classroom demonstration of gullibility. *Journal of Abnormal and Social Psychology, 44,* 118–23.

16. R. W. Clark (1984) *The survival of Charles Darwin: A biography of a man and an idea.* New York: Random House.

17. T. Gilovich (1983) Biased evaluation and persistence in gambling. *Journal of Personality and Social Psychology, 44,* 1110–1126.

18. R. Hastie & P. A. Kumar (1979) Person memory: Personality traits as organizing principles in memory for behavior. *Journal of Personality and Social Psychology, 37,* 25–38; E. T. Higgins & J. A. Bargh (1987) Social cognition and social perception. *Annual Review of Psychology, 38,* 369–425.

19. M. Ross & D. Holmberg (1990) Do wives have more vivid memories than their husbands of events in their relationship? Unpublished manuscript.

20. B. Zeigarnik (1967) On finished and unfinished tasks. In W. D. Ellis (Ed.), *A source book of Gestalt psychology.* New York: Humanities Press.

21. D. Goleman (1985) *Vital lies, simple truths: The psychology of self-deception.* New York: Simon & Schuster.

22. T. Gilovich & S. Madey (1990) Memory for one- and two-sided events. Unpublished manuscript.

23. Ibid.

24. E. Goffman (1963) *Behavior in public places: Notes on the social organization of gatherings.* New York: Free Press.

Chapter 5. Seeing What We Want to See

1. D. Kahneman, J. L. Knetsch, & R. Thaler (in press) Experimental tests of the endowment effect and the Coase theorem. *Journal of Political Economy;* R. Thaler (1980) Toward a positive theory of consumer choice. *Journal of Economic Behavior and Organization, 1,* 39–60.

2. D. O. Sears & R. E. Whitney (1973) Political persuasion. In I. deS. Pool, W. Schramm, F. W. Frey, N. Maccoby, & E. B. Parker (Eds.), *Handbook of communication* (pp. 253–89). Chicago: Rand-McNally.

3. D. Granberg & E. Brent (1983) When prophecy bends: The preference-expectation link in U.S. presidential elections, 1952–1980. *Journal of Personality and Social Psychology, 45,* 477–91.

4. R. C. Wylie (1979) *The self-concept (Vol. 2): Theory and research on selected topics.* Lincoln, NE: University of Nebraska Press.

5. W. B. G. Liebrand, D. M. Messick, & F. J. M. Wolters (1986) Why we are fairer than others: A cross-cultural replication and extension. *Journal of Experimental Social Psychology, 22,* 590–604; D. M. Messick, S. Bloom, J. P. Boldizar, & C. D. Samuelson (1985) Why we are fairer than others. *Journal of Experimental Social Psychology, 21,* 480–500.

6. J. M. Fields & H. Schuman (1976) Public beliefs about the beliefs of the public. *Public Opinion Quarterly, 40,* 427–48; H. J. O'Gorman & S. L. Garry (1976) Pluralistic ignorance—a replication and extension. *Public Opinion Quarterly, 40,* 449–58.

7. O. Svenson (1981) Are we all less risky and more skillful than our fellow drivers? *Acta Psychologica, 47,* 143–48.

8. "Word Watch" (1989) *Chance: New Directions for Statistics and Computing, 2,* p. 5.

9. College Board (1976–1977) *Student descriptive questionnaire.* Princeton, NJ: Educational Testing Service.

10. P. Cross (1977) Not *can* but *will* college teaching be improved? *New directions for Higher Education.* Spring, No. 17, 1–15. Reported in D. G. Myers (1990) *Social Psychology* (3rd Edition). New York: McGraw-Hill.

11. N. D. Weinstein (1980) Unrealistic optimism about future life events.

Journal of Personality and Social Psychology, 39, 806–820; N. D. Weinstein (1982) Unrealistic optimism about susceptibility to health problems. *Journal of Behavioral Medicine, 5,* 441–60; N. D. Weinstein & E. Lachendro (1982) Ego-centrism and unrealistic optimism about the future. *Personality and Social Psychology Bulletin, 8,* 195–200.

12. "Economic predictions: Personal future seems brightest." (1989) *Psychology Today,* October, p. 16.

13. D. T. Miller & M. Ross (1975) Self-serving biases in the attribution of causality: Fact or fiction? *Psychological Bulletin, 82,* 213–25; R. Nisbett & L. Ross (1980) *Human inference: Strategies and shortcomings of social judgment.* Englewood Cliffs, NJ: Prentice-Hall; P. E. Tetlock & A. Levi (1982) Attribution bias: On the inconclusiveness of the cognition-motivation debate. *Journal of Experimental Social Psychology, 18,* 68–88.

14. R. R. Lau & D. Russell (1980) Attributions in the sports pages. *Journal of Personality and Social Psychology, 39,* 29–38; C. Peterson (1980) Attribution in the sports pages: An archival investigation of the covariation hypothesis. *Social Psychology Quarterly, 43,* 136–41.

15. R. M. Arkin & G. M. Maruyama (1979) Attribution, affect, and college exam performance. *Journal of Educational Psychology, 71,* 85–93; M. H. Davis & W. G. Stephan (1980) Attributions for exam performance. *Journal of Applied Social Psychology, 10,* 235–48; T. M. Gilmour & D. W. Reid (1979) Locus of control and causal attribution for positive and negative outcomes on university examinations. *Journal of Research in Personality, 13,* 154–60.

16. R. M. Arkin, H. Cooper & T. Kolditz (1980) A statistical review of the literature concerning the self-serving attribution bias in interpersonal influence situations. *Journal of Personality, 48,* 435–48; L. Beckman (1970) Effects of students' performance on teachers' and observers' attributions of causality. *Journal of Educational Psychology, 61,* 76–82; P. E. Tetlock (1980) Explaining teacher explanations for pupil performance: An examination of the self-presentation interpretation. *Social Psychology Quarterly, 43,* 283–90.

17. M. G. Wiley, K. S. Crittenden, & L. D. Birg (1979) Why a rejection? Causal attribution of a career achievement event. *Social Psychology Quarterly, 42,* 214–22.

18. G. W. Allport (1937) *Personality: A psychological interpretation.* New York: Holt; F. Heider (1958) *The psychology of interpersonal relations.* New York: Wiley; M. Zuckerman (1979) Attribution of success and failure revisited, or: The motivational bias is alive and well in attribution theory. *Journal of Personality, 47,* 245–87.

19. D. T. Miller & M. Ross (1975) Self-serving biases in the attribution of causality: Fact or fiction? *Psychological Bulletin, 82,* 213–25; R. Nisbett & L. Ross (1980) *Human inference: Strategies and shortcomings of social judgment.* Englewood Cliffs, NJ: Prentice-Hall.

20. C. A. Anderson & M. P. Slusher (1986) Relocating motivational effects: A synthesis of cognitive and motivational effects on attributions for success and failure. *Social Cognition, 4,* 270–92; P. E. Tetlock & A. Levi (1982) Attribution bias: On the inconclusiveness of the cognition-motivation debate. *Journal of Experimental Social Psychology, 18,* 68–88.

21. R. B. Zajonc (1980) Feeling and thinking: Preferences need no inferences. *American Psychologist, 35,* 151–75.

22. Z. Kunda (1990) The case for motivated reasoning. *Psychological Bulletin,* in press.

23. Ibid., p. 10.

24. Z. Kunda & R. Sanitioso (1989) Motivated changes in the self-concept. *Journal of Experimental Social Psychology, 25,* 272–85; Z. Kunda, R. Sanitioso, & G. T. Fong (1988) Motivated changes in the self-concept. Paper presented at the meeting of the American Psychological Association, Atlanta, GA; R. Sanitioso (1989) Mechanisms for motivated changes in the self-concept. Unpublished doctoral dissertation, Princeton University.

25. P. Diaconis (1977) Statistical problems in ESP research. *Science, 201,* 131–36.

26. T. C. Schelling (1978) *Micromotives and macrobehavior.* New York: W. W. Norton, p. 64–65.

27. D. Dunning, J. A. Meyerowitz, & A. Holzberg (1989) Ambiguity and self-evaluation: The role of idiosyncratic trait definitions in self-serving assessments ability. *Journal of Personality and Social Psychology, 57,* 1082–1090; D. Dunning, A. L. Story, & P. L. Tan (1990) The self as model of excellence in social evaluation. Unpublished manuscript.

28. L. B. Alloy & L. Y. Abramson (1979) Judgment of contingency in depressed and nondepressed students: Sadder but wiser? *Journal of Experimental Psychology: General, 108,* 441–85; S. E. Taylor & J. D. Brown (1988) Illusion and well-being: A social psychological perspective on mental health. *Psychological Bulletin, 103,* 193–210.

29. R. P. Abelson (1986) Beliefs are like possessions. *Journal for the Theory of Social Behaviour, 16,* 222–50.

30. Ibid., p. 231.

Chapter 6. Believing What We Are Told

1. J. B. Watson & R. Raynor (1920) Conditioned emotional reactions. *Journal of Experimental Psychology, 3,* 1–14.

2. B. Harris (1979) Whatever happened to little Albert? *American Psychologist, 34,* 151–60.

3. H. J. Eysenck (1960) Learning theory and behaviour therapy. In H. J. Eysenck (Ed.), *Behaviour therapy and the neuroses: Readings in modern methods of treatment derived from learning theory.* Oxford: Pergamon Press.

4. C. W. Telford & J. M. Sawrey (1968) *Psychology.* Belmont, CA: Brooks/ Cole.

5. J. O. Whittaker (1965) *Introduction to psychology.* Philadelphia: Saunders.

6. E. R. Hilgard, R. C. Atkinson, & R. L. Atkinson (1975) *Psychology* (6th ed.). New York: Harcourt Brace Jovanovich; G. W. Kisker (1977) *The disorganized personality* (3rd ed.). New York: McGraw-Hill; B. Weiner (1977) (Ed.) *Discovering psychology.* Chicago: Science Research Associates.

7. E. G. Boring, H. S. Langfeld, & H. P. Weld (1948) (Eds.) *Foundations of psychology.* New York: Wiley.

8. T. L. Engle & L. Snellgrove (1969) *Psychology: Its Principles and applications (5th ed.).* New York: Harcourt, Brace & World; W. L. Gardiner (1970) *Psychology: A story of a search.* Belmont, CA: Brooks/Cole; J. O. Whittaker (1965) *Introduction to psychology.* Philadelphia: Saunders.

9. H. P. Grice (1975) Logic and conversation. In P. Cole & J. Morgan (Eds.), *Syntax and semantics* (Vol. 3). New York: Academic Press.

10. F. C. Bartlett (1932) *Remembering.* Cambridge: Cambridge University Press.

11. G. W. Allport & L. J. Postman (1947) *The psychology of rumor.* New York: Holt.

12. T. Gilovich (1987) Secondhand information and social judgment. *Journal of Experimental Social Psychology, 23,* 59–74.

13. F. Heider (1958) *The psychology of interpersonal relations.* Hillsdale, NJ: Lawrence Erlbaum; R. Nisbett & L. Ross (1980) *Human inference: Strategies and shortcomings of social judgment.* Englewood Cliffs, NJ: Prentice-Hall.

14. E. E. Jones & R. E. Nisbett (1972) The actor and the observer: Divergent perceptions of the causes of behavior. In E. E. Jones et al. (Eds.), *Attribution: Perceiving the causes of behavior.* Morristown, NJ: General Learning Press.

15. T. Gilovich (1987) Secondhand information and social judgment. *Journal of Experimental Social Psychology*, *23*, 59–74.

16. Ibid., Experiment 3.

17. J. W. Connor (1984) Misperception, folk belief, and the occult: A cognitive guide to understanding. *Skeptical Inquirer, 8* 344–54.

18. M. Fumento (1990) *The myth of heterosexual AIDS*. New York: Basic Books.

19. T. J. Moore (1989) The cholesterol myth. *Atlantic Monthly*. September, p. 37–70.

20. "It's not hysterical to aid missing children." (1985) *USA Today*. July 19, p. A10.

21. A. P. Weisman (1986) I was a drug-hype junkie. *New Republic*. October 6, p. 14–17.

22. D. E. Berlyne (1960) *Conflict, arousal, and curiosity*. New York: McGraw-Hill; M. Csikszentmihalyi (1975) *Beyond boredom and anxiety*. San Francisco: Jossey-Bass.

23. "Overheard" (1987) *Newsweek*. July 13, p. 13.

24. "Too late for prince charming?" (1986) *Newsweek*. June 2, p. 54–61.

25. J. Randi (1986) *Flim-flam: Psychics, ESP, unicorns and other delusions*. Buffalo, NY: Prometheus Books.

26. Cited in M. Fumento (1990) *The myth of heterosexual AIDS*. New York: Basic Books, p. 168.

27. M. E. P. Seligman (1970) On the generality of the laws of learning. *Psychological Review, 77*, 406–18; M. E. P. Seligman (1971) Phobias and preparedness. *Behavior Therapy, 2*, 307–20.

28. M. E. P. Seligman (1971) Phobias and preparedness. *Behavior Therapy, 2*, 307–20.

29. S. Sass (1989) A patently false patent myth. *Skeptical Inquirer, 13*, 310–12.

30. M. Hall (1965) The great cabbage hoax: A case study. *Journal of Personality and Social Psychology, 2*, 563–69.

31. Cited in M. Fumento (1990) *The myth of heterosexual AIDS*. New York: Basic Books, p. 3.

32. Ibid., p. 249.

33. Ibid., p. 324.

Chapter 7. The Imagined Agreement of Others

1. S. Freud (1956) Further remarks on the defense neuropsychoses. *Collected papers of Sigmund Freud*, Vol. 1. London: Hogarth Press.

2. D. S. Holmes (1968) Dimensions of projection. *Psychological Bulletin, 69*, 248–68.

3. L. Ross, D. Greene, & P. House (1977) The false consensus effect: An egocentric bias in social perception and attribution processes. *Journal of Experimental Social Psychology, 13*, 279–301.

4. Ibid.

5. Ibid.

6. W. D. Crano (1983) Assumed consensus of attitudes: The effect of vested interest. *Personality and Social Psychology Bulletin, 9*, 597–608; S. J. Sherman, C. C. Presson, L. Chassin, E. Corty, & P. Olshavsky (1983) The false consensus effect in estimates of smoking prevalence: Underlying mechanisms. *Personality and Social Psychology Bulletin, 9*, 197–207; W. Wagner & H. B. Gerard (1983) Similarity of comparison group, opinions about facts and values and social projection. *Archives of Psychology, 135*, 313–24.

7. S. J. Sherman, C. C. Presson, & L. Chassin (1984) Mechanisms underlying the false consensus effect: The special role of threats to the self. *Personality and Social Psychology Bulletin, 10*, 127–38.

8. K. Granberg & M. King (1980) Crossed-lagged panel analysis of the relation between attraction and perceived similarity. *Journal of Experimental Social Psychology, 16*, 573–81; D. R. Kinder (1978) Political person perception: The asymmetrical influence of sentiment and choice on perceptions of presidential candidates. *Journal of Personality and Social Psychology, 36*, 859–71; G. Marks & N. Miller (1982) Target attractiveness as a mediator of assumed attitude similarity. *Personality and Social Psychology Bulletin, 8*, 728–35.

9. D. Frey (1986) Recent research on selective exposure. In L. Berkowitz (Ed.) *Advances in experimental social psychology.* (Vol. 19; pp. 41–80). Orlando, Fl: Academic Press; D. O. Sears & J. L. Freedman (1967) Selective exposure to information: A critical review. *Public Opinion Quarterly, 31*, 194–213.

10. S. J. Sherman, C. C. Presson, L. Chassin, E. Corty, & P. Olshavsky (1983) The false consensus effect in estimates of smoking prevalence: Underlying mechanisms. *Personality and Social Psychology Bulletin, 9*, 197–207.

11. E. E. Jones & R. E. Nisbett (1972) The actor and the observer: Divergent perceptions of the causes of behavior. In E. E. Jones, D. Kanouse, H. H. Kelley, R. E. Nisbett, S. Valins, & B. Weiner (Eds.), *Attribution: Perceiving the causes of behavior* (pp. 79–94). Morristown, NJ: General Learning Press.

12. T. Gilovich, S. Jennings, & D. L. Jennings (1983) Causal focus and

estimates of consensus: An examination of the false consensus effect. *Journal of Personality and Social Psychology*, *45*, 550–59.

13. T. Gilovich (1990) Differential construal and the false consensus effect. *Journal of Personality and Social Psychology*, in press.

14. S. E. Asch (1948) The doctrine of suggestion, prestige, and imitation in social psychology. *Psychological Review, 55*, 250–76.

15. E. Goffman (1963) *Behavior in public places: Notes on the social organization of gatherings.* New York: Free Press.

16. J. Martin (1982) *Miss Manners' guide to excruciatingly correct behavior.* New York: Warner Books, p. 76.

17. E. Post (1960) *Etiquette: The blue book of social usage.* New York: Funk & Wagnalls, P. 46.

18. E. T. Higgins & W. S. Rholes (1978) Saying is believing: Effects of message modification on memory and liking for the person described. *Journal of Experimental Social Psychology, 14*, 363–78; M. Manis, S. D. Cornell, & J. C. Moore (1974) Transmission of attitude-relevant information through a communication chain. *Journal of Personality and Social Psychology, 30*, 81–94; D. Newtson & T. Czerlinsky (1974) Adjustment of attitude communications for contrasts by extreme audiences. *Journal of Personality and Social Psychology, 30*, 829–37.

19. E. E. Jones & V. A. Harris (1967) The attribution of attitudes. *Journal of Experimental Social Psychology, 3*, 2–24; M. Manis, S. D. Cornell, & J. C. Moore (1974) Transmission of attitude-relevant information through a communication chain. *Journal of Personality and Social Psychology, 30*, 81–94; L. D. Ross (1977) The intuitive psychologist and his shortcomings: Distortions in the attribution process. In L. Berkowitz (Ed.), *Advances in experimental social psychology* (Vol. 10, pp. 173–219). New York: Academic Press.

20. R. Paine (1967) What is gossip about? An alternative hypothesis. *Man: The journal of the royal anthropological institute, 2*, 278–85; J. Sabini & M. Silver (1982) *Moralities of everyday life.* Oxford: Oxford University Press, ch. 5; J. Suls (1977) Gossip as social comparison. *Journal of Communication, 27*, 164–68.

21. T. Hoopes (1969) *The limits of intervention.* New York: David McKay, p. 31.

22. I. L. Janis (1982) *Groupthink: Psychological studies of policy decisions and fiascoes.* Boston: Houghton & Mifflin, p. 39.

Chapter 8. Belief in Ineffective "Alternative" Health Practices

1. "Preying on Aids patients." (1987) *Newsweek*, June 1; "The AIDS underground." (1989) *Newsweek*, August 7.

2. R. M. Deutsch (1977) *The new nuts among the berries: How nu-trition nonsense captured America*. Palo Alto, CA: Ball Publishing; C. Hansen (1969) *Witchcraft at Salem*. New York: Braziller.

3. V. Herbert (1984) Testimony before United States Congressional hearing, "Quackery: A 10-billion dollar scandal." May 5, p. 88; "Preying on Aids patients." (1987) *Newsweek*, June 1.

4. Cited in W. E. Schaller & C. R. Carrol (1976) *Health, quackery, and the consumer*. Philadelphia, PA: W. B. Saunders, p. 169.

5. D. B. Bem (1972) Self-perception theory. In L. Berkowitz (Ed.) *Advances in Experimental Social Psychology*. (Vol. 6, pp. 1–62) New York: Academic Press.

6. W. A. Nolen (1974) *Healing: A doctor in search of a miracle*. New York: Random House.

7. P. B. Medawar (1967) *The art of the soluble*. London: Methuen, p. 14.

8. C. D. MacDougall (1983) *Superstition and the press*. Buffalo: Prometheus, p. 332.

9. Cited in W. A. Nolen (1974) *Healing: A doctor in search of a miracle*. New York: Random House.

10. R. Ornstein & D. Sobel (1987) *The healing brain: Breakthrough discoveries about how the brain keeps us healthy*. New York: Simon and Schuster, p. 32.

11. B. Dossey (1983) Holistic nursing: How to make it work for you. *Journal of Holistic Nursing, 1*, 32–34.

12. W. A. Nolen (1974) *Healing: A doctor in search of a miracle*. New York: Random House.

13. O. C. Simonton, S. Matthews-Simonton, & J. Creighton (1978) *Getting Well Again*. Boston: J. P. Tarcher, p. 220.

14. B. R. Cassileth, E. J. Lusk, T. B. Strouse, & B. A. Bodenheimer (1984) Contemporary unorthodox treatments in cancer medicine. *Annals of Internal Medicine, 101*, 105–12.

15. W. A. Nolen (1974) *Healing: A doctor in search of a miracle*. New York: Random House.

16. Cited in R. M. Deutsch (1977) *The new nuts among the berries: How nutrition nonsense captured America*. Palo Alto, CA: Ball Publishing, p. 263.

17. R. M. Deutsch (1977) *The new nuts among the berries: How nutrition nonsense captured America*. Palo Alto, CA: Ball Publishing; R. E. Nisbett & L. Ross (1980) *Human inference: Strategies and shortcomings of social judgment*. Englewood-Cliffs, NJ: Prentice-Hall; Pepper,

C. (1987) Quackery: The need for federal, state, and local response. *Skeptical Inquirer, 12,* 70–74.

18. S. Barrett (1987) Homeopathy: Is it medicine? *Skeptical Inquirer, 12,* 56–62.

19. "The irrational connection between diet and demeanor." (1989) *Psychology Today,* October, p. 14.

20. Cited in R. M. Deutsch (1977) *The new nuts among the berries: How nutrition nonsense captured America.* Palo Alto, CA: Ball Publishing, p. 272.

21. Ibid., p. 7.

22. K. M. Dillon, B. Minchoff, & K. H. Baker (1985–86) Positive emotional states and enhancement of the immune system. *International Journal of Psychiatry in Medicine, 15,* 13–17; H. Hall (1983) Hypnosis and the immune system: A review with implications for cancer and the psychology of healing. *American Journal of Clinical Hypnosis, 25,* 92–103; J. B. Jemmott & S. E. Locke (1984) Psychosocial factors, immunologic mediation, and human susceptibility to infectious diseases: How much do we know? *Psychological Bulletin, 95,* 78–108; J. K. Kiecolt-Glaser & R. Glaser (1988) Behavioral influences on immune function: Evidence for the interplay between stress and health. In T. Field, P. McCabe, & N. Schneiderman (Eds.), *Stress and Coping* (Vol. 2). Hillsdale, NJ: Erlbaum; D. C. McClelland (1989) Motivational factors in health and disease. *American Psychologist, 44,* 675–83.

23. B. Crary, S. L. Hauser, M. Borysenko, I. Kutz, C. Hoban, K. A. Ault, H. L. Weiner, & H. Benson (1983) Epinephrine-induced changes in the distribution of lymphocyte subsets in peripheral blood of humans. *The Journal of Immunology, 131,* 1178–81; A. A. Stone, D. S. Cox, H. Vladimarsdottir, & J. M. Neale (1987) Secretary IgA as a measure of immunocompetence. *Journal of Human Stress, 13,* 136–40.

24. B. R. Cassileth, E. J. Lusk, D. S. Miller, L. L. Brown, & C. Miller (1985) Psychosocial correlates of survival in advanced malignant disease? *New England Journal of Medicine, 312,* 1551–55.

25. B. Blattner (1981) *Holistic nursing.* Englewood Cliffs, NJ: Prentice-Hall, p. 35.

26. Cited in C. D. MacDougall (1983) *Superstition and the press.* Buffalo: Prometheus, p. 333.

27. "Handicapping Education" (1985) *Newsweek,* April, 29, p. 33.

28. "Letters to the editor" (1989) *New Age,* January/February. p. 12.

29. E. Smith (1988) Fighting cancerous feelings. *Psychology Today,* May,

p. 22–23; S. E. Taylor, R. R. Lichtman, & J. V. Wood (1984) Attributions, beliefs about control, and adjustment to breast cancer. *Journal of Personality and Social Psychology, 46,* 489–502.

30. S. Sontag (1978) *Illness as metaphor.* New York: Farrar, Straus, & Giroux, p. 55.

Chapter 9. Belief in the Effectiveness of Questionable Interpersonal Strategies

1. R. M. Arkin & A. H. Baumgardner (1985) Self-handicapping. In J. H. Harvey & G. Weary (Eds.), *Attribution: Basic issues and applications.* (pp. 169–202). New York: Academic Press.
2. T. Gilovich, S. Madey, & S. Currall (1990) The general ineffectiveness of feigned self-handicaps. Unpublished manuscript.
3. E. E. Jones & C. Wortman (1973) *Ingratiation: An attributional approach.* Morristown, NJ: General Learning Press.
4. M. Kundera (1984) *The unbearable lightness of being.* New York: Harper & Row, p. 185.
5. R. E. Nisbett & L. Ross (1980) *Human inference: Strategies and shortcomings of social judgment.* Englewood Cliffs, NJ: Prentice-Hall. Chapter 3.
6. R. M. Dawes (1988) *Rational choice in an uncertain world.* San Diego: Harcourt, Brace, Jovanovich.

Chapter 10. Belief in ESP

1. N. D. Grace, H. Muench, & T. C. Chalmers (1966) The present status of shunts for portal hypertension in cirrhosis. *Journal of Gastroenterology, 50,* 684–91. See also D. Freedman, R. Pisani, & R. Purves (1978) *Statistics.* New York: W. W. Norton.
2. J. Randi (1986) *Flim-Flam.* Buffalo: Prometheus Books.
3. J. Beloff (1980) Seven evidential experiments. *Zetetic Scholar, 6,* 91–94. Cited in J. E. Alcock (1981) *Parapsychology: Science or magic?* New York: Pergamon Press, p. 144.
4. B. Wolman (1977) (Ed.) *Handbook of parapsychology.* New York: Van Nostrand.
5. National Research Council (1988, January) *American Psychological Association Monitor,* p. 7.
6. R. Hyman (1985) A critical historical overview of parapsychology. In P. Kurtz (Ed.), *A skeptic's handbook of parapsychology.* Buffalo: Prometheus Books.
7. S. Krippner (1977) *Advances in parapsychological research I: Psychokinesis.* New York: Plenum.

8. J. B. Rhine (1934) *Extra-sensory perception.* Boston: Bruce-Humphries.

9. Ibid.

10. J. L. Kennedy (1939) A methodological review of extrasensory perception. *Psychological Bulletin, 36,* 59–103.

11. B. R. Bugelski & S. Bugelski (1940) A further attempt to test the role of chance in ESP experiments. *Journal of Parapsychology, 4,* 142–48.

12. A. T. Oram (1954) An experiment with random numbers. *Journal of the Society for Psychical Research, 37,* 369–77. See also A. Hardy, R. Harvie, & A. Koestler (1975) *The challenge of chance.* New York: Vintage Books.

13. Quoted in R. Hyman (1985) A critical historical overview of parapsychology, p. 50. In P. Kurtz (Ed.), *A skeptic's handbook of parapsychology.* Buffalo: Prometheus Books.

14. Ibid.

15. C. E. M. Hansel (1966) *ESP: A scientific evaluation.* New York: Charles Scribner's Sons. G. R. Price (1955) Science and the supernatural. *Science, 122,* 359–67.

16. R. G. Medhurst (1968) The fraudulent experimenter: Professor Hansel's case against psychical research. *Journal of the Society for Psychical Research, 44,* 217–32.

17. C. Scott & P. Haskell Fresh light on the Shackleton Experiments. *Proceedings of the Society for Psychical Research, 56,* 43–72.

18. B. Markwick (1978) The Soal-Goldney experiments with Basil Shackleton: New evidence of data manipulation. *Proceedings of the Society for Psychical Research, 56,* 250–77.

19. D. Marks & R. Kammann (1980) *The psychology of the psychic.* Buffalo: Prometheus Books.

20. Cited in J. E. Alcock (1981) *Parapsychology: Science or magic?* New York: Pergamon Press, p. 135.

21. Ibid.

22. Gallup Opinion Index (1978) Political, social, and economic trends. *155,* 1–5.

23. A. Greeley (1987, January 17) From here to the hereafter. *San Jose Mercury News,* p. C–1.

24. R. J. Lederer & B. Singer (1983) Pseudoscience in the name of the university. *Skeptical Inquirer, 7,* 57–62.

25. J. Randi (1977) The media and reports on the paranormal. *The Humanist, 37,* 45–47.

26. D. Marks & R. Kammann (1980) *The psychology of the psychic.* Buffalo: Prometheus Books, p. 151.

27. P. Kurtz (1986) *The transcendental temptation*. Buffalo: Prometheus Books.

28. Cited in J. E. Alcock (1981) *Parapsychology: Science or magic?* New York: Pergamon Press, p. 24.

29. Quoted in R. Hyman (1985) A critical historical overview of parapsychology, p. 70. In P. Kurtz (Ed.), *A skeptic's handbook of parapsychology*. Buffalo: Prometheus Books.

30. J. E. Alcock (1981) *Parapsychology: Science or magic?* New York: Pergamon Press.

31. C. Evans (1973) Parapsychology—What the questionnaire revealed. *New Scientist, 57,* 209.

32. Cited in J. E. Alcock (1981) *Parapsychology: Science or magic?* New York: Pergamon Press.

33. J. Randi (1981) Selective test selection. *Skeptical Inquirer, 5,* 12–13.

34. L. W. Alvarez (1965) A pseudo experience in parapsychology. *Science, 148,* 1541.

35. S. J. Gould (1982) *The panda's thumb: More reflections on natural history*. New York: W. W. Norton.

36. F. Bacon (1960/1620) *The new organon and related writings*. New York: Liberal Arts Press.

37. J. E. Alcock (1981) *Parapsychology: Science or magic?* New York: Pergamon Press.

38. W. Allen (1972) *Without Feathers*. New York: Random House.

39. J. Randi (1982) Nostradamus: The prophet for all seasons. *Skeptical Inquirer, 7,* 30–37.

40. National Research Council (1988, January) *American Psychological Association Monitor*, p. 7.

41. T. S. Kuhn (1962) *The structure of scientific revolutions*. Chicago: University of Chicago Press.

Chapter 11. Challenging Dubious Beliefs

1. D. R. Lehman, R. O. Lempert, & R. E. Nisbett (1988) The effects of graduate training on reasoning: Formal discipline and thinking about everyday-life events. *American Psychologist, 43,* 431–42.

2. M. W. Wagner & M. Monnet (1979) Attitudes of college professors toward extra-sensory perception. *Zetetic Scholar, 5,* 7–16.

Index